COLLEGE
(UN)BOUND

COLLEGE (UN)BOUND

THE FUTURE OF HIGHER EDUCATION
AND WHAT IT MEANS FOR STUDENTS

JEFFREY J. SELINGO

NEW HARVEST
HOUGHTON MIFFLIN HARCOURT
BOSTON / NEW YORK

For Hadley and Rory, and their future

For information about permission to reproduce selections from this book,
write to Permissions, Houghton Mifflin Harcourt Publishing Company,
215 Park Avenue South, New York, New York 10003.

www.hmhbooks.com

Library of Congress Cataloging-in-Publication Data is available.
ISBN 978-0-544-02707-7

Printed in the United States of America
DOC 10 9 8 7

Some material in this book has appeared, in slightly different form,
in the *Chronicle of Higher Education.*

CONTENTS

INTRODUCTION

Bernardsville is an affluent village of nineteenth-century colonial homes, a small town center, and modern strip malls located in northern New Jersey, just thirty-five miles from midtown Manhattan. It's the type of American bedroom community where the college-educated settle, start families, watch their children grow up on the town ball fields, and then send them off to college after graduation from Bernards High School.

With a rich selection of Advanced Placement courses and the exclusive two-year International Baccalaureate curriculum, the 750-student high school is often ranked among the best public schools in the state. In the fall of 2005, Samantha Dietz entered her senior year at Bernards. She was a member of the debate club, Harvard Model Congress, and worked for the student newspaper. She took Advanced Placement psychology, as well as several International Baccalaureate courses, including English, French, and environmental science. She maintained a 3.9 grade-point average. And like almost all of her senior class, she was bound for college the following fall.

Dietz would be the first in her family to go to college. Her parents had solid jobs in technology, despite having only high-school diplomas. They didn't push her to go to college, but Dietz's teachers and guidance counselors did, especially to four-year colleges. She applied to more than half a dozen schools: Rutgers University, Drew University, Fairleigh Dickinson University in New Jersey; Hofstra University in New York; and Allegheny College and Bucknell University in Pennsylvania. She was accepted to all but Bucknell, where she was put on the wait list.

When decision time came in the spring, Dietz closely examined the financial-aid offers from each of the colleges. For her, the choice would be strictly about the bottom line. Fairleigh Dickinson offered her the most financial aid, nearly all of it in grants that wouldn't have to be paid back. Its campus was about twenty minutes away, so she could live at home and save on room and board. With Fairleigh Dickinson's financial package, Dietz's tuition bill would be about half of the university's $25,000 list price at the time. Her decision was easy.

What Dietz failed to examine was Fairleigh Dickinson's graduation rate. In 2006, only 38 percent of its students graduated within six years, a rate well below all of the other schools she had considered. The two other local schools on her list, Rutgers and Drew, graduated more than 70 percent of their students within six years. Though Fairleigh Dickinson was giving Dietz a boatload of money, her chances of emerging at the other end with a degree were pretty dismal.

Dietz took a full slate of classes her first semester. To pay tuition, she waitressed and helped manage a restaurant near her house. She worked twenty-five hours a week, mostly on nights and weekends. "By Thanksgiving, I was exhausted. I had no downtime," she recalls. She was doing well in school, with mostly B's in her classes. "I felt like I was killing myself for nothing," Dietz says. "This was money I could be saving and starting my life. I was managing a restaurant, handling finances and employees. I was learning a lot less about the real world in school and paying so much for it."

Toward the end of the semester, she received a letter from the university announcing that state funds to private colleges in New Jersey were at risk of being cut. It was a warning: She would likely need to pay even more the following fall.

So she dropped out of college.

The Dropout Crisis

The story of Samantha Dietz is not unique. It reflects a broad, national trend in American higher education, where some 400,000 students drop out every year.[1]

For most of the twentieth century, the United States bragged that it had the best colleges and universities in the world—and rightfully so. Since the end of World War II, when colleges and universities threw open their doors to returning GIs, helping to create a vast middle class that defined a generation, these institutions have been the envy of the world and a symbol of American greatness. They attracted the most talented students from other countries, and graduated young Americans who were the best educated in the world.

Not anymore. Over the last thirty years — and particularly in the first decade of the new millennium — American higher education has lost its way. At the very top, the most elite and prestigious institutions remain the best — the world still clamors to get into Harvard, Princeton, Yale, Berkeley, Stanford, Amherst, Williams, and a few dozen other household brands.

But at the colleges and universities attended by most American students, costs are spiraling out of control and quality is declining just as increasing international competition demands that higher education be more productive and less expensive. Only slightly more than 50 percent of American students who enter college leave with a bachelor's degree. Among wealthy countries, only Italy ranks lower. As a result, the United States is now ranked number twelve among developed nations in higher-education attainment by its young people.[2] As the baby boomer generation leaves the workforce, the country risks having successive generations less educated than the ones that preceded them for the first time.

Such trends carry significant economic risks for the United States. For every dollar earned by college graduates, those who drop out without a degree earn sixty-seven cents. Since the turn of the century, average wages for high-school graduates — who today make up about half of the adult population — have fallen considerably to just over $19,000, below the federal poverty level for a family of four. Nothing short of winning the lottery helps ensure a young person will achieve the American dream quite like a college degree. A four-year college credential is the best ticket — and perhaps the only ticket — for kids from the poorest families to get ahead. For children from families at higher income levels (defined as $61,000 and above), a degree helps them make it to the top themselves.

In 2010, four years after Dietz quit Fairleigh Dickinson, she signed up for a class at nearby Raritan Valley Community College. Since then, she has taken one class a semester, paying about $500 a course. She wishes her counselors in high school had encouraged her to consider community college, instead of mocking two-year institutions as places for students who couldn't hack it on a four-year campus.

Now, Dietz is twenty-four years old and working for a real estate company. Her job doesn't require a degree, but she thinks she'll eventually get one. She has heard the statistics on the long-term payoff of a degree, but for the moment Dietz feels she is better off than many of her high-school friends who went to college. "They graduated and are in worse situations," she says. "They are back to waitressing or nannying, not doing anything with their degree. They are living at home and in tons of debt. I'm in a much better situation."

A Risk-Averse, Self-Satisfied Industry

American higher education is broken.

Like another American icon — the auto industry in Detroit — the higher-education industry is beset by hubris, opposition to change, and resistance to accountability. Even the leaders of colleges and universities think we're in trouble. More than one-third of them say American higher education is headed in the wrong direction.[3]

In 2006, in its final report from a year-long study, a federal commission studying the future of higher education warned of the dangers of complacency. "What we have learned over the last year makes clear that American higher education has become what, in the business world, would be called a mature enterprise: increasingly risk-averse, at times self-satisfied, and unduly expensive," it said. "History is littered with examples of industries that, at their peril, failed to respond to — or even to notice — changes in the world around them, from railroads to steel manufacturers."[4]

Change comes very slowly to higher education. Many institutions in the United States were established more than two centuries ago, with a handful dating back to the days before the American Revolution. Tradition is important at these colleges. A confluence of events — flagging state support for public colleges, huge federal budget deficits, and falling household income — now makes it necessary to consider new approaches.

Ideas for change are everywhere. Almost every day a report about innovation in higher education or an invitation to a meeting about its future lands on my desk. In April 2012, I made my way to one of the largest of those gatherings, the Education Innovation Summit at Arizona State University.

The summit was notable for who wasn't there. As I scanned the name tags of the 800 or so attendees, I found very few were actual educators—the college presidents, professors, or others who spend their days on campuses immersed in the business of higher education.

This gathering at an office park for start-ups run by Arizona State had attracted educational entrepreneurs, CEOs, and investors to hear talks about the future of education and see demonstrations from more than a hundred companies promising to bring massive change to the tradition-bound industry.

Kicking off the meeting with a call to arms was Michael Crow, the hard-charging leader who, in his ten years as president, had transformed Arizona State from a sleepy public university to a test bed for new ideas. Lecturing the group on what ails higher education, he summed up its problems in a word most of us had never heard—filiopietism. Translation: Higher education is clinging to tradition. Too few students are going to college, not enough are graduating, and the whole thing costs too much. Quoting his father, a US Navy sailor, Crow called this a "piss-poor performance."

Although Crow is derided in some academic circles for his business-like approach to higher education, he found a sympathetic audience in this gathering. For this crowd, the lack of an academic pedigree is exactly what's needed to reform the outdated methods of traditional colleges, and of course, profit at the same time. Investors are lining up to cash in on the college of tomorrow. Venture capitalists poured some $429 million into education companies in 2011. That same year, in the midst of a worldwide economic slump, 124 education start-ups received financial backing, the most since 1999, during the height of the dot-com boom.

The new business ideas that are changing higher education range from rethinking how high-school students apply to college (think Facebook, with colleges making friend requests to prospective applicants), to how courses are delivered (150,000 students in an online class), to how learners are certified (think of a badge like those given in the Boy

Scouts, instead of a diploma). Each new idea raises the anxiety level of administrators on traditional college campuses that have had a monopoly on the credential market and want to maintain it.

In other industries, "those who don't innovate go out of business," Jennifer Fremont-Smith tells me under the ninety-degree Scottsdale sun during a break in the program. She is cofounder of Smarterer, a Boston-based start-up that offers technology for validating technical skills on everything from social media to Microsoft Office programs. "Higher ed," she adds, "shouldn't be different."

Despite the technological advances of the past two decades, the revolution in the way college education is delivered is just beginning. For the most part, the residential college experience of today is much like it was ten or twenty years ago — the classrooms, dorms, dining halls, and quad. Though laptops and iPads are ubiquitous in lecture halls, students can take classes online, the dining halls have sushi, and nearly everyone has a smartphone, the basics of going to college and getting a broad education or training in a profession remain largely unchanged.

At least for now.

A college has many purposes, from research and discovery to maturing students. At its core, one of the purposes is information delivery, and in recent years other long-established content providers from music to journalism to books have been transformed by technology, resulting in the decline of the middleman — record stores, newspapers, bookstores, and publishers. Are colleges next? Talk of a coming disruption to the traditional college model has reached a fever pitch in some corners of higher education — each day seems to bring news of innovations with the potential to transform how we get a college degree, just as iTunes forever changed how we buy music.

If every revolution has a turning point, perhaps that defining moment came for higher education in the fall of 2011. A Stanford professor, Sebastian Thrun, and Google's director of research, Peter Norvig, offered their graduate-level artificial intelligence course online for free. They thought the class might appeal to 500 students, perhaps a thousand. It ended up attracting 160,000 students from 190 countries, prompting the label "Massive Online Open Course," or MOOC. The 22,000 students who finished received an official "Statement of Accomplishment." Thrun then asked the top thousand students who had perfect or near-perfect scores on their assignments to send him their résumés. He promised to pass the best ones on to tech companies throughout Silicon Valley. After the course ended, Thrun turned his focus to a company he started, Udacity, which offers low-cost, online classes.

Two other Stanford professors also opened their courses to the world for free that fall and attracted 200,000 students. The success of the Stanford classes touched off a string of announcements in the following months by MIT, the University of California at Berkeley, the University of Pennsylvania, the University of Michigan, Princeton University, and dozens of others that they would attempt to deliver a piece of their brand-name education to the masses online. In less than a year, one of those efforts, Coursera, has enrolled 2.5 million students, offered 215 courses, and partnered with more than 30 universities.

At the same time, new ideas to substantially lower the cost of a traditional college degree were emerging. The most notable effort was at the University of North Texas. There, leaders called in the management consulting firm Bain & Company, famous for helping corporate America restructure its operations, to assist the university in designing the college of the future for its branch campus in Dallas. The model shaped by Bain called for a limited number of majors tied to the needs of the local economy (such as business and information technology), classes offered year-round, and hybrid courses (a combination of online and face-to-face classes). For students who graduate on time, a bachelor's degree would cost about $18,000.

The new University of North Texas campus and massive online courses like Thrun's are precisely the type of disruptive forces that Clay Christensen envisions displacing traditional players in higher education. Christensen, a Harvard Business School professor, is the father of the disruptive innovation theory that argues that the most original new products take root at the bottom of the market and eventually move up market, displacing established competitors. Think of cell phones replacing landlines and digital cameras replacing film. Christensen has written several best-selling books on the theory. He believes higher education is the next industry ripe for this kind of change, and in 2011 he laid out his arguments in the book *The Innovative University*. I met him that summer at a day-long seminar he held for those leading change in higher education. "We need new models because the cost of higher ed is becoming prohibitive," he told me. "The history of innovation tells us those new models are not going to come from within higher ed. They will come from new entrants."

As a reporter, I've heard plenty of people over the years make similar sweeping statements about coming change, only to see nothing happen. In each decade since the 1970s, the end of higher education as we know it has been predicted, usually during a deep recession that made people question the need for college. In 1976, *Newsweek* magazine ran a famous cover of two college graduates donning their caps and gowns while holding a shovel and jackhammer. The headline: "Who Needs College?"

Of course, those predictions now seem greatly exaggerated, furnishing current college leaders with an abundance of overconfidence. The truth about change is that we tend to overestimate its speed while underestimating its reach.

This moment in higher education is ripe for change. States have increasingly rolled back their financial support for higher education, leaving their public universities, which already educate eight in ten Americans, scrambling for cash at a time when more students are trying to get in. By some measures, state taxpayer support for higher education hasn't been this low since 1965, when there were some sixteen million fewer students in the system.[5] Overall, student debt has surpassed trillion dollars while, since the late 1970s, the annual costs at four-year colleges have risen three times faster than the rate of inflation. Some $110 billion in student loans was borrowed in 2011 alone. Some 50 million Americans now hold some kind of student loan, slightly more than the number of people on Medicare and almost as many as receive Social Security benefits.

The massive run-up in student-loan debt has raised plenty of comparisons to the bubbles of the last fifteen years in tech stocks and housing prices. Could higher education be the next bubble to burst? Some economists dismiss this idea, pointing out that a college degree is not an asset like a house or a stock, which can be flipped and will lose value if people can't or don't want to buy it on resale. Still, a kind of bubble could exist if students overvalue degrees from some colleges — and I believe this is already happening. The worth of a degree is often measured by the salary a graduate receives, especially when they come from elite colleges and go on to lucrative employment at Wall Street banks and consulting firms. But these kinds of employers recruit only at top colleges. The question remains: Is a degree from Podunk U worth $50,000 a year? Even if you go $30,000 or $40,000 into debt to get a diploma and then have trouble getting a good job?

Heavy debt burdens for recent college graduates might make good news stories, but they rarely generate more than a collective sigh from the public and politicians who largely see a college education as a private good paid for by the person who benefits from it most, the graduate. As one state lawmaker told me when I asked him if he worried that the average debt of graduates in his state had hit the $25,000 mark, "So what? That's the price of a new car." Under the hood of that new shiny car, however, are societal shifts causing a growing divide between the haves and have-nots in higher education. The wealthiest colleges are spending ten thousand dollars more per student on instruction than less affluent schools that dedicate about as much money to their students as high schools do. Even as more of our citizens need an education past high school, elite colleges are making themselves even more exclusive, proudly boasting each spring about the smaller and smaller percentage of applicants they have accepted (in 2012, Harvard rejected nine in ten applicants, including at least 1,800 high-school valedictorians).[6] At the 200 colleges that are most difficult to get into, only 15 percent of entering students in 2010 came from families in the bottom half of incomes in the US (under $65,000). Nearly seven in ten students on those campuses come from the top income group (above $108,000).[7]

The result is that the US higher-education system is becoming less of a meritocracy. In the last decade, the percentage of students from families at the highest income levels who got a bachelor's degree has grown to 82 percent, while for those at the bottom it has fallen to just 8 percent.

No Longer a One-Size-Fits-All Experience

Eighteen years ago, just as the Internet was taking off, I graduated from Ithaca College, a traditional, residential college with 6,000 students (I didn't have an e-mail address until my sophomore year). Sixteen years from now, my youngest daughter will go to college, and I can only imagine what her experience might be like. One of the reasons I decided to write this book is to help students better understand the various pathways to a degree and also to assist parents like me sort through the hype and the reality about the future of higher education.

Unlike the disciples of Clay Christensen — the "disrupters," as they are known — I don't believe that scores of colleges will simply disappear in the future and be replaced by online imitations. Sure, by my estimates only 500 or so of the 4,000-plus colleges and universities in the United States are truly safe because they have stable finances or large endowments.

Unlike newspapers and bookstores, colleges are mostly protected from market forces by large government subsidies and a complex regulatory environment that does not allow you or me to simply start a new college from our bedroom like we can a website that puts a newspaper out of business. Although as many as a thousand colleges are at risk of closing or merging in the decade ahead because of poor finances, the vast majority of colleges will adapt. Colleges are like cities, as so many people have reminded me throughout the research for this book. They evolve as needs change, although many of them will struggle through this next evolution.

If you're a parent who went to college, don't assume your children will follow the same route. Technology has given students so many more choices about how and where to get a college credential. One difficulty I've encountered is that we no longer have a shared vision in this country about what a college education should consist of. Even college students today can't be described in a single way. The people we think of as traditional college students, eighteen- to twenty-four-year-olds, make up a little more than a third of enrollments at colleges across the country. These students have different interests and learning styles from each other, so for some a four-year liberal-arts college is best, while for working adults an online degree is often the better option.

We think of American higher education as a cohesive system, but there is nothing uniform about it. Colleges and universities provide a wide variety of educational and social services and bring them together in one package, which usually is delivered at one physical location. That system is collapsing under an unsustainable financial model.

In its place is emerging a collection of providers. In the face of these new competitors, a portion of traditional higher education is trying to remake its model. One of the most significant efforts we'll visit is at Carnegie Mellon University, where professors in specific academic subjects and researchers versed in the science of how students learn have teamed up to build elaborate online courses that are already reshaping how content is delivered in college and university classrooms.

The technological revolution in how information is distributed and consumed holds the promise to scale higher education to serve more students and cut costs. At the same time, the rush to embrace technology as a solution to every problem has created tension on campuses over whether the critical role higher education plays in preparing the whole person to be a productive citizen in a democratic society is at risk. Indeed, in an increasingly complex world, the foundation of learning—a liberal-arts education—is more important than ever.

The Lost Decade

This is a book about the future of higher education. The first part will explain how we got to this point. This is not meant to be an exhaustive history. Indeed, I believe that colleges lost their way in just the last decade and were consumed by the ego-driven desire of their leaders to keep up with competitors and rise in the rankings. I call the period from 1999 to 2009 the "Lost Decade." It's the time when a boom in high-school graduates gave colleges the opportunity to prepare for what's coming next: fewer government dollars and a more diverse pipeline of students lacking academic skills but needing lots of financial aid. Like day traders in the dot-com boom and those who flipped homes during the housing bubble, college leaders spent the last decade chasing high-achieving students, showering them with scholarships to snatch them from competitors, and going deep into debt to build lavish residence halls, recreational facilities, and other amenities that contribute nothing to the actual learning of students. *More* was the guiding principle of the Lost Decade—more buildings, more majors, more students, and of course, more tuition. To keep tuition dollars rolling in to support the whole enterprise, students were not exposed to a rigorous academic experience that would have prepared them for the working world, but instead were treated like customers to be pleased and placated. The era of *more* is finally coming to an end. It began unraveling after the financial crisis of 2008, and now the disrupters have colleges looking in their rearview mirrors.

The second half of this book will describe how the traditional college is becoming unbound — its students less tethered to one campus for four years and its functions, from courses in a fifteen-week semester to majors, no longer in a one-size-fits-all package. Think of it as the unbundled cable package where you're allowed to pick and choose your channels. In these later chapters, we'll go on a campus tour of potential new pathways to a credential. I'll take you inside one of the massive online courses. We'll enter the student swirl, in which an increasing number of students are getting degrees by transferring between colleges. I'll explain the idea of competency-based education, where students learn at their own pace and are certified when they master a concept. We'll look at how professors are flipping the classroom to improve the traditional lecture. And we'll explore other alternatives, including online and hybrid courses. For those still interested in the traditional route, I'll provide ideas on how you can compare the return on investment between institutions and determine the value of a $200,000 bachelor's degree at a private college. We'll explore a decision too often left until the last minute for too many students: picking a major in an economy where what may be the fastest growing jobs in the future don't yet exist. This is not meant as a guidebook about individual schools, but you will find examples of colleges that are experimenting with innovative ideas and profiles of several colleges where, right now, the future of higher education is unfolding.

Throughout, I'll argue that you don't need to be looking for a college as much as you need to look for what and how you want to learn and decide what you're preparing for afterward. On campus tours, colleges emphasize the bells and whistles: the fancy dorms, climbing walls, and technology-filled classrooms. Don't let them distract you. Smart students should focus their attention on the quality of teaching, the portability of their credits, and the value a degree or other credential will provide them in the job market. The more questions students and parents ask about these matters, the more attention schools will pay to them, and, in the long run, the more successful the American higher education system will be.

Part I

HOW WE GOT HERE

1

The Great Credential Race

NEW YORK CITY PROCLAIMS itself the center of the financial, media, and publishing world, but with an economy built on technological innovation, its mayor, Michael Bloomberg, worries it's missing one key ingredient: a world-class science and engineering university.

In late 2010, the mayor set off to change that. He offered prime land and $100 million to a university that would build a new campus in the city. This announcement spawned an all-out competition among more than a dozen top schools around the world, including Stanford, Cornell, and Carnegie Mellon universities, the University of Toronto, and the Indian Institute of Technology. The new campus "has the potential to help catapult New York City into a leadership position in technology and diversify its economic base," Stanford's president, John Hennessy, wrote in a letter accompanying its proposal. Stanford and others pitched ideas that called for $2 billion in new construction over thirty years and spots for 2,000 graduate students.

Cornell eventually grabbed the top prize in a contest with the pomp and circumstance of a city trying to land a new auto factory or sports team. For New York City, the economic, civic, and cultural stakes were just as high. Despite the tear-filled nostalgia that the image of college evokes — tree-shaded quads, ivy-covered neo-Gothic buildings, and fall football weekends — the truth is that in the last two decades higher education in the United States has evolved into a big business. Consider these numbers: Today, there are some 5,300 colleges and universities in the US, everything from beauty schools to Harvard. They bring in $490 billion in revenues each year. They employ more than 3.5 million people. They hold $990 billion in assets, including cash, investments, and campuses that are essentially minicities. And they spend $440 billion on goods, services, and people each year.

Their influence goes beyond money and people, of course. American higher education helps shape public opinion through its research and experts, both featured frequently in the news media. Its leaders, from presidents to prominent faculty, travel in exclusive circles with politicians, corporate CEOs, and famous journalists. During the height of the Occupy Wall Street Movement, a chart in the New York Times showed who is in the top 1 percent of American incomes.[1] It included 9,300 college managers and 31,672 college professors, about equal to the number of hospital managers and accountants. Sure, not every college president makes a million dollars (only forty-five do) and not every professor has a cushy job for life (only 25 percent of faculty at four-year colleges have tenure), but employment in American higher education is certainly more lucrative and prestigious for those at the top than their counterparts in K–12 education, who make up less than 1 percent of the top earners in the country.

In a growing number of towns and cities throughout the United States, colleges have replaced manufacturers and other private businesses as the top company. In Rochester, New York, the University of Rochester is the largest employer, with 20,000 workers in a city that gave birth to several American business icons: Kodak, Xerox, and Bausch & Lomb. Cities from Philadelphia to Charlotte are promoting themselves as havens for "meds and eds" in an effort to attract other industries, and, most important, residents with college educations (and higher salaries, of course).

Higher education is the linchpin in the economies of American metropolitan areas that are pulling away from the rest of the country. College graduates are concentrated in a smaller number of cities than ever before: The difference between the most and least educated metro areas is now double what it was in 1970.[2] Mesa, Arizona — a suburb of Phoenix with a population larger than that of Atlanta; St. Louis; and Minneapolis — has followed New York City's lead and has asked colleges to set up shop there. "You look at comparable metro areas," says Mesa's mayor, Scott Smith, "and there are a variety of institutions that offer a variety of services and options, not only in education for the citizens, but also for medicine and business."[3] So far, the city has landed branch campuses of Westminster College in Missouri, Benedictine University in Illinois, and Wilkes University in Pennsylvania.

Becoming the modern equivalent of the steel or auto plant has not been without costs. As colleges have become more central to city and regional economies, they have lost focus on what had been and should be their primary mission — teaching students and researching the next big discoveries. More than ever, American colleges and universities seem to be in every business but education. They are in the entertainment business, the housing business, the restaurant business, the recreation business, and, on some campuses, they operate what are essentially professional sports franchises. As colleges have grown more corporate in the past decade, they have started acting like Fortune 500 companies. Administrative salaries have ballooned, and members of boards of trustees are chosen for their corporate ties, not for their knowledge of higher education. Colleges now view students as customers and market their degree programs as products.

Selling College

Zakiya Muwwakkil was one of those customers, a participant in the great credential race. The Jacksonville, Florida, native graduated from Florida A&M University in 2003, with a bachelor's degree in philosophy and religion. Muwwakkil had picked those majors with plans to go to law school, but by her senior year in college she had changed her mind. "Law school wasn't the best fit," she said. Even so, her mentors and advisers encouraged her to go on to graduate school in order to make herself more marketable to employers. The following year Muwwakkil received a master's degree in peace and justice studies at Fordham University and landed a job at a nonprofit in New York City. As she continued to look for better jobs, she realized that she would either be doing the work of a dozen people or that the positions didn't pay well. "I kept thinking that if I continued to go to school I'd be more competitive for some of the top positions," she said.

Muwwakkil headed off to Columbia University's Teachers College for a master's in international development. That was followed by a doctorate in 2010 from Fordham. Muwwakkil now lives back in Jacksonville, where she is teaching part-time at a local college. With more than $100,000 in student loans, she now regrets some of her decisions. Now the advice she gets is from potential employers, who tell her to leave one or two of her degrees off her résumé. "They tell me I look overqualified," she said.

Living in New York, Muwwakkil was bombarded with advertisements for degree programs. You can hardly go anywhere these days and not see or hear an advertisement for college. Throughout Concourse B at Denver International Airport, nearly every other advertisement greeting passengers is for a higher-education institution: Colorado State University, the University of Wyoming, Colorado Mesa College, and the University of Northern Colorado. Airline magazines are filled with promotions for executive MBA programs. At least once an hour on the all-news radio station in Washington, DC, listeners hear about the degree in cybersecurity offered by a University of Maryland campus. Sunday newspapers are filled with details on certificate programs in the latest hot job fields, such as social media and sustainability. Anyone checking e-mail on Google will see ads pop up for the creative writing program at Southern New Hampshire University or the political management degree at George Washington University.

Colleges have adopted the selling techniques used in marketing toothpaste, movies, and cars. Universities have doled out big dollars in recent years to develop branding campaigns, pitching their wares to potential students. American University paid $675,000 in an effort to brand itself as Home of the American Wonk. When it became a university, Loyola College of Maryland spent nearly a million dollars on its marketing campaign. And Boston University invested some $500,000 to brand its image from a local and regional school to a world-class research university.

While marketers say the primary purpose of these campaigns, and the uptick in advertising in general, is to differentiate academic programs and colleges from competitors, these promotions have produced a beneficial byproduct: an almost insatiable demand for college credentials. Last decade saw a surge in the number of students enrolled at every level of higher education — undergraduate, graduate, and professional schools. Today, more than 18 million students attend two- and four-year colleges, and another 2.9 million are pursuing graduate degrees or are enrolled in law, medical, or business schools. In all, the number of students in higher education is up by more than a third since the late 1990s.

The demand for degrees in the last decade was driven partly by a boom in the number of college-age Americans. But the real boost was the race for more and more credentials by those looking to gain any edge in a competitive job market. For the unemployed or those stuck in dead-end jobs, the constant barrage of advertisements by colleges seems to offer a way to stand out in a pile of job applications. The bachelor's degree, *the* symbol of success and *the* ticket to the middle class for the post–World War II generations, has slowly become the new high-school diploma. The number of people with college degrees holding jobs has swelled, even in professions not requiring them. By 2008, more than one in five clerical and sales workers had a college degree. Ten percent of service workers had one, as did one in twenty laborers.[4]

Colleges pounced on the demand by creating a bevy of new majors. In 2010, when the US Education Department updated its list of academic programs used in various higher-education surveys, more than three hundred majors were added to a list of 1,400 from a decade earlier. A third of the new programs were in just two fields: health professions and military technologies/applied sciences. Other fast-growing fields include biology/biological sciences and foreign languages/linguistics, perhaps a response to the September 11, 2001, terrorist attacks. The 1990s saw similar growth in the number of majors. Indeed, nearly four in ten majors on today's government list didn't exist in 1990.

You'd recognize many of these new majors just by glancing at the list of undergraduate programs at almost any college these days. Take Lasell College, a 1,600-student campus outside of Boston. Besides the usual history, English, and sociology majors, it also offers bachelor's degrees in athletic training, sports management, and graphic design. Jim Ostrow, vice president for academic affairs at Lasell, admits that the programs are vocational in name and were created largely in response to the career focus of today's parents and students who are paying more than $100,000 for four years of tuition. They want a practical return on their investment. "I don't think there is anything more vocational about a degree in sports management than there is a degree in English," Ostrow says. "We're not sacrificing the arts and sciences core that emphasizes writing, oral presentations, and critical thinking. That's important for an educated public and it's what employers want."

The massive proliferation of majors seems extraordinary, even for an economy transformed by the Internet and technology. The workforce is filled with people who didn't major in sports management, video-game design, or entrepreneurship, or earn advanced degrees in their field. Why are such credentials needed now?

The most common answer is that colleges created the new majors in response to employers who want graduates with more specific and technical skills. Anthony Carnevale, a labor economist, argues that in the past, people could choose a specific industry and move through many jobs, from the mailroom to management, to the CEO's office. Business history is filled with stories like those of Jack Welch or Bob Iger, who both started at the bottom in their companies (GE and Walt Disney, respectively) and went on to become CEOs. These days the detailed knowledge required for any job within a company is so extensive, Carnevale maintains, that people choose an occupation and now move through different industries. "We work in occupation silos," says Carnevale, who is also the director of the Center on Education and the Workforce at Georgetown University. "Once you're in that silo, it's almost impossible to move across to a different one without getting an education in that occupation."

Of course, tailoring majors for employers assumes they always know what they want in graduates and that colleges can quickly respond to those needs. Neither is the case in my experience. Another, more skeptical viewpoint, is that colleges need new degree programs to attract more students and distinguish themselves from competitors down the street, just as brands need to release new products to juice demand (think the iPod, the Gillette Fusion razor, or new car models). "This is all about a quest for more revenue," argues Richard Vedder, an economics professor at Ohio University and director of the Center for College

Affordability and Productivity. "It isn't Harvard, Yale, or Princeton creating these programs. You'll find a large percentage of them at schools desperate for revenues."

Vedder is a frequent critic of how colleges operate and he served on a federal commission during President George W. Bush's second term that studied the future of higher education. A few days after I talked with Vedder, an ad in the local newspaper grabbed my attention: "Your Ideas? Our Program. Wanted: Thinkers, Doers, Creators, Entrepreneurs, Intrapreneurs. Apply now: MA in Media Entrepreneurship. 20 month executive program. Saturdays and weeknights." This program at American University is a perfect example of a new product designed to drive demand for a communications degree at a time when jobs in the field are hard to come by. But how do you learn entrepreneurship when a big part of it is risk taking, an innate quality? How do you teach media entrepreneurship when even astute media watchers can't predict the digital future of the industry?

I went to an information session at American to get a sense of the prospective students and the kinds of questions they are asking. This open house is for master's programs in communications, and about two dozen would-be students show up on a sunny May morning for the spiel about the degrees. We're eventually split into smaller groups by program, and seven of us head downstairs to a classroom to hear more about the new Media Entrepreneurship degree. Amy Eisman, one of the program's architects, tells us that the university's board of trustees signed off on the degree a few months earlier, after two years of planning and various other approvals. It's one of only two in the country. "We've had great interest so far," she says. Then we go around the room and introduce ourselves. Most of the prospective students seem to be in their late twenties and early thirties. Many hold jobs but are looking for additional skills to help them stand out and get ahead. Almost all of them have a business start-up idea that they hope the program can help them develop.

Eisman walks through the ten courses needed for the degree, a mix of business-school and communications classes taken on nights and weekends over twenty months. The last course, she explains, is a capstone course in which students present a project or proposal to a "panel of potential investors and industry leaders." She's careful to point out that the "potential investors" are not there to actually invest. Just in case these students think the program is their best shot to win cash for their business ideas, it's not *American Idol*. Next it's time for questions, and many concern the courses. Some want to take business courses or other communications classes than those listed. They want an à la carte menu to personalize their education around their needs. This is 2012, after all—we can buy single songs on iTunes. These prospective students would probably be better off taking a few business or law courses or maybe investing the tuition dollars in their idea, but then they wouldn't have the credential. After forty-five minutes of questions, no one has asked about the price. So I flip through the various papers and brochures they provided, finally coming across the one I need. Tuition is listed per credit hour, but a quick calculation yields the bottom-line number: $41,970. A list of fees follows, easily pushing the total price over the $42,000 mark.

These prospective students are not alone in their hunt for a master's degree—the fastest-growing credential in higher education. In 2009, about 693,000 were awarded, a number that has doubled since the 1980s. The number of people with a master's degree is now about equal to those with at least a bachelor's degree in 1960. Just as the bachelor's degree has become the new high-school diploma, the master's degree is turning into the new bachelor's degree, and it's probably only a matter of time before the doctorate is the new master's degree. It's called credential creep or credential inflation, and it's rampant in almost every career field. In today's economy, another degree is sometimes necessary. In many cases, though, a few courses might be all that's needed. But because a full-fledged degree is the only signal to the job market that an employee is ready, it's the path many are forced to take. Call it the tyranny of the degree.

Probably the best illustration of credential inflation is in health care, where nearly every job requires more credentials than were needed twenty or thirty years ago. For decades, a bachelor's degree was sufficient to become a pharmacist, a physical therapist, or a nurse practitioner. Now a doctorate has replaced the bachelor's as the minimum a pharmacist needs to practice. And in the coming years, physical therapists and nurse practitioners will need the same credential—despite little evidence that additional education results in better care for patients.

Colleges aren't the only ones profiting from credential creep. As states try to fill gaps in their budgets, they have turned to collecting increased fees by requiring that more professionals, from interior designers to athletic trainers, get a license. Many states require applicants to take courses or get a credential just to sit for a licensure exam. Often you can take the exam only if you attended an accredited program, a requirement put into place in many states after lobbying by professional associations — the same groups that make money by accrediting specific academic programs at colleges.

Accreditation in higher education is an arcane subject, but students and parents need to understand the differences between the two types of accreditation: regional and specialized. Regional accreditors deal with the entire institution and give it a stamp of approval every decade. Without regional accreditation, a college will cease to exist because its students are not eligible to receive federal grants and loans. The specialized accreditors look at specific subjects from teacher education to landscape architecture to business schools. This type of accreditation is particularly problematic because it's not required and doesn't help students find high-quality programs, yet it adds to the cost of college.

As the number of majors has increased, so have the specialized accreditors looking after them. There are some sixty-one different specialized accreditors now in higher education. Some colleges have actually made it a goal to apply for approval by as many of them as they can, even though the entrance fees for each one can run around $25,000.[5] And that fee doesn't include the cost of the changes often required by the accreditors, from the number of full-time faculty with doctorates to the condition of the facilities where the programs are housed. Paul LeBlanc, the president of Southern New Hampshire University, calculated that the cost of getting his business school accredited by the Association to Advance Collegiate Schools of Business would end up being more than $2 million annually. He decided it wasn't worth it.[6]

Few presidents are willing to follow LeBlanc's lead. They think accreditation bolsters the reputations of their schools and that students care about it. But accreditors protect higher education, not prospective students. While specialized accreditors might say they operate in the interest of the consumer, as membership organizations they are run by the very same people they are supposed to police. Few of them explain to the public why they took actions against a college or rejected its application. Yet colleges trumpet positive decisions from these accreditors.

One of my favorite examples of this accreditation phenomenon came in a recent press release from the Stevens Institute of Technology in New Jersey. The institute heralded the fact that it was "the only university in the tri-state area with PMI accreditation," a designation from the Project Management Institute (another vocational major that has grown in recent years). Stevens used the occasion to highlight the expansion of its project-management program with — what else? — another master's degree.

Keeping up with the Joneses

Higher education also suffers from mission creep. Every college has a mission about the students it aims to enroll and the public it wants to serve. But too many colleges, unhappy with their mission, aspire to move higher in the pecking order. Prestige in higher education is like profit is to corporations.[7]

In my fifteen years at the *Chronicle of Higher Education,* I've seen this horserace play out daily. Hundreds of college presidents have come through our Washington offices, accompanied by an army of public-relations staff, piles of slick brochures, and inch-thick strategic plans. The sales pitch would usually go something like this: We want to be in the top ten of (fill-in-the-blank) ranking and to achieve that goal, we plan on some combination of the following: Build a new medical school, start a cutting-edge academic program, capture more federal research dollars, lure star faculty, attract better students in places we never recruited before, and so on.

They are angling for news coverage of their grand ambitions so colleagues at other schools will know that so-and-so university is getting more exclusive. Free media coverage is enough for some colleges and universities, but others go further, creating advertising campaigns that tout their accomplishments. Texas Tech: "Becoming the next great National Research University." The University of North Texas: "Investing in 15 research clusters." Lehigh University: "Research Matters."

Every spring the print edition and Web site of *The Chronicle* is stuffed with more of this kind of advertising. Why? Because that's the time of year when influencing a key group of readers really matters. It's in April that college presidents, provosts, and admissions officers receive a survey from *U.S. News & World Report,* which asks them to rate institutions on a scale of one to five for the magazine's annual college rankings issue. The results from this survey count from 15 to 25 percent of a college's overall ranking in *U.S. News.* Some presidents believe that changing their brand perception among their counterparts is easier than improving the other measures that go into the rankings, such as student selectivity, faculty-student ratio, or financial resources.

The measures counted by *U.S. News* and other rankings drive colleges to focus obsessively on what the schools that scored above them are spending and whom they are accepting, instead of what students actually learn in the classroom. The effort by these colleges and universities to move up in the rankings is essentially a fool's errand. Count up the presidents who said over the years that they wanted to move into the top tier of some ranking, and you'll find fifty schools trying to fit into twenty spots. The truth is that the list of the best colleges and universities in the United States has remained virtually unchanged for the last century. In the case of the *U.S. News* rankings, the magazine's criteria works against public universities. In 1989, for example, five of the top twenty-five national universities were public. By 2011, only three were (Berkeley, UCLA, and Virginia). Every college able to significantly improve its rank during that time was private.[8]

The rankings game among colleges is pervasive and is not played just with prospective students. Another contest waged within higher education is to better yourself in the rankings of universities receiving the most federal research dollars. Number one on this list is Johns Hopkins University, which rakes in $1.58 billion a year in federal grants. Universities believe that ranking high on this list helps attract star faculty and even more research dollars.

The competition to move up in the research rankings has real costs to students and their families. It matters so much to some universities that they have spent tuition dollars to gain an advantage. Around a quarter of the top hundred universities on the list have doubled their own spending on research in the last decade. But get this: Nearly half of them ended up *falling* in the rankings. Among those that dropped the most: Stony Brook University, the University of Utah, and New Mexico State, which together spent an additional $157 million of their own money on research over the decade.[9]

A surefire way to grab more research dollars and boost a university's prestige is to build a medical school. More than a dozen medical schools opened in the last decade, after the number held steady for some twenty years. Nowhere has the growth spurt been bigger than in Florida. In the late 1990s, estimates showed that the state was going to face a deficit of some 200,000 doctors in the next twenty years. Medical experts suggested that the quickest and cheapest solution would be to increase enrollments at the existing medical schools and then add residency slots at local hospitals, a key part of a doctor's training.

But several university presidents and their local politicians had a different strategy. They saw the addition of a medical school to a university as both a legacy for them and a signal to the rest of higher education that they had arrived. So they first lobbied the state's higher-education board and then the legislature to create new medical schools. First up was Florida State University. When the higher-education board rejected its proposal for a new medical school, lawmakers overruled it and instead abolished the board. A few years later, two more aspiring universities, Florida International and Central Florida, persuaded a new state board and the legislature to build medical schools on their campuses — at a cost to taxpayers of $500 million over ten years. By the time those two schools welcomed their first classes, Florida was in the midst of a full-blown economic crisis brought on by the crash of its housing market. During the next three years, the state slashed financial support to its public colleges by 11 percent, resulting in higher tuition, fewer courses, and staff cuts. But Florida had its new medical schools — at an annual operating cost of $20 million each.[10]

While medical schools might be a pricey addition to a university on the move, a law school isn't. They don't require expensive lab facilities, and students can be stuffed into large lecture classes. Indeed, law schools add to both a university's status *and* its bottom line. They are so profitable that some pass on as much as 30 percent of their tuition revenues to other parts of the university, subsidizing money-losing departments, such as English or history. As a result, universities can't get enough of them. Despite a tough job market and a glut of lawyers in most states, law schools keep adding spots for students. Some 52,000 students enrolled in law school in 2010, the largest first-year law class in history (enrollments have since dropped). Meanwhile, the American Bar Association (ABA) has accredited eighteen new law schools in the last decade or so. Another half dozen are awaiting accreditation, are about to open, or are on the drawing board.[11]

The evidence university presidents or state politicians peddle to support their case for creating these law schools would probably get any actual lawyer thrown out of a courtroom. Take Texas as an example. Even as the cash-strapped legislature there was talking about closing four community colleges in 2011, they approved a new law school in downtown Dallas for the University of North Texas. A state report commissioned in advance of the report found that Texas already produces more lawyers than it has job openings. It also noted that building a new law school would cost nearly $55 million over five years, while expanding the current public law schools by the same number of students would cost $1.3 million. Still, university officials, backed by a group of powerful local politicians, prevailed with their argument: Dallas has two law schools, both private, and Houston, a smaller metro region, has three law schools, including a public option. A similar me-too argument was used by the University of Massachusetts when it won approval in 2009 to create the state's first public law school, after acquiring the Southern New England School of Law, a struggling private institution an hour south of Boston. The problem was that Southern New England twice failed to obtain accreditation from the ABA, a requirement for an institution's students to sit for the bar exam in forty-two states. It took more than three years after the merger and millions of state dollars in improvements for the new University of Massachusetts School of Law to receive provisional accreditation from the ABA.

Why are supposedly well-educated, reasonable-minded university leaders ignoring the evidence and pushing to add more academic programs, more schools, and more credentials? Bruce Henderson, a psychology professor at Western Carolina University, has been studying this phenomenon for twenty years among his type of school: former state teachers colleges that have made the leap in the last half century to become full-fledged universities with a wide array of master's and even doctoral programs. You know these schools — places like Central Michigan University, Eastern Kentucky University, and St. Cloud State University in Minnesota. They're often called regional public universities or comprehensive universities and have long been considered the undistinguished middle child of public higher education — squeezed on one side by flagship research universities, on the other by community colleges. While they educate the bulk of teachers in most states, that primary mission has been cast aside in recent decades as they added dozens of master's and PhD programs that soaked up money and personnel, hired faculty members who pushed for research opportunities, and pumped money from undergraduate programs into expensive graduate programs. The result? Institutions that look like lesser versions of their states' flagship universities, with much smaller endowments, low-quality programs, and poor graduation rates. What Henderson has found in his research is that everyone from the president on down through the faculty at these universities wants to re-create the schools where they trained as academics, yet they're not working with the same caliber of students. "We all got our doctorates at research universities, we learned how to behave there, and we wanted to teach at places where we could clone ourselves," said Henderson, who received his PhD from the University of Minnesota. "When I came to Western Carolina I was in shock. It took me a few years until I realized I could either adapt or sit here and be unhappy."

The price of trying to move up the food chain is not limited to schools trying to gain legitimacy in research. It affects all colleges, perhaps nowhere more than in their price. Aspirational schools are known to shower financial aid on accomplished students in the form of merit scholarships in an attempt to woo them away from better schools. That's good news if you have a strong academic record in high school. But it's bad news if you're a B student, especially if you have financial need. To pay for new merit scholarships, these schools have raised the overall sticker price of tuition for everyone to gain more money from those who could afford to pay and cut back on need-based aid to students who can't. This strategy has worked for a handful of colleges — George Washington, Boston, and New York Universities, namely — but at a terrible cost to some students who have taken on a tremendous amount of debt in order to enroll at these hot schools.

Even where the strategy hasn't worked, the shift in institutional dollars from need-based aid to merit aid continues. In the mid-1990s, both public and private colleges gave out twice as much need-based aid as merit aid, according to the United States Department of Education. Now, the proportion of students receiving merit aid from public and private colleges actually outnumbers those receiving need-based aid, and the average amount of merit aid from the school also exceeds the average need-based grant. You're probably thinking that financial aid should be based on merit — the thing is, it was always based on merit. Students had to get accepted to a school before they received aid, and they had to maintain a certain GPA once enrolled to keep it. The change now is that this merit aid goes disproportionately to students from upper-income families, who could afford to pay more of the cost of college and would go to college no matter what. All this in an effort to gain position for greater prestige.

The race for that ever-elusive prestige plays out all over campus. Professors, especially those hoping for tenure, increasingly devote more of their time to research, and, at bigger universities, their graduate students. Often this comes at the expense of undergraduates who are paying the bills that help subsidize graduate education. In a typical week, faculty members spend about eleven hours on advising, preparing for class, and in actual classroom time.[12] To attract academically talented students they wouldn't otherwise get, schools add pricey programs aimed at them — from honors colleges to enhanced study-abroad options. There is nothing wrong with a college or university growing and evolving their missions. But as with individuals who try to differentiate themselves by earning another credential, the vast majority of schools that try to stand out end up looking like everyone else trying to do the same thing.

Best in the World?

Whenever we talk about the education system in the United States, we seem to talk about the failures of K–12 education and the successes of higher education. Sure, we complain about how much college costs, but we have largely adopted the belief that American colleges and universities are the best in the world. I'm not quite sure how this status is determined, given that the United States now ranks twelfth in the percentage of twenty-five- to thirty-four-year-olds with postsecondary credentials among the seventeen countries in the Organisation for Economic Co-operation and Development. As recently as 1995, the United States ranked first.

Perhaps it's just a sign of the times. Modesty, it seems, is out of style. In a thought-provoking talk at the Washington Ideas Forum that I attended in the fall of 2011, *New York Times* columnist David Brooks maintained that we live in an era of "expanded conception of self." That attitude, he believes, results in the trends we have witnessed in recent years toward increased consumption, polarization, and risk. "We have moved from a culture of self-effacement to one of self-expansion," Brooks said.

The Brooks lecture was a fitting endnote to a spirited conversation I had earlier the same day at the forum with a dozen education, business, and think-tank leaders on the state of the American higher-education system. After two hours of talking, there was no more agreement on how to improve the system than when we had walked into the room. Indeed, the diversity of constituencies represented in the room couldn't even settle on what the system *should* be doing.

Higher education is feeling good about itself these days because it remains in demand. Why offer classes at more convenient times when you're getting a record number of applicants? Why hold the line on rising costs when students are willing to take on more debt? Why collect better job-placement data to provide to prospective students when they're still flocking to mediocre graduate programs? As Brian Kelly, the editor of the much-maligned rankings at *U.S. News,* put it that day, "colleges seem immune to the pressures facing every other sector of the economy."

But look underneath the facade that has been built in the last decade by adding more degree programs, more law and medical schools, and more research capacity, and you will begin to see a more sordid reality. What you witness are campuses where the students are customers first, classrooms are filled with adjunct professors who rush off to their next job after class, and students spend very little time engaged in studying or learning.

2

The Customer Is Always Right

THE DEAN OF BASIC SCIENCES at Louisiana State University had a problem. Students at the Baton Rouge campus had one week left to withdraw without penalty from a large intro biology course for nonscience majors, and 60 percent of them were failing. Not one student had earned an A so far. Another 20 percent had already dropped out. The dean decided to take an extraordinary step. He removed the professor, Dominique Homberger, from the course. He said later that if every course at the university had the dropout rate of Homberger's, the university would never graduate any students. The dean told the tenured professor, who had taught at LSU since 1979, that he was acting in the "best interest of the students." The new professor for the course retroactively gave each student a twenty-five-point bump on their first exam.[1]

The Homberger case at LSU in the spring of 2010 set off alarm bells on campuses nationwide. For many faculty members it was yet another example of deteriorating standards, grade inflation, and — perhaps most of all — their diminishing power in the classroom, where students increasingly are gaining the upper hand. For others, LSU's decision was one more sign that the era of rigor on campuses is coming to an end. Out are the days of professors telling students on the first day of class to look at the person on their left, then their right, and know that only one of them would still be there at graduation. Now professors know that students expect convenience, ease, and entertainment.

Colleges are turning into businesses where customers — in this case, students — expect to be satisfied. They have come to regard their professors as service providers, just like a cashier at the supermarket or a waiter in a restaurant. This way of thinking represents a major power shift in the classroom from professors to the students. This shift results from four key developments in higher education during the Lost Decade:

Rising Prices. Annual tuition increases outpaced inflation during that decade, as sticker prices skyrocketed 68 percent at public four-year colleges and 39 percent at private colleges. In 2003, only two colleges charged more than $40,000 for tuition, fees, room, and board. By 2009, 224 had crossed that mark, and another fifty-eight passed the $50,000 plateau. While most students received discounts on those rates in the form of scholarships and grants, the rising prices have forced families to realize that college is a major purchase and investment — not just a rite of passage. As a result, once students are on campus, they put a price tag on everything, including the classroom experience.

Part-time Professors. The Hollywood image of the college professor dressed in a tweed jacket and hanging out with students after class is as outdated as the jacket itself. About half of all professors at four-year colleges teach part-time as adjuncts (and the number is even higher at community colleges). Some adjuncts are working professionals who want to teach on the side and earn a little extra cash (and I mean a little, about $2,500 per class at many colleges). Many adjuncts, however, have a PhD and would like full-time academic jobs with tenure. In a bid to save money and increase their flexibility in a changing economy, colleges are hiring fewer full-time faculty and more and more adjuncts. Adjuncts, hired semester by semester, depend on positive student evaluations at the end of the term to get their contracts renewed. One way to ensure a good evaluation is to be an easy grader.

Revolving Door. Institutions began focusing on keeping students in school and moving them through quickly. The number of students who return for their sophomore year and the number who eventually don a cap and gown are important metrics in the *U.S. News* rankings.

As a result, colleges pay much more attention to improving those figures. To do this, they look to attract better students in the first place, or carefully track how students are doing in classes. College leaders are not the only ones paying attention. State lawmakers are, too, and in Louisiana, Ohio, Tennessee, and several other states, they reward public colleges that graduated a higher percentage of their students.

The Millennials. The generation of Americans born after 1982 started college at the beginning of the Lost Decade. This group is often referred to as the "Me Generation" because they are considered to be most concerned with putting their own needs first.

The classroom has become one giant game of favor exchanges between students, professors, and administrators. When they each play their parts, everyone comes out a winner. Students receive better grades, adjuncts keep their job year after year, full-time professors win tenure or have to spend less time dealing with students complaining about bad grades, and administrators are rewarded with more money and higher rankings. Stephen Hampe, an adjunct professor who has taught psychology at Utica College and several City University of New York and State University of New York campuses, said that course evaluations now look eerily similar to customer satisfaction surveys from department stores. They ask questions such as "Did the instructor meet your needs?" and "Was the information presented in a style you found useful?" And students often include comments about how enjoyable the material was or how fun the course was, but they say little about how much they learned or the challenges of the course. "When I was a student in the 1980s," Hampe said, "the concern was whether the instructor served the class as a whole. Today, every student has come to expect personalized service."

As students have come to think of themselves as customers who need to be satisfied, they have begun to view the professor at the front of the room as a performer. Much like when they go to a concert or a movie, they want to be engaged, persuaded, and entertained. The expectation of professor as performer has only increased as more distractions make their way into the classroom. In the past, students had few alternatives beyond reading a newspaper and sleeping in class. Now they come armed with electronic devices, all connected to the outside world thanks to the campus wireless network. The *Harvard Crimson,* the student newspaper at Harvard University, has coined a term to measure how interesting a professor is — "the Facebook index." Students at Harvard told the newspaper that they turn to browsing Facebook or the Internet in class when the professor repeats what is in the textbook or goes off on a tangent that isn't interesting or relevant. And this is at what is supposedly the best university in the United States. A writer for the *Crimson* argued that if Harvard (or any school, for that matter) didn't respond to this competition for student attention, it risked making the educational experience irrelevant. "Professors need to start thinking of themselves as service providers who must constantly innovate to serve students better, servicing students' curiosity and their desire to apply knowledge to create impact."[2]

Is that an unrealistic expectation? Most students and their parents probably don't think so, but many professors do. Siva Vaidhyanathan, a media-studies professor at the University of Virginia who speaks and writes frequently about higher education, told me that he doesn't "owe the student a special level of performance because a student paid the bill." He thinks that academe is one place that should be insulated from the demands of the marketplace.

For one thing, professors face unique challenges in the classroom. Some are best in front of 300 students in a lecture hall; others are at the top of their game with a dozen students around a table. Yet many institutions require professors to perform in both arenas. Some are only as good as the appeal of their material. It's easy to make media studies interesting, less so math. Vaidhyanathan is a regular on the speakers' circuit as author of *The Googlization of Everything (and Why We Should Worry).* I asked him if those audiences should have expectations of him that might seem unreasonable for his students in class to have. "Yes," he said. "I have a very different relationship with them. I don't have a responsibility to take them through a checklist on a syllabus. I don't have to cover a certain amount of material. And I don't have to grade them."

No matter, students are increasingly rating professors. Using consumer-friendly Web sites like RateMyProfessors, students grade instructors on a scale of one to five on everything from easiness to clarity (or a chili pepper if they're "hot"), in the same way they give ratings and reviews on a recent hotel stay on TripAdvisor. Instructors who are hard graders typically don't score high on RateMyProfessors, said Reiko Goodwin, an anthropology professor at Fordham University. "Generally speaking, 95 percent of the students only care about the grades," the twenty-year veteran said. "They do not seem to be interested in gaining knowledge."

The early adopters of the customer philosophy in higher education were for-profit colleges. Led by the likes of the University of Phoenix, the for-profits touted convenience first (evening classes in office parks near major interstates), and watched as their enrollments shot up. Today, one in ten college students is enrolled in a for-profit college, such as DeVry University, Everest College, and Grand Canyon University.

While the for-profits operate in different ways, they often share common business strategies. They employ mostly adjuncts, who teach from a curriculum planned at corporate headquarters by a small group of faculty members. They have virtually no campuses; only classrooms in office buildings. They hold classes year round and enroll students on an almost monthly basis (not just in the fall, spring, or summer). They compress classes into a short time period (so students can navigate around work schedules) or have students meet on their own and count it toward class time. And they have built robust online operations, which collect and analyze millions of pieces of data about students' online behavior to personalize how they are taught.

Because for-profits serve mostly working adults, they pitch convenience and flexibility in their advertisements. Bottom line: You can juggle multiple demands. Professors at traditional colleges say this mindset has seeped into their classrooms as well. "The expectations about how much work or how much rigor or how much time is largely influenced by the marketing of schools that tell students they can do it all, but never actually talk about the work they will need to do," said Lance Eaton, an adjunct who has taught some ninety courses at five different colleges in the Boston area. As traditional colleges look for new ways to save money or take advantage of online learning, they are increasingly taking pages from the for-profits' playbook. The convergence between the two models may accelerate in the future, especially as students come to campus with greater expectations of how technology can personalize their education (as I will explain in a later chapter).

Where Everyone Deserves an A

Perhaps college has always been an extended vacation, and today's parents just like to tell tales of the all-nighters they regularly pulled to prepare for that big exam. What is more probable, however, is that the heightened focus on the student as customer is leading to a systematic dumbing down of college campuses. The evidence, from grades to achievement tests to graduation rates, is pretty damning — students are skating through college, if they make it through at all.

"Students tell me that they *deserve* an A because they did all their assignments," said Deborah Louis, an adjunct professor at Eastern Kentucky University, repeating a refrain I hear frequently from professors. The A is now the most common mark given out on college campuses nationwide, accounting for 43 percent of all grades. (In 1988, the A represented less than one-third of all grades.)[3] With little sense of what to make of grades anymore, graduate schools and employers have stopped using them as the leading indicator of success. Even within schools, there is little consensus on what a particular grade means. How two students perform taking the same course with different professors really depends on the luck of the draw. An analysis of some large lecture courses at LSU in the wake of the Homberger case found that in American History, for example, one professor gave A's to fewer than 5 percent of his students, while a colleague awarded them to 30 percent of his.[4] But this grade inflation is not limited to less prestigious schools. Indeed, studies have found that grade inflation has existed at high-end schools for several decades (and is most prevalent at private schools in general). Back in 2001, the *Boston Globe* reported that a whopping 91 percent of the graduating class at Harvard that year had received honors.[5] That's like everyone getting a trophy just for showing up.

Perhaps students are getting smarter? Not so, say the results of various standardized tests over the past several decades. Perhaps students are working harder and, as a result, getting better grades? In fact, college students say they're actually working a lot *less* and still getting better grades. The problem is that while the price of a degree is increasing, the amount of learning needed to get that piece of paper is moving in the opposite direction. We don't know for sure how much students learn in college. As much as we spend on higher education, no bottom-line evaluation method exists for measuring what actually happens in the classroom and how that eventually translates into the value of the degree. Think about it: Before we buy a car, we can find various measures on everything from gas mileage to results of safety tests. We can turn to objective sources to check comparisons of similar vehicles and see which cars hold their value over time. But when it comes to potentially one of the most expensive purchases in a lifetime, the attitude from colleges has always been that we should just trust them on the quality of their product.

Faith in that assurance is flagging. There are now ways to measure learning, chief among them the Collegiate Learning Assessment. Known as the CLA, the essay-only test gives students a set of materials and asks them to synthesize evidence and write a persuasive argument. More than five hundred colleges use the exam to measure their curriculum and teaching, although few release the results, or even averages, publicly. Maybe there are reasons they don't want the public to know the truth. A few years ago, two researchers tracked a representative sample of 2,300 students at twenty-four colleges and universities who took the CLA three times in their college careers: at the beginning of their freshman year, at the end of their sophomore year, and finally, before graduation. The findings of this groundbreaking study resulted in the 2011 book *Academically Adrift,* which received plenty of attention in faculty lounges on campuses but, given its roots as an academic research study, didn't receive as much attention as it should have among the general public.[6]

Most in higher education probably preferred it that way. The book's bottom line: 45 percent of students in the study made no gains in their writing, complex reasoning, or critical-thinking skills during their first two years of college. After four years, the news wasn't much better: 36 percent failed to show any improvement. "American higher education is characterized by limited or no learning for a large proportion of students," wrote the authors, Richard Arum and Josipa Roksa. For many undergraduates, "drifting through college without a clear sense of purpose is readily apparent."

The main reason for this, the researchers found, was a lack of rigor. Through surveys they learned that students spent about twelve hours a week studying on average, much of that time in groups. Most didn't take courses that required them to read more than forty pages a week or write more than twenty pages over the course of an entire semester. Students who studied alone did better, as did students whose teachers had high expectations or assigned a significant amount of reading or writing. Those who majored in the humanities, social sciences, hard sciences, and math did the best. And the majors that did the worst? Education, social work, and the most popular major on US college campuses: business.

To determine how these students fared after college, the authors later resurveyed more than nine hundred of them after graduation. Not surprisingly, the students who scored the lowest on the CLA also struggled in life after college. They were three times more likely than those scoring at the top to be unemployed, twice as likely to be living at home with parents, more likely to have run up credit card bills, and less likely to read the news or discuss politics.[7] "You can't assume that in sending off a student to a typical college that they're going to get a rigorous education," said Arum, a father of four teenagers ready to go off to college. "You can't trust these institutions to police themselves."

Why Does College Cost So Much?

If students are graduating from college having learned little, what are they paying for? If college is nothing more than a long break before adulthood, why does it cost so much?

I get asked these questions all the time. I often turn to Jane Wellman, a self-described data geek whose tiny Delta Project produces the best reports detailing where colleges get their money and how they spend it. In 2011, when President Obama was considering what efforts the federal government should undertake to promote college affordability, he called ten college presidents, the head of a prominent education foundation, and Wellman to the White House. Wellman sat across from the president in the Roosevelt Room that day and helped frame the conversation on the thorny questions surrounding rising tuition prices.

The Delta Project, named for the mathematical symbol for change, opened shop in 2006. Wellman's research has busted plenty of myths about college costs (don't blame faculty salaries and tenure, for instance) and has shown that public institutions, particularly community colleges, have been hurt the most by state governments slashing budgets for higher education. In 2012, I appeared with Wellman at a conference in California on the future of higher education in the Golden State just before she was about to move on to a new job in higher education. I asked her what she had learned in her six years at the Delta Project about why college is so expensive.

Wellman was blunt and had a stack of PowerPoint slides ready to back up any point she made. I was just beginning the research for this book, and after fifteen years of covering this topic thought I knew it all. But Wellman made me quickly realize that I'm no different than many parents, students, politicians, and even college professors and administrators in my assumptions about what is driving tuition higher. Wellman's research illustrates that we're not always paying for what we think we are.[8]

Employee Benefits. About 40 percent of payroll costs are eaten up by employee benefits, and most of that goes to health insurance. Put another way, about a dime in every tuition dollar coming in the door is going back out in health care benefits.

Support Staff. Not only are health care costs absorbing tuition dollars, but many of those dollars go to people who will never step into a classroom. "Our campus has spent two decades hiring people to solve problems or deliver new solutions," said Frank Yeary, a vice chancellor at the University of California at Berkeley. "We threw people at problems, rather than technology." Ask college presidents why their institutions cost so much and they will talk about the need to pay highly skilled, highly educated professors. But the fact is that on many four-year campuses, faculty make up less than half of all employees, and, over the Lost Decade, spending on student services, administration, and maintenance increased much faster than spending on instruction. At the biggest public research universities spending on student services went up 19 percent, administration 15 percent, and operations and maintenance 20 percent. On instruction? Just 10 percent. "We don't need as many procurement, IT, or payroll offices as we have now," Wellman said. That's exactly what big public campuses like Berkeley and the University of North Carolina at Chapel Hill discovered when they called in Bain & Company to review their business operations in recent years. At both schools, Bain identified more than $100 million in annual savings, mostly in nonacademic areas.

Amenities and Personalized Attention. The climbing wall has become the poster child in the debate over rising college costs. It's the one feature critics seem to point to when talking about the student recreational centers constructed over the Lost Decade (more on this in a bit). The most absurd frill is the Lazy River, essentially a theme park water ride where students float on rafts. The University of Alabama has one. So does Boston University. Texas Tech University boasts on its Web site that its "student leisure pool" is the "crown jewel," representing "the largest leisure pool on a college campus in the United States. With a 645 foot long lazy river as the center piece of the design." At private colleges during the Lost Decade, spending on student services rose anywhere from 25 to 33 percent. By the end of the decade, private research universities were spending almost $3,400 per full-time student on services such as intramural sports, career services, student organizations, and counseling. Indeed, as students have come to expect a personalized experience, schools have added hosts of advisers to help them. Such positions now make up nearly a third of professional jobs on campuses, and more than three times the number of administrative positions.[9] Besides costing a great deal, these professionals hired to help students actually cheat them out of chances to learn through their own problem solving.

It costs so much because it can. For much of the Lost Decade, there was huge demand for higher education. The basic laws of business tell us that when demand outstrips supply, prices go up. At least until recently, students and parents have been willing to pay *any* price to go to *any* college.

College budgets are incredibly complex and make it nearly impossible to follow the money. How much do colleges spend on marketing and advertising? That's a metric most Fortune 500 companies can provide in a minute. Not so in higher education. "Good luck in getting that number," Elizabeth Scarborough said. Scarborough is a guru of higher-education marketing and chief executive of SimpsonScarborough, a branding firm. A college's marketing budget is often spread across campus, she explained, in admissions, fundraising, and athletics. It's not a line item in the budget.

That lack of transparency is the primary reason the public doesn't trust colleges to spend tuition dollars wisely. It's difficult to track money because a college campus is like one big trading floor. Money is constantly moving from parts of the operation that make money to subsidize those segments that lose money. For instance, colleges make a profit on large lecture courses because they squeeze hundreds of students paying a flat tuition rate into a classroom with one faculty member and a few teaching assistants. The excess revenue from that class helps cover the additional costs that come with offering small seminars to seniors or lab courses to science majors. "The reality is that English has been subsidizing chemistry as long as there has been chemistry," Wellman said.

Some colleges charge more than their real costs for room and board and funnel that surplus to other operations. And then there's tuition discounting. That's the practice of setting a high tuition price and then giving a percentage of it back as student aid. The practice of tuition discounting is the reason going to college is like traveling on an airplane. You have no idea how much the student sitting next to you is paying, although there's supposedly one sticker price for everyone. Wellman has figured that most of the increase in tuition prices at private colleges since the Great Recession has gone to pay for discounts. The *average* discount for first-year students at private colleges is now a staggering 42 percent. That's quite a sale for financially needy students or those highly sought by the college (academic superstars, athletes, tuba players), and paid for by those wealthy enough to cover full freight although they get nothing extra for paying so much more.

What's more, the annual financial figures that colleges report to the federal government don't quite capture what's being spent and where. Take the category of instruction as one example. You would think that money for instruction is what is spent on academics overall. The figure is dominated by faculty salaries, but doesn't include what schools channel to advising students. And the numbers provided to the government are never audited, making it impossible to know how often schools make simple errors or outright fudge the numbers. In my experience, schools seem to frequently discover problems with their data only when they are highlighted in some major report or in the news media. Over a ten-year period, George Mason University, for instance, appeared to experience an eye-popping surge in the number of administrators and professional staff—a 121 percent growth in the ratio between staff members and students. After this figure appeared in the news media, university officials were quick to correct the number with the Department of Education. The university had discovered that when it switched to a new computer system some employees were inadvertently classified incorrectly. Such incidents make me wonder how many other numbers are just plain wrong.

The Resort Campus

Perhaps the ultimate sign that higher education is now in the business of pleasing the customer can be seen simply by walking around any campus these days. The traditional college campus has always been a place of beauty. The father of American landscape architecture, Frederick Law Olmsted, once said that a well-designed campus helps to shape the tastes, inclinations, and habits of students. But I doubt that Olmsted ever imagined that college campuses would evolve into the resorts they are today.

As recently as the early 1990s, when I was a freshman in college, dorm rooms were as sterile as those in a hospital, a 193-square-foot box with white cinderblock walls that, in my case, I shared with two other guys. The bathroom was also shared—with an entire floor. By the time I was a sophomore, I had moved to a newly constructed dorm. I still had a roommate and the walls were still cinderblock, but the room did come with one luxury: a private bathroom.

That was just before colleges began a decade-long amenities arms race to build more luxurious and outlandish facilities that had nothing to do with classroom education. Their goal was to keep up with the Joneses, their competitors across town or in other states, and, as college presidents tell the story, to meet the demands of a new generation of parents and students. This climbing-wall era coincided with the arrival of the Millennials on campus, many of whom never had to share a bedroom with a sibling or a bathroom with their parents. Why should they have to do so when they go off to college?

Colleges responded by constructing new campus housing. The *dorms* of the past were replaced by *residence halls*, often with multiroom suites shared by a few students, some with private bedrooms and bathrooms as part of the deal. The old-style dorms still exist on many campuses with some upgrades, but new buildings have sprouted up everywhere from regional public colleges to wealthy urban private institutions, like Boston University. Indiana University of Pennsylvania replaced all of its student housing in recent years at a cost of $270 million. The new suites include wireless Internet, microwaves, refrigerators, and carpeting. "It is essential to provide students with a living environment that meets their needs and interests," said Rhonda H. Luckey, vice president for student affairs.[10] Boston University built a twenty-six-story glass-and-steel tower near the banks of the Charles River with walk-in closets and floor-length mirrors, so nice that the *Boston Globe* reported "parents' jaws dropped in disbelief" when their children moved in. "Students want beauty, and they should have beauty," said Kenneth Elmore, the university's dean of students.[11]

Of course, the amenities arms race didn't stop with new residence halls. During the last decade, cranes and construction workers filled campuses as student unions, dining halls, recreational centers, and performing arts spaces were erected almost as quickly as they were designed. Gettysburg College spent $27 million on a 55,000-square-foot recreational center with a bouldering area. Drexel University devoted $45 million to an 84,000-square-foot recreation center, complete with a walking and jogging track. The University of Memphis paid $50 million for a 169,000-square-foot campus center that houses a theater, food court, and a twenty-four-hour computer lab. And California State University at Northridge spent ten years planning a $125 million performing-arts center that opened in 2011.[12]

To show off these new attractions to prospective students and their parents, colleges remade the campus tour. Admissions officers have long called the tour the "golden mile" or the "million-dollar walk" because few things matter as much in where a student eventually ends up as the campus visit. As a result, schools have increasingly tried to sell an experience on the tour rather than simply convey information, which is often easier to do on the Web anyway.[13] Consultants who go undercover charge thousands of dollars to point out what is wrong—from walking backward (slows down the tour) to showing nondescript buildings that every campus has (like the library)—and help colleges overhaul their tours. The best known of these consultants, Jeff Kallay, took his experiences from visiting Disney World dozens of times and applied them to the campus tour. His company, TargetX, has worked with nearly 200 schools, including Hendrix College (students and their parents now get a personalized pamphlet and itinerary), American University (guests are given passes that identify them as VIPs), and York College of Pennsylvania (guides introduce faculty members they pass on tours).

Students and parents remain willing customers, Jane Wellman said, "happy to have their tuitions raised for better dorms, high-speed Internet, and better food." There's no pressure on colleges to declare a truce. Even so, if Harvard replaced all of its dorms with rooms that were comparable to a jail cell, I doubt students would refuse to go there. In the end, the quality of the academics is what matters.

When a *New York Times* reporter asked the director of campus recreation at the University of Houston, Kathy Anzivino, if she could ever imagine some "pinnacle of amenities that universities simply cannot surpass, some outer limit so far beyond the hot tubs, waterfalls, and pool slides," she couldn't picture any. "There's got to be one, but what it is, I don't know," she told the newspaper.[14]

Maybe that's because no outer limit exists, at least not yet. If you don't believe me, there is a campus in North Carolina you really should see. To say that High Point University is unlike any school I have ever visited is an understatement. For one, the campus tour is by golf cart. When you start the tour, faint sounds of classical music are piped in from hidden outdoor speakers as you pass life-size statues of Galileo, Jefferson, and Aristotle. The stunned looks on the faces of parents and students continue at almost every turn: There's a first-run movie theater, a steakhouse, outdoor hot tubs, and free food all over campus, including a roaming ice cream truck (part of the $39,800 list price). The university has perhaps the only director of WOW in the country, whose job it is to please current and prospective students and, of course, to oversee the concierge desk. Yes, this really is a college, not a Ritz-Carlton. At the concierge desk, students can get restaurant recommendations, send out dry cleaning, and drop off library books. All this is the vision of Nido Qubein, a motivational speaker and multimillionaire, who became president in 2005. Since then, he has spent an astonishing $700 million to refurbish and expand the campus. Even more is planned: new dorms, a health sciences school, a college of pharmacy, and a sports arena. The total price tag for those improvements is expected to reach $2.1 billion by 2020. Moody's Investors Service has downgraded the university's debt rating to junk status and calls it one of the most highly leveraged universities in the country. The over-the-top services for students have resulted in plenty of free publicity for the university, although not all of it welcomed by High Point leaders. A *BusinessWeek* profile of High Point in 2012 questioned how the school can avoid "financial calamity" given its debt, more than $165 million (the school only has $105 million in revenues a year). The headline that accompanied the piece summed it up well: "Bubble U."

High Point undoubtedly occupies an extreme position in the amenities race, but it's not alone in facing a mountain of IOUs for its ambitions. The colleges most heavily engaged in improvements over the Lost Decade didn't pay for them out of their endowments or through private donations. They borrowed money, often stretching themselves beyond their limits, hoping their plans would someday pay off and that the current financial model of higher education would continue forever. Both trustees and presidents thought, "build it and they will come." Meanwhile, the debt taken on by colleges has nearly doubled since 2000 — to more than $300 billion. While these extravagant facilities made college leaders as ecstatic as a toddler showing off a shiny new toy on Christmas and gave students a taste of the high life, few paid much attention to the real cost in terms of borrowed dollars. Even less notice was paid to the unintended consequences of these amenities on what students actually learn. The climbing walls, food courts, and movie theaters offer plenty of alternatives to studying.

I'm not arguing that college shouldn't be fun. But college students spend very little of their time on academics, which is the reason, after all, they are there in the first place. The students in the *Academically Adrift* survey reported spending on average twenty-six hours a week attending classes, labs, and studying. More than half of their time, an estimated eighty-six hours a week, was spent on socializing and recreation, distractions the colleges readily provided. Predictably, the researchers found that the more time students spent in activities outside the classroom, including work, the smaller their gains on the Collegiate Learning Assessment test. Most worrisome is the fact that students who can least afford college are most harmed by the partying that pulls down grades — and tend to lack a post-graduation safety net. In a study of fifty-three freshmen women at Indiana University, Elizabeth Armstrong, a sociologist from the University of Michigan, found that affluent students typically can draw on family resources after college to make up for their weak academic records as undergraduates.[15]

More than anything, the customer-is-always-right mentality has fostered a sense of entitlement among college students. High Point might be the only college with a concierge desk, but with a plethora of professional counselors and advisers at their disposal, students everywhere expect to have their problems solved by someone else. The luxury accommodations not only add to the sense of entitlement, but offer few opportunities for students to learn how to get along with different people and manage conflicts. That's a skill previous generations quickly acquired when randomly matched to live with people in close and communal quarters. Now, many colleges allow students to match themselves using sophisticated social networking tools.

Colleges are not only graduating a generation of students less prepared for the rigors of the world, but like the institutions themselves, they will be saddled with debt.

3

The Trillion-Dollar Problem

WHEN KELSEY GRIFFITH first visited Ohio Northern University as a high school senior she was immediately sold on the campus. The private university, affiliated with the United Methodist Church, with 3,600 students was just the right size and provided the marketing courses and vibrant sorority life the peppy eighteen-year-old was seeking. For Griffith, attending Ohio Northern would mark the beginning of the road out of her rural hometown of Ottawa, about thirty minutes away in northwest Ohio.

Griffith came from a modest background. She was one of five girls. Her father was a paramedic. Her mother was a preschool teacher. Tuition and fees at Ohio Northern — some $30,000 at the time — were a bit steep and probably would have scared her away if not for the university's admissions materials and pitches that frequently reminded her to "get over the sticker shock."

"I was really stubborn," Griffith recalled. "I wasn't going to let anyone tell me I couldn't go because my parents didn't make a lot of money."

The fact is that someone along the way — perhaps even the university itself — should have told her she simply could not afford an Ohio Northern degree. But by the time her financial-aid offer arrived in the spring of her senior year, she had made her decision. She barely noticed that the package was top-heavy with student loans. When she met with financial-aid counselors at the school, they focused on the benefits of attending a private college rather than outlining the monthly payments she would face after graduation.

Year after year, her financial-aid package was filled with loans, and not until her last year did the school increase her scholarship so she wouldn't have to take on even more debt. By the time she graduated in May 2012, Griffith had racked up an astonishing $120,000 in loan debt. Without a full-time job, Griffith moved back home and worked three different jobs to afford the $900 monthly payments. "Debt wasn't tangible to me when I was a student," Griffith said. "It didn't seem like it would be that big of a deal."[1]

While Griffith's level of debt is unusual (fewer than 1 percent of undergraduate borrowers owe more than $100,000 in student loans after graduation), what is not uncommon is how emotion steered her college choice. The college search starts as early as middle school for some students these days. By the time they reach their junior year of high school they often have their hearts set on a particular campus. But unlike other major purchases in life—a home, a car—many families know little about what they will actually pay for college and, more important, exactly how they will finance it until a few weeks before a final decision needs to be made. During this period—March and April of the senior year of high school—the sales rhetoric from colleges turns to cold-blooded financial reality. Under pressure, families sometimes make bad financial decisions: students because they don't know any better and parents because they don't want to disappoint their sons and daughters.

The weekend Kelsey Griffith graduated from Ohio Northern, her story landed her on the front page of the *New York Times,* part of a series of articles the newspaper published on the burdens of student borrowing. The total amount of outstanding student-loan debt in the United States had just passed the $1 trillion mark that spring, even as other household borrowing—credit cards and auto loans, in particular—was shrinking. Big, round numbers attract attention, and this significant milestone came on the heels of the Occupy Wall Street protests the previous fall and President Obama's warning to colleges about rising tuition prices in his State of the Union address that winter. The topic of student loans seemed to make headlines on an almost daily basis.

To accompany its series, the *Times* created a nifty interactive graphic on its Web site that allowed readers to plug in the name of a specific school to see the average amount of debt its students had racked up by graduation, as well as the percentage of students who had taken out loans. I entered the names of a few random schools. Rochester Institute of Technology. Nothing. It wasn't in the system. The University of North Carolina at Chapel Hill. Again, nothing. Drexel University. Nothing.

Was I doing something wrong? I had failed to read the fine print: *The data on student debt is self-reported by the schools, and many institutions don't participate.* The information came from an annual survey conducted by several organizations, including *U.S. News & World Report,* Peterson's, and the College Board. The problem was that some colleges chose not to respond or left the debt questions blank. Indeed, only about half of the four-year colleges in the country reported figures for both average debt and the percentage of students with loans. After the *New York Times* report, Ohio Northern announced it would no longer respond to the survey.

How could so many schools fail to respond with numbers vital to prospective students attempting to weigh the true cost of schools they were considering? Why not share these important numbers? In some ways, schools don't want families to know too much, too soon, about the price they'll actually pay and the amount of financial aid they'll really get.

As with Kelsey Griffith, colleges want to hook prospective students on emotion first in hopes they will enroll at any cost. In an attempt to build more financial awareness into the college search, Congress recently mandated that schools include a net-price calculator on their Web sites so that students can estimate early on what a college would cost after grant aid. Be sure to look for the calculator on the Web sites of the colleges you're considering. Some colleges try to hide that as well.

The best numbers we have on student debt exist only for broad groups of borrowers. The United States Department of Education, for instance, can tell you how much students borrow by type of institution (public or private), by family income, or one of several other measures. Those figures come from a survey the department conducts every four years. Other organizations, including the College Board and the Federal Reserve Bank of New York, also release figures on student-loan borrowers, but again they don't break the numbers out for individual schools. We know from those surveys that about two-thirds of bachelor's degree recipients take out loans to attend school, either from the federal government or private banks. That's up from 45 percent since the early 1990s. The average debt for all borrowers in 2011 was around $27,000. One in four borrowers owes more than $28,000, and about 10 percent of borrowers owe more than $54,000.[2]

On the surface, those numbers might not seem a reason for panic. But they hardly tell the whole story about student-loan debt in the United States. That story is embedded in the numbers about individual schools, at least where it's available. Let's return to that *New York Times* interactive. This time I plug in Princeton University. For the Class of 2011, only 23 percent of graduates had debt, averaging just $5,225. In the last decade, Princeton, along with many other wealthy, elite schools, eliminated loans as part of their financial-aid packages. So if Princeton students take out loans, as some obviously do, they only need the money for expenses beyond tuition. Contrast the debt level of Princeton's Class of 2011 with that from Ohio Northern University. There, 85 percent of students graduated with debt averaging nearly $49,000.

Right out of the gate, graduates from Ohio Northern are $44,000 deeper in debt than those from Princeton. That equals about $430 in higher payments *a month* for ten years, assuming a generous interest rate of 3.4 percent. The value of a college degree is based on more than getting a job afterward, but as you consider how you're going to pay back your loans, what you might earn in those first years after college is an important factor. The median starting salary of Princeton graduates is $56,900, according to payscale.com. For Ohio Northern graduates, the median starting salary is $44,800. The gap widens considerably after ten years in the workforce, when Princeton graduates make about $37,000 more a year than those from Ohio Northern. Another way to look at it: The monthly payment on a student loan eats up only 1 percent of a Princeton graduate's monthly paycheck but 13 percent of an Ohio Northern graduate's salary.

Princeton is a much more selective institution than Ohio Northern and its graduates go on to some of the best jobs in the private and public sectors around the world. Not everyone has a desire to go to Princeton or will get accepted even if they do. Some Ohio Northern graduates do go on to earn much more than Princeton graduates. The comparison between the two might be an extreme example, but weighing potential debt against potential earnings is a calculation few families seem to make during the college search process, including Kelsey Griffith's.

After the story on Kelsey appeared in the *New York Times,* Don Heller, an expert on student aid and a dean at Michigan State University, wondered why she decided to go so far into debt to attend Ohio Northern. He noted that eleven public universities in Ohio offer bachelor's degrees in marketing. Two of them, Bowling Green and the University of Toledo, have a net price that's $6,000 to $7,000 less per year than Ohio Northern.

"I understand that she may have felt that Ohio Northern was a 'good fit,' but the reality regarding price and the amount of borrowing required has to be part of that fit," Heller wrote on his blog. "In the end, it is up to the student and his family to decide whether to accept an offer of admission, and corresponding financial aid offer, or not."

Are families being irresponsible by taking on too much debt to pay for school? Are colleges clear enough with prospective students about how much they'll need to pay back after graduation? How much student debt is too much? If schools had more of a stake in how many of their graduates eventually pay off their loans, would they allow students to borrow so much? And does the wide availability of student loans take pressure off schools to hold down their prices?

How did we become so dependent on loans to finance higher education in the first place? Can we reverse that trend, or force schools to become more affordable? These questions and more are ones we need to answer as we design a system for financing higher education in the future.

The Days of Low Tuition Are Over

Students and parents have complained about rising tuition prices for decades, but worries about the escalating debt burden of graduates is a relatively recent phenomenon.[3]

For much of the first half of the 1900s, average tuition rates at public colleges — which educate 80 percent of American students — were well under $100 a year. Financial-aid programs were rare because low tuition made getting a college degree relatively easy. The end of World

War II marked the beginning of what is commonly referred to as the "golden age of higher education" with the passage of the G.I. Bill. It provided tuition benefits of $500 a year, plus $75 a month for living expenses—well above what was needed to pay for tuition at most colleges. As a result of the G.I. Bill, college enrollment surged from 1.5 million students before World War II, to more than 2 million after the war.

Throughout the 1950s and early 1960s, many states tried to maintain low tuition at public schools to help increase the number of students going to college. Lawmakers reasoned that low tuition was the fairest and easiest mechanism to achieve that goal—it required little paperwork and provided the same subsidy to every taxpayer. But by the late 1960s, the slow and steady pace of tuition increases that had marked the post-war period began to speed up. Baby boomers accelerated demand for a college education, and schools responded by spending massive amounts of money on new buildings and new faculty. By 1971–72, the first year the College Board began to track tuition rates, the average cost of a public four-year college was $376, or 44 percent higher than in 1964.

Until the mid-1960s, the federal role in higher education was limited. That changed with the passage of the Higher Education Act in 1965. This sweeping legislation established, for the first time, government-guaranteed student loans. In 1972, an update to the law created a new direct grant to needy students (later renamed the Pell Grant), and added incentives to encourage states to set up their own financial-aid programs. By 1979, every state was operating its own grant programs for students, and taxpayer dollars to the programs grew significantly during the 1980s and 1990s.

But during this twenty-year period states started to pull back on the amount of money going directly to public colleges. Many states adopted the philosophy of "high tuition, high aid," meaning public colleges would raise tuition for everyone and the state would redirect dollars from the colleges to the neediest students. Some states, most notably California and North Carolina, maintained "low tuition, low aid" models, continuing to funnel generous state subsidies to their public colleges. As late as 2001, when I covered North Carolina as a reporter for the *Chronicle of Higher Education,* tuition and fees across the University of North Carolina system were about $2,000 a year (by 2012, tuition at the flagship Chapel Hill campus was around $7,000).

To keep pace with rising tuition at both public and private colleges, the federal role in financing higher education grew. At the same time, there was a shift in how the federal government helped families pay for college. In 1980, more than half of financial-aid dollars were in the form of grants (meaning they didn't need to be paid back). Today, the reverse is true. About 40 percent of all financial-aid dollars are in the form of loans. In the 1980s, as tuition rose year after year at a rate that exceeded inflation, the top education official in the Reagan administration began to wonder if the federal government was indirectly causing higher tuition prices by providing a boost in federal aid each year. In a seminal essay in the *New York Times* in 1987, William J. Bennett, the secretary of education, touched off a firestorm of debate when he suggested that "increases in financial aid in recent years have enabled colleges and universities blithely to raise their tuitions."[4] His reasoning was that if families didn't have access to financial aid, they would refuse to pay higher prices, in the same way consumers can control prices in other markets. The theory, known as the Bennett hypothesis, has been tested by dozens of researchers over the past twenty-five years with conflicting results.

This much is clear: Despite the strict limits Congress put on the amount students can borrow from the federal government, the overall amount of money loaned to students and their families to pay for college has more than doubled since 2000. That's because, contrary to popular thinking, the term "student loan" doesn't refer to one type of product. There are many types of student loans, and when families max out on one they tend to move to others, usually with less generous financial terms.

The student-loan process is a complex maze confusing even to those of us who have covered the industry for years. I can't imagine the plight of parents and students who are thrown into the labyrinth anew each year.

Take a small group of seniors and their parents I met at a high school outside of Orlando in the spring of 2012. It was little more than a week before the May 1 deadline when they had to commit to a college, and they gathered early on a weekday morning to go over their financial-aid options with several counselors. After years of searching for just the right college, it had come down to a last-minute decision for these families. Many of them had waited for the results of appeals to their financial-aid offers from some of their first-choice schools. Now it was time to decide.

After a short discussion as a group, the parents and students broke into private sessions with the counselors.[5] As we sat down, Matt, a burly seventeen-year-old with an interest in science, explained to me that his top picks were in the metropolitan Northeast: Drexel, Villanova, Fordham, and Hofstra universities. On a small table, the counselor spread out the financial-aid offers. As he went through them one by one, he glanced at his own homemade cheat sheet, and I quickly discovered why. Deciphering financial aid letters is almost impossible. Each uses different formats, difficult-to-understand abbreviations or mixes together loans and grants, blurring the lines between the two and creating confusion. The worst offenders suggest students are getting a great deal. No one polices these practices. Unlike when we buy a car or a house or sign up for a credit card, there are no standardized disclosure forms schools are required to hand out.

Each of the offers for Matt included a Stafford loan. Some of the letters clearly spelled out that it's a loan, while others simply used the term "Stafford," followed by the words "subsidized" or "unsubsidized." Matt's mom was already confused. She asked the counselor to explain the difference, although I couldn't believe this was the first time she had seen the loans listed in such a way. The counselor explained that Matt is allowed to borrow the maximum $5,500 in federal Stafford loans his first year. Of that, up to $3,500 is subsidized by the federal government, meaning he won't be charged interest on it while he's in school or during the six-month grace period after graduation. Interest will accumulate on the other $2,000, the unsubsidized part. The counselor reminded them that the overall limit on what Matt could borrow in Stafford loans in four years was $27,000, less than what it cost to attend any of the schools on his list for just one year.

The counselor consulted his cheat sheet again — an Excel spreadsheet that neatly separated loans from grants and scholarships. Segregating them made it simple to compare offers. Matt's mom asked why all the offers factored in loans before they got to the bottom line of what Matt and his family would be expected to contribute. "Why, if we have to take out more loans to make up the gap?" she wondered. The counselor nodded his head. It's in this confusion where over-borrowing for college begins.

The loan column on the counselor's spreadsheet breaks down the types of loans. Two of the schools, Drexel and Villanova, include a Parent PLUS Loan in the financial-aid package. Drexel's parent loan is more than $15,000 for the first year. The counselor explains that Matt's mom must apply for this separately and is ultimately responsible for paying it back, not Matt. These government-backed loans have become a popular way in recent years for parents to pay for their children's college educations; the amount of Parent PLUS loans has doubled in the last decade. In some cases, parents have nowhere else to turn. Because of the housing bust, parents can't easily tap money from their home-equity credit lines as they did during the Lost Decade. A crackdown on private loans to students has also made those more difficult to obtain for some borrowers. The Parent PLUS Loan, with an interest rate close to 8 percent, is essentially the last choice for parents desperate to send their sons and daughters to their first-choice school. The result has been a huge run-up in the size of these loans at some schools. Drexel, for instance, saw the average size of its Parent PLUS loan nearly triple since 2000 to some $24,000.

After a few more questions from Matt's mom, the counselor is getting antsy. We've been here for about ten minutes, and he knows a line of students and their parents are waiting outside. Matt still hasn't made up his mind. As a parting gift, the counselor gives Matt his spreadsheet. In the hallway, Matt's mom starts asking me questions she didn't get to ask the counselor. It's clear she is worried about the size of the parent loans. "What if we need to take those out all four years?" she asks. They could be in the hole for more than $60,000. She explains that Matt is the oldest of three children and that she and her husband recently increased their contributions to their retirement plans at work. Now she is considering stopping those contributions altogether. I explain that I'm far from an expert on paying for college, but most financial planners discourage parents from forgoing retirement savings to pay for their children's college education. After all, you can't take out a loan to pay for retirement.

When I catch up with Matt a few weeks later, he tells me that he decided to go to Fordham because it offered the best deal for his parents. "I was worried about them," he says. "They need to put my sisters through college, and I want them to retire some day."

As Matt told me about the frustrations of his college search, I wondered why so few people in the process are helping students and their parents, especially when it comes to financial matters. Instead of being resources for Matt and his family, financial aid offices at colleges have become another cog in the wheel that brings students in the door. And for a period during the Lost Decade, some administrators actively colluded with banks to profit off their students.

Selling Financial Aid

On a hot and muggy July 4th weekend in 2005, more than 3,000 financial-aid officials from colleges around the country converged on New York City for their national association's annual meeting. The gathering at the Hilton New York was typical of an industry convention. Over lunch in the Hilton's Grand Ballroom, the running back of the New York Giants, Tiki Barber, indulged the audience with stories from the professional football field, drawing leadership lessons from his long career as one of the NFL's best running backs. In the bowels of the hotel in midtown Manhattan, hundreds of sessions, spread out over the four days, were filled with technical advice for financial-aid administrators, from how to run a more efficient office to complying with federal regulations. In between the panel discussions, conference goers passed the time in an exhibit hall where dozens of companies set up booths to market their wares, enticing those walking by with everything from free pens to raffles for big-ticket items: televisions, computers, Bose headphones, or a lobster dinner.

What made this meeting stand out — at least compared to most other higher-education conferences — was what happened over the several nights of the meeting. A group of college officials were wined and dined at the Rainbow Room on the sixty-fifth floor of Rockefeller Center. Groups of financial-aid counselors were treated to front-row orchestra seats at sold-out Broadway shows, including *Wicked* and *The Producers,* courtesy of banks and other lenders. The hot ticket was for a dinner cruise up the East River, where two hundred attendees got a prime viewing spot for Macy's annual fireworks display. "Along with the big show, dinner and premium beer, there will be dancing, a DJ, giveaways, and a whole lot of fun," advertised the brochure for the event. The menu included artichoke and Parmesan torte, filet mignon with a port-sweetened demi-glace, truffled mashed potatoes, and a Valrhona chocolate torte with caramel ice cream. The cruise cost more than $70,000 and was paid for by J. P. Morgan Chase & Company.[6]

The bankers were all after the same thing: securing a spot on a school's coveted preferred-lender list. As college costs rose throughout the Lost Decade, the limits on what students could borrow from the government failed to keep pace. That left students looking for alternatives. For those who couldn't borrow against their homes or didn't have enough equity, one of the few remaining options was a private loan. Between 2000 and 2005, private lending to college students quadrupled. Until then, private education loans had mostly gone to graduate students and those enrolled in medical, law, and business schools. (In other words, those who could eventually afford the payments on the high-interest, unregulated loans.)

Getting a mention on the preferred-lender list was like gold to a lender. This is the list colleges give to guide students looking for a loan. Students weren't required to choose a lender on the list, but some 90 percent did. Besides the freebies at the conference, lenders supplied temporary employees to financial-aid offices or kickbacks. In a few cases, the financial-aid administrators themselves owned stock in the companies they recommended or sat on the corporate boards. At the University of Texas at Austin, officials kept track of lender treats like ice cream, happy hours, and birthday cakes.

While students benefited in some instances (when the lenders offered discounted loans in exchange for getting on the list), in most cases the cozy relationships tipped the financial-aid scale even further in favor of the school. A year after that extravagant New York convention, one lender was so frustrated by its attempts to break into the student-loan market that it took out a two-page ad in the Sunday edition of the *New York Times* accusing financial-aid offices of taking "kickbacks" and "payola" from banks. The ad caught the attention of the New York State attorney general's office, which opened an extensive investigation into the $85 billion student-loan industry. The two-year inquiry uncovered deceptive marketing practices and routine, widespread kickbacks. The investigation resulted in settlement agreements with fifty schools and lenders totaling some $20.8 million.[7]

The probe painted the banks and the colleges as the bad guys in the story of college graduates drowning in debt. But families are not always innocent victims in these tales. Take the case of Natasha van Doren.[8] Her daughter, Mariah, had her heart set on going to Southern New Hampshire University, but Natasha couldn't afford the $500 deposit to secure a spot in the freshman class. So she wrote an e-mail to Paul LeBlanc, the university's president, asking for him to waive the fee. Most presidents get such personal appeals every year, but LeBlanc worried that if she couldn't afford to pay a small deposit, how would she ever pay the tuition bill? LeBlanc took a look at Mariah's financial-aid offer. As part of her package, she would have to borrow $7,000 her first year. Even then, Mariah still had a $10,000 gap that she would probably have to fill with additional loans. LeBlanc thought that Southern New Hampshire was too much of a financial stretch and told Mariah's mother so in an e-mail message:

> I know Mariah really wants to attend SNHU and we are offering her a lot of grant money to help (around $12,000), but might it make sense for her to attend a much more affordable two-year college for her first two years and then transfer in? She would still have two years with us and finish with an SNHU degree, but would be in much better shape financially. I urge you to reconsider — not because we wouldn't love to have Mariah here, but because her enthusiasm for this place might be clouding her thinking about the financial implications. Also, I have worries about your ability to find the needed $10,000 of additional funding even if we waive the deposit.

LeBlanc spotted how emotion was driving a financial decision, but Natasha van Doren was not pleased with the response. She tried again, writing to LeBlanc:

> Does this mean that my appeal did nothing? I always hear schools say that there is always a way to pay for school. How the school expects a family that pays 75% of their income on rent to pay $10,000 is crazy.

LeBlanc wrote back, once more suggesting community college and telling her he couldn't attend his first-choice college because of money (his father was a stone mason, his mother a factory worker):

> Sometimes the math just doesn't add up. It is precisely because we cannot expect someone paying 75% of their income to rent to manage the cost of an education here that I raised my concerns. We do you and her no favor if we put her in a worse predicament two years from now or even if she graduates, but with a crippling amount of debt (and I do not trust high school kids, however mature, to realistically assess the impact of that debt).

Natasha van Doren called LeBlanc's advice "harsh" and ignored it. Natasha had attended a community college and didn't think it was the right fit for her daughter. By the time she scraped together the deposit, there were no more spots for housing Mariah at Southern New Hampshire. So she ended up going to Marlboro College, a private four-year school in Vermont, where she expected to take on some $10,000 in debt her first year.

You won't find many college presidents like LeBlanc who would recommend that you *not* attend their school. John Sexton is another one who tried it, this time on a much larger scale, but also without much success. Sexton is the president of New York University, one of the most expensive schools in the country, with an annual price of nearly $60,000. It's also located in one of the most expensive cities in the world. Because it has a large student body and a relatively small endowment, it can't provide generous financial-aid packages like many of the schools it competes against. The *average* debt of its class of 2010 was some $41,000.

At a dinner I attended with Sexton in Albany, he said a quarter of NYU students work two jobs while going to school full-time. "If you're working that much, you're not taking advantage of the fullness of our education," said Sexton, pounding his fist on the table for emphasis.

The white-bearded, former law-school professor is an intense, funny man, and like LeBlanc, comes from a modest background that shapes his thinking about the growing debt of his students. Of course, he can also afford to lose some students because he has a line of others willing to take their spots. Despite its price tag, NYU is one of the hottest colleges in the country. In the 1970s and early 1980s, it was known as a commuter school. Today, it regularly tops the *Princeton Review*'s dream school list and breaks application records almost every year, rejecting two out of three applicants.

Like a good lawyer giving a closing argument, Sexton never seems to lose his train of thought. He begins to rattle off ideas about how colleges could help high school students balance their dream college against the financial reality of paying for it. He once proposed telling students in their acceptance letters that NYU might not be the right financial fit for them. But others thought that was too negative a message to convey in what is supposed to be one of the happiest moments in life. Instead, the university started systematically calling some students right after they got their financial-aid offers. It focused on those who were first in their family to go to college or who had a big gap between what NYU offered and what the family was expected to pay. Nearly 2,000 calls were made.

"And it had no impact," Sexton says, letting his face drop to express his disappointment. "These are difficult discussions to have in some families. The parents don't want to let down their kids."

After one year, the university stopped calling students. The NYU and Southern New Hampshire cases raise numerous questions about how far a school should go to warn students about the debt they are about to take on, and whether universities that fail to advise their students—or in some cases potentially mislead them—are ultimately responsible for the choices their students make. It's a debate playing out right now among law-school graduates, and how that turns out could have an impact across all of higher education.

Employment Data That Doesn't Add Up

When Katherine Cooper was applying to law schools in the summer of 2006, she paid close attention to one particular column in the *U.S. News* law-school rankings: graduates known to be employed nine months after graduation. "I wanted reliable work after graduation," said the Washington state native.[9]

Cooper applied to a dozen law schools, but with average LSAT scores she was rejected from most of them. A couple of acceptances came through, including one from New York Law School. The school is often confused with the more prestigious one affiliated with New York University a mile away in lower Manhattan. That's probably to its benefit. New York Law School is ranked in the bottom third of all law schools in the country, yet it charges more than Harvard, with a price tag of some $48,000 a year. In 2009, in the midst of a massive slowdown in hiring at law firms, the school *expanded* its incoming class by almost a third.[10]

Cooper arrived there in the fall of 2007. By the spring, she had applied for dozens of summer associate positions. Not one bite. The following year, even with better grades, the best she could get was an unpaid internship at MTV Networks. In the spring of 2010, she graduated with north of $100,000 in student loans and no job prospects. So she turned the tables on New York Law School and became a plaintiff in a growing spate of lawsuits filed against a dozen law schools, accusing them of deceiving prospective students with inflated job-placement and salary statistics. "I was at the lowest of my lows," she said.

The case was ultimately dismissed. A judge ruled that applicants had plenty of information available to them about their chances of getting a job. That may be true, but a question remains whether that information should be trusted, especially when it comes from the schools themselves. A quick look at the *U.S. News* law-school rankings shows relatively high employment rates and six-figure median salaries for nearly every school, even those outside the top twenty-five. The survey is an invitation to distort the numbers. Graduates count as "employed after nine months" even if they're not in a law-related job or a permanent one. One year, Georgetown University's law school created temporary jobs in admissions and advertised them to alumni "still seeking employment" in order to skew the numbers. The positions lasted just six weeks, conveniently right around the time the employment survey was being conducted.[11]

Soon after several of the lawsuits against the law schools were filed, I met with a higher-education lawyer who formerly worked for a big private university in the Northeast. I asked him whether he thought these cases had any merit. After all, none of these schools actually promised jobs. He compared the lawsuits to those brought against the tobacco companies. Consumers were warned of the dangers of using cigarettes, yet they still prevailed in their class-action suits and the tobacco companies paid billions of dollars to the states to prevent further lawsuits. As student-loan debt grows, he predicts that so too will the chorus of complaints from students about the implicit promises schools make in their admissions pitches. Some students might be willing to go to court if they feel wrongfully deceived.

Right now, colleges offer these loans to students and then essentially wash their hands of them. It's up to the students to pay them back. Colleges are only on the hook when too many of their graduates default on their loans within two years of graduation (soon to be three years). When this happens, schools lose their eligibility to participate in federal student-aid programs, essentially a death sentence for any institution. But few schools are actually kicked out of the federal programs. Students may struggle with paying off loans for years after graduation, yet the schools keep giving loans to a new generation of students.

Would colleges be more cautious of how many loans they offer to students if the schools themselves had a bigger stake in the outcome? What if colleges were lending out their own dollars, like a bank? Most banks lend money based on a formula, using your current salary, assets, other debts, and of course, your credit score. A student loan for college is about the only one you can get where it's truly a promise to repay. That's why the government guarantees the loans. Otherwise, no bank would make such a deal.

Then the question turns to how much student debt is too much. Banks can easily calculate how much to give you in a mortgage because they know how much you earn and the price of the house you want to buy. When it comes to higher education, they could use predictive measures of a student's income after graduation, such as major, college, and grade-point average, argues Mark Kantrowitz, the publisher of two popular financial-aid Web sites, FastWeb.com and FinAid.org. The federal government suggests that no more than 15 percent of your income should go toward paying off student-loan debt. Another rule of thumb — your total undergraduate borrowing should be limited to what you might expect to make your first year after graduation. By that measure, many college graduates seem to be doing well: Average debt is about $25,000 and first-year salaries are around $36,000.

Economists often remind us that education debt is good debt. Taking on a student loan seems like a good investment, when placed next to the lower unemployment rate for college grads and the lifetime payoff of a bachelor's degree. Of course, don't tell that to recent college grads who are unemployed or working in jobs that don't require a bachelor's degree. Compared to earlier generations, today's college graduates compete in a global economy, so they might be more limited in how much they can earn. While a college degree might make good economic sense, one at any cost doesn't. Education debt may be good debt, but even too much of a good thing can hurt you.

Excessive borrowing is the biggest problem facing higher education, and it hurts everyone. For graduates, it means a decade or more of making choices with that debt hanging over their heads, governing the types of careers and jobs to pursue, when to get married, when to buy a house, and when to have kids. If the students overborrow, it's likely that the parents did, too, or they are helping out with the payments now. Research from the Federal Research Bank of New York shows that Americans aged fifty and older still owe $139 billion in student loans. More than 15 percent of those loans are delinquent.[12] Some were loans taken on by people who went back to school later in life, but many were loans they signed or cosigned for their children and grandchildren. Student loan debt is now an intergenerational problem, with ripple effects throughout the economy and social policy.

One petition that has generated hundreds of thousands of signatures on Facebook and even a bill in Congress is a proposal to forgive all student-loan debt. That's not the answer. Students or their parents at most income levels should have a stake in paying for college. They are, after all, getting something in return.

While economists are confident that a college degree is worth more than just a high school diploma, "there is less evidence that an expensive college degree is worth it compared to a cheap one," says Justin Wolfers, an associate professor of business and public policy at the University of Pennsylvania. "Going to college is worth it, [but] doing so expensively might not make a lot of sense."

That means big trouble for expensive colleges where students graduate with higher-than-average amounts of debt. Those institutions have been helped by the association of higher price with quality in many people's minds, the wide availability of loans, and the willingness of students and families to take on major debt. But the current structure of higher education is beginning to crumble and will eventually be replaced by a radically different system.

Part II

THE DISRUPTION

4

The Five Disruptive Forces That Will Change Higher Education Forever

THE PRESIDENT OF the University of Virginia, Teresa Sullivan, arrived in her office late on a Friday afternoon for what she expected would be a routine meeting with two members of the university's governing board, including its chair. It was early June, and the historic, pristine campus designed by its founder, Thomas Jefferson, was quiet for the summer, the calm before the storm that was about to erupt. Sullivan had just returned from a day-long retreat. The board chair, Helen Dragas, got down to business. She told Sullivan that the board was unhappy with her performance leading the 193-year-old university with 21,000 students, a $2.6 billion budget, and 7,900 employees. They were worried that she was moving too slowly to position the top-rated school in a rapidly changing world, particularly when it came to online education. The chair told the president she needed to resign or else the board would force her out.

Two days later the news was announced: Sullivan was stepping down after just two years on the job. In a statement, Sullivan cited a "philosophical difference of opinion" with the board. The abrupt resignation of the popular leader shocked the campus community. Over the next two weeks, opposition to the board's decision mounted. Faculty, students, and alumni expressed their unhappiness in droves on Twitter and Facebook. Protests and meetings were held almost daily on the Charlottesville campus. Donors threatened to withhold financial support. During a marathon twelve-hour board meeting, Sullivan addressed the group and released a fourteen-page document critical of the swift change the members reportedly wanted. "Corporate-style, top-down leadership does not work in a great university," she wrote. "Sweeping action may be gratifying and may create the aura of strong leadership, but its unintended consequences may lead to costs that are too high to bear."

The student newspaper acquired e-mails that were sent between the board leaders in the weeks leading up to the resignation and posted summaries on Twitter. The messages revealed a lack of deliberation on Sullivan's firing as board members exchanged a series of newspaper columns on the pressures facing higher education. In one of them, about the growing number of elite universities offering free online courses, the board chair noted: "why we can't afford to wait." Virginia's governor weighed in, telling the board to resolve the leadership crisis, or he would force them all to resign. A few days later, the board voted to reinstate Sullivan.[1]

The drama that unfolded at the University of Virginia in the summer of 2012 reveals the pressures facing colleges and universities as the financial and historical foundations of higher education swiftly shift beneath them. The public debate over the future of Jefferson's university characterizes similar discussions at colleges across the country — mostly behind closed doors and mainly between presidents and governing boards — about the path that would lead to a stable and successful future and how quickly they need to move to get there.

September 15, 2008: The Beginning of the End

The roots of this crisis were planted nearly four years earlier, on September 15, 2008, when Lehman Brothers filed for the largest bankruptcy in US history. The collapse of the venerable Wall Street investment firm touched off a global financial crisis, sending the US stock market and home prices into a tailspin and the economy into a deep recession.

For American higher education, the day marked the beginning of the end of a decade of remarkable excess. Within months, the largest university endowments shed billions of dollars, and massive deficits opened in state budgets, leading to unprecedented budget cuts at elite schools, including Duke and Harvard Universities and the University of California at Berkeley. It would take many more months for the ripple effects of the financial crisis to reach all campuses. For colleges that depended on tuition for the bulk of their revenue, the collapse had come at an almost perfect time. Classes had started for the semester a few weeks earlier, and tuition bills were mostly paid.

But by early 2009, nearly every college started to feel the pain. The first sign came from parents asking colleges to reconsider their financial aid packages for the spring semester. Colleges dipped into rainy day funds to fulfill the requests, but students transferred nonetheless, usually to attend colleges closer to home where they could save money on room and board.

The second sign came when public colleges suddenly faced gaping budget holes after the spigot of dollars from the state slowed to a trickle. These cuts came even as more students started to look at state schools as a cheaper alternative to private colleges. The public colleges either turned them away (the twenty-three-campus California State University system slashed enrollment by 16,000 students) or increased tuition (prices went up by about $2,000 at the average state school in the four years after the economy collapsed).

The third sign came from small private colleges. To keep their seats filled with freshmen, the schools began to inch up their discount rates, the percentage they knock off the sticker price through financial aid. In 2009, almost two-thirds of colleges said they changed their aid policies, nearly all of them because of the economy.[2]

Despite the tough times, many in higher education believed the recession was merely a temporary dip. They had survived past downturns. The conventional wisdom was that they would survive this, too. One reason for the optimism? Applications continued to flood schools in record numbers. As long as the pipeline of students continued to flow, everything would be fine.

Beneath the surface of rising application totals, serious problems lurked. By the spring of 2012, fewer colleges were touting their number of applications. The focus, instead, was on two other figures: discount rates and yield (the percentage of accepted students who send deposits to enroll). These are the numbers that keep admissions deans, financial officers, and presidents up at night. And that summer, at college admissions officer meetings in New York and Minnesota, I heard plenty of worry about increasing discount rates and declining yields and their implications for the future.

The schools fortunate enough to hit their enrollment target did so by discounting tuition at rates that approached 50, 60, and in one case 70 percent. While there is no rate that automatically triggers an alarm, a rule of thumb in recent years is that a rate above 50 percent puts considerable pressure on the bottom line. Other colleges resisted raising their discount rate and missed their enrollment goal. Now they were paying the price in another way: fewer students, less tuition revenue, and possibly a deficit, because most schools set a budget before they know exactly how many students will enroll. Admissions officers from those schools told me they were considering whether to boost their discount rate the following year in order to maintain enrollments.

This strategy can easily turn into a death spiral. Year after year, colleges increase published tuition prices in an effort to keep pace with their rising discount rates. They succeed in sustaining enrollment levels but spend heavily to snag those students, so their revenues barely grow or actually drop. Their options for survival are limited. They don't have large endowments they can dip into. They can't lower their academic standards to enlarge their pool of potential students without exposing themselves to new risks. If they are located in the Northeast or Midwest, demographics are not in their favor.

The result is a higher-education system in financial crisis, with an urgent need for radical change in order to serve the next generation of college students — or, in some cases, simply to survive. The decade ahead for colleges and universities will be much different than the Lost Decade. And at the center of this disruption is a perfect storm of financial, political, demographic, and technological forces.

Force #1
A SEA OF RED INK

Birmingham-Southern College is something of an anomaly in the Deep South. It is a small, private liberal-arts college in the heart of Alabama, a state with only a handful of private institutions and home to two large public universities well-known for their prowess on the football field, the University of Alabama and Auburn University.

In an effort to get noticed, Birmingham-Southern, with only 1,500 students, embarked on an ill-fated attempt in 1999 to move up to compete at the highest level of college athletics, Division I. Over the next eight years, its fourteen teams competed in three Division I championship events.[3] During that time they earned a distinction off the field: a running deficit of $6 million, nearly 15 percent of the college's overall budget.

In 2007, after the college's bond rating was repeatedly downgraded, eventually to junk status, the school pulled the plug on Division I athletics. By then, with enrollment flagging, the college was in the midst of a plan to upgrade facilities to bring in more students and revenue. When the economic crisis hit in late 2008, Birmingham-Southern was already in a financial hole. Rather than stop digging, it went deeper. The college's financial department increased the discount rate more than it disclosed in internal financial reports. To cover the extra costs, officials borrowed. The president and the board were kept in the dark, and financial statements were never audited. By the time the bogus accounting was discovered, the college faced a deficit of $13 million. It cut millions in expenses, laid off dozens of professors, reduced salaries, and eliminated five majors.[4]

Birmingham-Southern's situation was the result of a confluence of bad decisions exacerbated by the economic downturn. But it was not alone among colleges trying to paper over money troubles during the recession. One-third of all colleges and universities in the United States face financial statements significantly weaker than before the recession, and according to one analysis, are on an unsustainable fiscal path. Another quarter of colleges find themselves at serious risk of joining them.[5] "Expenses are growing at such a pace that colleges don't have the cash or the revenue to cover them for much longer," says Jeff Denneen, head of the higher-education practice at Bain & Company, the global consulting firm that, along with private-equity firm Sterling Partners, performed the financial analysis. "A growing number of colleges are in real financial trouble."

Other forecasts predict a similar future of red ink for more colleges. The number of schools on a Department of Education watch list has grown by more than a third since 2007.[6] A database maintained by an association of small private colleges shows more than half are carrying long-term debt above a level considered healthy. Moody's Investors Service, which examines the finances of hundreds of colleges that issue bonds through public markets, has put a negative outlook on the entire higher-education sector. "We're seeing prolonged, serious stress," says Karen Kedem, an analyst at Moody's.

What is significant about the move by Moody's is that it typically rates only schools with strong balance sheets to begin with. Reading a college's bond-rating report is like reading a person's credit report: It is a financial checkup that gives insight into strengths and weaknesses that you will never find in any college guidebook, but probably should. Take this line from a Moody's report when it downgraded Drew University in New Jersey in 2012: "The rating is based on persistent operating deficits and thin cash-flow driven by a decline in enrollment and net tuition per student coupled with rising debt service payments and transition of several key members of university leadership."[7] Translation: The private college is operating in a hole, it is discounting tuition too much, and it is not attracting enough students, especially those who will pay more in tuition.

For colleges and universities, a financial metric perhaps more important than the discount rate is the so-called net tuition per student. That is the actual cash added to the college's bottom line from a student's tuition bill after grant aid is subtracted. Like any business, a college needs cash on hand to pay employees, bills, and debts; cash that net tuition helps supply. But in recent years, net tuition revenue has either been flat or falling at 73 percent of colleges.

Net tuition is under pressure because colleges, particularly private schools, lack the market power to raise their prices significantly in a down economy, given the discounting they are already using to attract students. Business and law schools are no longer the cash cows they once were for their parent institutions. Meanwhile, employees expect raises, and other costs continue to rise. "This is a perfect storm where you have a number of challenges at the same time over a long period of time," says Kedem, the Moody's analyst.

Add to these money troubles another revenue stream that is dry-ing up: research dollars from Washington. The federal government accounts for about 60 percent of grants awarded to research universities. Most of that comes from the National Institutes of Health, where spending has been flatlined by tight federal budgets. In the future, what is left will mostly go to research powerhouses like Johns Hopkins University and the University of Washington. That will leave those schools that attempted to become research universities during the Lost Decade with a series of bad choices: Continue to spend limited tuition dollars on research, go further into debt, or be stuck with a bunch of empty labs.

Carrying debt, even too much of it, is fine for colleges as long as they have a plan for paying it back. For the last decade, investing in a college's debt has been a fairly safe bet, because a school had a steady stream of students and income. Despite the evidence to the contrary, some colleges still think the tough times are a temporary inconvenience — that eventually they will again be able to pass on their additional costs to students or get more money from the state and federal governments. But the most informed and realistic of higher-education leaders realize they are now living in a new normal. Unless they suddenly find alternative revenue sources (the silver bullet everyone is looking for), these colleges either need to cut costs quickly or face the prospect of a long, painful path to closure.

Force #2
THE DISAPPEARING STATE IN PUBLIC HIGHER EDUCATION

As she approached her thirtieth birthday, Brooke Roberson decided it was time for a career change. She had a bachelor's degree in electronic communications from the University of North Carolina at Chapel Hill and had worked for a small business for seven years after graduation. Her real passion was helping people, and nursing seemed a natural fit. Roberson researched programs in the area around her Raleigh, North Carolina, home and settled on Wake Technical Community College. She enrolled in the prenursing classes needed to qualify for the nursing program. Her first semester, she found getting into classes difficult. They were all at capacity, but she diligently checked her computer every day hoping for spots to open up. They did. By the next semester, she had learned to sign on as soon as registration opened.

In the last semester of prerequisites, Roberson put in her application and crossed her fingers. "It's so competitive," Roberson says. "I didn't think it would be this competitive. There are just not enough spots." The semester before, there were 230 *qualified* applicants for seventy spots. Wake Tech divvies out the spots based on points students accumulate through the classes they take and the grades they earn. To improve her chances and get more points, Roberson is taking two additional classes this semester, Nutrition and Development Psychology. I ask Roberson what she will do if she doesn't get into the nursing program. "I'll have to apply to other places," she says, though she has been told almost every program in the region has the same wait.

North Carolina, like many states, faces a nursing shortage. But Wake Technical is unable to expand its nursing program to accommodate students such as Roberson in part because its allowance from the state has been cut by nearly a quarter in the last three years, even as enrollment has grown by almost a third. The number of spots in the nursing program remains stuck at three hundred, with hundreds of other students waiting in the prenursing program.

Public colleges like Wake Technical are the workhorses of American higher education. Three of every four college students in the United States attend a state school. For generations, they were seen as access institutions designed to provide a college education to the majority of Americans. Some of them were among the finest universities in the country—the University of California at Berkeley, the University of Virginia, the University of Michigan—providing a high-quality education at a cut-rate price, courtesy of state taxpayers.

For the last twenty-five years, however, states have been slashing higher education appropriations during each downturn in the economy and never fully restoring the money when good times returned. This retreat hastened after the financial collapse in late 2008. Since then, nearly every major public university has started to look more like a private institution. The clearest indicator of this is that students now pay more toward their instruction at many public universities than the state does. Indeed, the state often holds one of the smallest pieces of the budget pie. Just 6 percent of the University of Virginia's budget comes from the state. At the University of Michigan, it's 7 percent. Berkeley is one of the lucky ones at 11 percent.

Across the country, twenty-nine states gave less to colleges in 2012 than they did in 2007. Lawmakers cannot charge prisoners a fee for their room and board, but they can charge students tuition. Higher education remains the largest single chunk of discretionary spending in the state budget. That means it is not mandated by the federal government or the state constitution, like public K–12 education or Medicaid. Higher education is often at the end of the line when lawmakers dole out money. In recent years, not much has been left to give to colleges. Students have had to pick up more of the bill for their education.

Among public institutions, community colleges like Wake Technical have been hit the hardest. With more than eight million students, community colleges make up the largest type of college in the United States, although they remain almost invisible to the media and the public. They educate their students on about a third of the resources of public four-year colleges. Their programs tend to be closely aligned to the local and regional economy, and they offer programs that can quickly train people for new jobs. In other words, they are key to filling the skills gap that keeps millions of jobs begging for workers.

"We know from employers where the jobs are, we just need the resources to do something about it," says Stephen Scott, the president of Wake Technical Community College. We're standing outside the college's gleaming new health sciences building. With the facility close to opening, the college went ahead and expanded the nursing program. But opening spots in the program is dependent not only on classroom space and faculty members. To train its students, the college also needs clinical positions in hospitals and other health care providers in the region. Those spots, too, are limited. High-tech equipment in the new health sciences building will allow students to get more hands-on training at school and require less time in the field, which Scott says should ease demand a bit.

The $16 million, 100,000-square-foot facility was built with borrowed money, thanks to a bond measure the county voters approved a few years earlier. The college is about to go to the voters again to ask for more money. It is also in the midst of its first private fundraising campaign with a $10 million goal. Employers, who rely on the graduates to become workers, are being asked to pony up more as well. Scott has worked at public colleges his whole career, thirty-five years. He's never seen it this bad. "We can't count on the state anymore," Scott says.

Across the country, state disinvestment in higher education has been swift and has largely gone unnoticed by the public. With state lawmakers unlikely to return to paying for the majority of a resident's college education, public institutions face a choice: Significantly cut costs (and give up part of their mission to serve the needs of the state) or continue to raise tuition and price their education out of the reach of some residents. If the current trends continue, by 2022 states will begin getting out of the business of supporting public higher education, leaving their colleges to scour the globe looking for a shrinking share of full-paying students.[8]

Force #3
THE WELL OF FULL-PAYING STUDENTS IS RUNNING DRY

Newark, Delaware, is a quintessential American college town, with an historic main street lined with boutique shops, local restaurants, and, of course, plenty of bars. Its convenient location along Interstate 95 and the Northeast Amtrak train corridor has long made the University of Delaware, the town's big draw, a popular destination for out-of-state students. In recent years, however, the university has also become a trendy spot for students from one country in particular: China. In 2007, the university enrolled just eight Chinese students. Just four years later, the number passed the 500 mark.

The university, with 21,000 students, is not alone. The number of Chinese undergraduates studying at American colleges has tripled in three years to 40,000. They now account for the largest group of foreign students at colleges in the United States. While colleges publicly say that recruiting in China (and other foreign lands) is mostly about diversity, privately they will admit to an equally compelling reason: to bring in more revenue. Foreign students typically pay full freight and don't require financial aid. The world's most populous country has an expanding middle class willing and able to pay American tuition bills. College fairs in China attract crowds of 30,000 prospective students who then flood foreign schools with applications. Ohio State drew 2,900 undergraduate applications in 2011 from China. Mount Holyoke College, a prestigious women's school in Massachusetts, received more than 600 applications, enough to fill its entire freshman class.[9]

While foreign students bolster the bottom line at both private and public colleges, another group of applicants helps the finances at public colleges: out-of-state students. These students usually pay twice as much as their in-state counterparts, so many public colleges have aimed to increase their numbers of out-of-staters to make up for cuts in government aid. The University of Arizona and the University of Oregon now enroll more freshmen from California than six California State University campuses do.[10] Of course, when every state is engaging in the same strategy, the result is a national game of swap. California residents go to Oregon, Oregon students go to Washington, and so on.

As public colleges mine for new sources of students, they are often running into private colleges doing the same thing. The demographic boom that fueled the growth at so many colleges in the last decade hit its peak in 2008, when the number of public high school graduates passed the three million mark. Since then, that number has been declining and is expected to reach its low point in 2014 before climbing again. In the Northeast, the number of high school graduates will continue to drop through 2022. That spells trouble for hundreds of Northeastern colleges that get the bulk of their students from in-state or neighboring states. It is the major reason why some of those schools have spent heavily in recent years to expand their reach. Take the University of Scranton in Pennsylvania. Traditionally, it has pulled students from three states: Pennsylvania, New Jersey, and New York. Now the Jesuit university is buying advertising space on kiosks in the Tysons Center shopping mall in Northern Virginia. It hopes that the Washington, DC, suburbs and other secondary markets will provide up to 10 percent of its students in the coming years.

This search for students able to pay higher prices is already showing signs that the well is running dry. In the United States, the economic crisis has left the median American family with no more wealth than it had in the early 1990s. With household budgets tight, families are taking another look at the public colleges in their own backyard. Moody's notes that, among the schools it rates, the number of students accepting offers of admissions from schools has been dropping at a fast clip since 2008. This is occurring even as these schools are spending more to enroll students. The trend, Moody's said, is particularly serious at the lower-rated private colleges "which are increasingly competing with lower-cost public colleges and feeling the most pressure to slow tuition increases and offer more tuition discounting."

What's more, experts predict a drop in the number of affluent, well-prepared high school graduates — the type of students that every college is after. One such expert, Dan Lundquist, who headed up admissions at Union College and recruited students for the University of Pennsylvania, describes the coming bust using the image of a funnel of students. At the top is the total number of eighteen-year-olds, some 4.3 million in 2009. The ones that filter out at the bottom are those with above-average SAT scores and family incomes over $200,000 a year, who also want to attend small, private colleges in the mid-Atlantic or Northeast regions. That number in 2009, according to Lundquist? Just 996 students.

That figure will shrink further, Lundquist believes, as the pool of wealthy parents willing to pay high tuition prices gets smaller. When he shows the data to college presidents or trustees, he says, "there is nervous laughter.

"They know they're limping from year to year by nipping around the edges on their costs," Lundquist says. "But no one seems willing to make the hard decisions. It's just easier to kick the can down the road."

Across the world, American universities are facing increased competition for students. While the United States is still clearly the leader in attracting students from other countries, everyone else is quickly catching up. In Asia, governments are pouring money into new elite universities and research. "Asians have studied very carefully the reasons why Western populations are now successful," says Kishore Mahbubani, author of *The New Asian Hemisphere*. "They realize that unless you create good universities and attract the best minds in the world, you can't move into the next phase of development."[11]

Even as American universities battle for students in every corner of the world, they also face new competitors at home chipping away at the corner they've had on the market.

Force #4
THE UNBUNDLED ALTERNATIVES ARE IMPROVING

The thirty-five-year-old slight Bangladeshi man bounds to the stage in a ballroom at the JW Marriott in Los Angeles. In front of him is an audience of nearly 800 top college leaders, gathered here for the annual meeting of the American Council on Education. Known as ACE, it is the umbrella organization for dozens of higher-education associations, and its yearly conference is the place where traditional colleges promote and defend themselves. In recent years, the group has tried to remain relevant by introducing its membership to those who want to remake conventional higher education. In 2011, the association invited Clay Christensen, the Harvard business professor and author of *The Innovative University*. And in 2012, here is Salman Khan.

The night before, Khan was profiled on *60 Minutes* as "teacher to the world." His Khan Academy is a free online tutoring Web site with more than 3,000 short educational videos on math, science, and history. To these fifty- and sixty-something academics dressed mostly in suits, Khan, tieless and in khakis, looks more like one of their graduate students. Never mind that; among the millions of high school students Khan has helped through a difficult math class he is much better known than many of the colleges these presidents head. Khan asks the audience how many of them haven't heard of the Khan Academy. About a fifth of the people in the room put up their hands.

Framed by an elegant PowerPoint presentation he has presented to thousands around the world, Khan walks the college administrators through the history of his namesake academy. In 2004, he was working as a hedge fund analyst in Boston when his cousin in New Orleans needed help with seventh grade algebra. He tutored her from a distance through short videos that he ended up putting on YouTube. Thousands of other people found them and started using them, including Microsoft's founder, Bill Gates. Encouraged by the positive feedback he received, Khan quit his day job and started the academy as a nonprofit, with backing from Gates, Google, and other tech giants. That was 2009. Back then, hundreds of students viewed the videos in a given month, he explains. On this day, just three years later, Khan Academy lessons are viewed by more than four million people *a month*.

The pace of building something this big, this fast, is a strange concept to many at the gathering. On most campuses, it can take years to get a new major up and running, because so many disparate groups, from academic departments to faculty committees to trustees, must sign off on the decision. Colleges and universities are extraordinarily complex institutions with multiple purposes: teaching, research, preparing students for life and career, and of course, providing support services, from campus organizations to athletics to residential life. It is the coordination required for this complexity that leads to higher costs, Clay Christensen tells me. Most industries, he says, focus on one business model at a time. The typical state university or research institution is the amalgamation of three different business models: a consulting firm that offers solutions (the university's research function), a manufacturer that adds value to a raw material (the teaching function), and an online auction site that facilitates networks (the life and career function).

What Christensen encourages, and what the disruptors like Khan are actually doing, is unbundling those services and driving down costs by focusing on just one model. Plenty of entrepreneurs and for-profit companies already help colleges manage student services — everything from dorm-room assignments to advising. Montclair State University in New Jersey outsources much of its student-affairs division to thirty-nine companies, services that years ago were performed by college employees.[12]

The real unbundling opportunities surround the content and delivery functions of a university. The Khan Academy is one example of a new generation of high-quality online learning alternatives quickly remaking the idea that a college education must be delivered at one physical location by professors who create and curate their own courses. Khan argues that an unbundled university will allow students to mix-and-match their college experience by taking classes both online and in person from various providers. Unbundling will help colleges and professors build courses for free (or close to free) with the best content from around the world.

Also unbundled: the credential from the college. Right now, colleges have a corner on the credential market, and a credential is *the* ticket to most good jobs. That's why colleges can charge whatever they want for that piece of paper. What if higher education lost its grip on the credential business? The day when other organizations besides colleges provide a nondegree credential to signify learning might not be far off. One interesting project on this front is an effort to create "digital badges," which would allow people to demonstrate skills and knowledge to prospective employers without necessarily having a degree.

Think of Boy Scout merit badges for professionals in a fast-changing job market where degrees often cannot keep pace. Badges could give recognition to, for example, informal learning that happens outside the classroom; "soft skills," such as critical thinking and communication; new literacies, such as aggregating information from various sources and judging its quality; or digital video editing or social media skills. And in a digital age, the badge could include links back to documents and other artifacts demonstrating the work that led to earning the stamp of approval.

This interesting but somewhat fringe idea is slowly gaining influential fans, among them Secretary of Education Arne Duncan (he calls badges a "game-changing strategy") and the John D. and Catherine T. MacArthur Foundation (sponsor of a $2 million contest to develop a badge system).

Under a badge system, colleges would no longer be the sole providers of a credential. While badges could be awarded by traditional colleges, they could also be given out by professional organizations, online education providers, companies, or community groups. The Khan Academy already offers users a chance to earn "challenge patches" in geometry, calculus, and probability after watching enough videos and passing standardized tests administered on the site. The big question, of course, is whether employers would view badges as credible, especially when compared against a traditional college diploma. Probably not, at least at first. But employers express plenty of dissatisfaction with the current crop of college graduates, especially those from lower-tier schools. For some technical jobs, employers might prefer a system that can show them what students studied, as well as samples of their work.

Perhaps the most appealing aspect of these alternatives is the low price. A credential from a free online course might cost twenty-five or thirty dollars. These alternatives have the potential to reduce costs and improve the learning experience for students. Unbundled learning and badges will not replace the traditional college and diploma anytime soon, but they serve as a great option for the next generation of students who are accustomed to using technology in their daily lives and unwilling to navigate the current one-size-fits-all system.

Force #5
THE GROWING VALUE GAP

> "It's not enough for us to increase student aid. We can't just keep subsidizing skyrocketing tuition; we'll run out of money. States also need to do their part, by making higher education a higher priority in their budgets. And colleges and universities have to do their part by working to keep costs down. Recently, I spoke with a group of college presidents who've done just that. Some schools redesign courses to help students finish more quickly. Some use better technology. The point is, it's possible. So let me put colleges and universities on notice: If you can't stop tuition from going up, the funding you get from taxpayers will go down."
> President Barack Obama
> State of the Union address
> January 24, 2012

Higher education rarely gets mentioned in a major political speech, let alone a State of the Union address. But with public anxiety over rising college costs at an all-time high, tapping into those worries is a smart political strategy in a presidential election year.

College graduates struggling in a tough economy or overwhelmed by student-loan debt are questioning the value of their degrees, and delaying other life decisions, such as getting married or buying a home. One in four college graduates who make less than $50,000 a year now say their degree was a bad deal, according to a survey by the Pew Research Center. Some 75 percent of Americans say college is out of reach for most people, up from 60 percent just two decades ago.

No matter a person's race, income, education level, geographic location, the answer is usually the same: Higher education is too expensive. The number one reason by far that young Americans are not going to college or not finishing their degree is a lack of money. "I hear questions from families now that I never heard before, like 'Is it worth it?'" says Ann Kirschner, a dean at the City University of New York. "Because of sticker shock, the idea of the degree has been very much called into question."

Colleges continue to return to the same well-worn playbook to defend their prices, arguing that very few people pay the sticker price. But even with financial aid, the amount families pay for college has skyrocketed more than 400 percent since 1982.[13] It is not just about pure costs anymore, as Kirschner observed. In the Pew survey, about half of Americans think that the higher education system is doing a poor or fair job in providing *value* for the money spent.

Most college presidents are tone-deaf to those concerns. Three-fourths of them say higher education is providing a good or excellent value, according to the Pew survey. For some presidents, it is easy to ignore public and political consternation over college prices. Elite institutions can continue to charge almost anything, because they have enough qualified applicants to easily fill their incoming classes ten times over.

For the majority of colleges, however, the time has come to prove their worth. Already, we are seeing evidence of price-sensitive families trading down; choosing less expensive institutions, including community colleges and local public universities. That trading down will inevitably result in more students trying out alternatives to traditional higher education.

In the face of several stinging reports about the limited learning that goes on during the undergraduate years, prospective parents and students want to know if the academic experience will be rigorous enough to justify the cost and reap the rewards in the job market. Sure, the climbing walls, the new dorms, the fancy food in the dining hall, and the sports teams will continue to be sales tools employed by many colleges to reel in students. How rigorously colleges prepare students for the workforce, as well as mature them for life, will play a greater role in the calculation of value. And on that front, many colleges don't measure up. The alternatives, because of their largely virtual format, fall short on helping students mature, but they do demonstrate student learning better than individual courses at most colleges. For some students, especially older ones, what they need most is to prove they have specific skills.

It is hard to exaggerate how big a role the value gap will play in the future of higher education. For decades, colleges have traded on the value of their degree in the employment markets and social circles to push up prices. That financial strategy has come to a screeching halt.

Mass Consolidation?

The collapse of higher education's business model has been predicted many times before. Yet more colleges have opened their doors in the past fifty years than have closed. That fact provides a false sense of security for academics and contributes to the hubris of American higher education. Just because we believe that colleges are a public trust and shouldn't fail doesn't mean they won't. Failure is not unprecedented in higher education. In the years before the Civil War more than seven hundred colleges closed for economic reasons or because of new competitors entering the scene.[14]

Will we see mass consolidation, downsizing, and closures in the higher education industry in the coming years as we have in the music, newspaper, and publishing industries? I don't foresee hundreds of colleges closing down. But with no end in sight to rising prices, higher education cannot hold off the forces of technological and economic change much longer. During discussions that resulted in the Bain/Sterling financial analysis I mentioned earlier, the authors and I often talked about how colleges succumbed to the "Law of More" in the last decade by building and spending more under the assumption they would prosper. Instead, they should have followed Moore's Law. It's a principle from the tech industry that says the number of transistors on a computer chip will double approximately every two years. Silicon Valley has maintained that pace since the 1970s and has been seen as an innovative force in the American economy.

Technology has rapidly transformed nearly every industry. While colleges have spent millions to outfit campuses with wireless technology, purchase the latest computing power, and hire IT staff, technology has failed, until now, to improve quality, bring greater efficiency, and lower costs, as the next two chapters will detail.

5

A Personalized Education

EVERY DAY, IN ALMOST everything we do, we leave a trail of data. Beginning in the mid-1990s, retailers started to collect and analyze these bits of information by encouraging us to sign up for the loyalty cards that now fill our key chains. Each time we go through the checkout line and the card is swiped, another piece of our life story is added to the store's database, including when we shop, what kind of cereal we buy, and how often we purchase toothpaste. These statistics are then used to personalize our experience, from the coupons cash registers spit out to the types of catalogs we receive in the mail.

Because people spend more time online than in stores, the number of data points has ballooned. Companies like Netflix and Amazon suggest movies or products by comparing us to similar customers. Google and Facebook target advertisements based on what we're reading in our e-mail messages or in wall posts from friends. As the volume of available consumer data swells and more mathematicians and scientists specialize in analyzing the information, the value of massive amounts of information becomes more apparent to every sector of the economy.

The modern data flood is a powerful tool to improve decision making, from whether a doctor should order an expensive medical test for a sick patient to how much insurance companies should charge for coverage in hurricane zones. Until recently, data science was largely absent from the high-stakes decisions made in higher education. Think about it: We have used this technology for years to help us with mundane choices like picking our next movie from Netflix, but not to help a student select the right college or pass a class needed for a degree.

That mindset is beginning to shift, and the change has huge implications for how students will choose colleges, pick majors, make course selections, and even find partners for discussing a problem in a math class. Decades after the personal computer arrived on college campuses, the promise of technology to better match students and colleges as well as improve learning and lower costs is finally close to a reality. "We're moving from a model where we forced one teaching method on hundreds of students in a class to a model where we can personalize the education of every student on a campus," George Siemens told me. Siemens leads the Technology Enhanced Knowledge Research Institute at Canada's Athabasca University and is an evangelist for using data analytics in the classroom. "The way we learn should be our most personalized experience because no two people process information the same way."

A Tutor Is Always Watching

When I first walked into the remedial math class at Arizona State University, it reminded me of a computer lab you might find on any college campus. I quickly discovered as I glanced at a student's screen that this was no ordinary math course. It's powered by Knewton, an adaptive learning technology that watches a student's every click and then adjusts on the fly what it delivers next. The software does "the dirty work," the company's forty-four-year-old founder, Jose Ferreira, explained to me, by working on basic skills so that professors can spend their limited time with students on higher-level concepts. There are no lectures here. The faculty member acts more like an adviser, helping a student when he gets stuck.

I watch as Alejandro Corona, a freshman business major, navigates through videos and word problems, with Knewton behind the scenes tracking his moves. As he answers questions, he racks up points. When he gets stuck on a problem related to linear functions, he's pulled into a tutoring lesson. His screen reminds me of Facebook, and the software has the feel of a video game. He follows his progress on a car-like dashboard that tells him the next recommended activity. When he masters a concept by collecting enough points, he gets an electronic badge — ranging from Iron to Diamond. Collect six of those, and he can take the final exam, even if the semester is far from over. The course moves as fast as he does. Here in the middle of October, about half the class has already finished. With Knewton, Corona said, "I get to focus on what I don't know and don't have to sit through classes with students asking questions about problems I know the answer to."

Arizona State started using Knewton in 2011 for thousands of students enrolled in three freshman math courses. What most interested Arizona State's Executive Vice Provost Phil Regier about Knewton was its potential to improve remedial math. Every year, Regier said, about one in ten first-year students arrive on campus unprepared to do college math, so they need to take an extra course to brush up on the concepts they should have learned in high school. The university hasn't had much success with these students in the past. Most of them either couldn't get out of the remedial class or ended up later failing their first math course.

With Knewton, professors can keep closer tabs on student progress by scrolling down a class roster, quickly seeing who is on-track (in green) or off-track (in red). They can easily look across the class and see which concepts most students are struggling with and can pair students with classmates at similar stages. So far, the results are encouraging. Among the first group of students who used Knewton for remedial math, half of them finished four weeks early, allowing them to move on to their next class. Overall, pass rates in the course rose from 66 percent to 75 percent in the first year alone.

Math is only the beginning of a grand plan for personalized education at Arizona State, an impersonal place with 72,000 students. The day I talked with Regier he had just returned from a meeting where the discussion centered on the next courses to adopt the Knewton platform: psychology, biology, and two economic classes, with perhaps another course or two to come. Regier's hope is that Knewton can help guide more students through these introductory courses so they are no longer viewed as places where freshmen sink or swim.

Arizona State, like many other universities, is losing too many students before graduation (only 60 percent of the university's students graduate within six years). "We're doubling down on technology because it changes the pedagogy," Regier said. This is a place where every senior administrator seems in lockstep with the president, Michael Crow, and his vision that technology will improve learning. Arizona State's provost, Elizabeth Phillips, is a psychology professor by training and she can't wait until Introduction to Psychology is taught using Knewton. Right now, the current course introduces a term a week, "then you're done and you know nothing." With Knewton, she said, the concepts can be put in a logical order depending on how well the student knows the terms already covered.

For Knewton's Ferreira, learning technology is the realization of a dream he had in 2001 while at Kaplan, the giant test-prep company, where he wanted to develop an online course that would adapt to students. The project never got off the ground, but Ferreria realizes now that the technology was not quite ready. What has changed in a decade? The explosion in mobile technology and improvements in broadband video allow the cheap and easy streaming of lessons and permit companies like Knewton to grab data from students anywhere, at any time.

With millions of dollars in venture capital behind Knewton, Ferreira was one of the rock stars of the Education Innovation Summit at Arizona State. He's not alone in thinking about mining vast amounts of data to shape a student's educational experience. Students spend hours a week engaged in learning, both in the classroom or just about anywhere else thanks to wireless networks, mobile phones, and tablets. Think about the data they leave behind. "Google collects in the tens of actionable data per user, per day," said Ferreria. "Amazon collects in the ones. We're collecting thousands of data points per student, per day."

If you think such a data-driven approach to the future of higher education is reserved for large state universities like Arizona State, think again. Even tradition-bound, elite universities are getting in on the game. Take Harvard University. In several courses there, professors are extending data mining beyond the individual student to help spur better classroom discussions. When students enter class, they sign on to the system known as Learning Catalytics using their laptop or mobile device. As a professor poses questions and students answer them electronically, the software monitors the back-and-forth. When it's time for discussion, the software pairs students with right and wrong answers through prompts that display on the student devices. This technology allows students to be partnered with others they might actually learn from, rather than just a friend or the person sitting next to them, explained Brian Lukoff, who teaches calculus at Harvard and is one of the company's cofounders. Eventually, he said, the system will learn which pairings improve learning the most.

The experiments at Arizona State and Harvard are part of a broader rethinking of how education will be delivered in the future by flipping our long-held beliefs about what happens inside and outside of the physical classroom. The Internet allows any of us to watch lectures by star professors from around the world as many times as we need to master a concept. So why take a class with a mediocre professor droning on, especially if we never have a chance to ask him to repeat a section of the lecture we didn't quite understand?

This is where the idea of flipping the classroom comes in: Students amass information outside of class largely through online materials and class time is spent processing that information and working through problems with the professor or other students. The basic concept is not new, of course. Literature classes have been taught this way for decades. Read the book outside of class and discuss its characters and themes in class. What is new is that professors across a range of disciplines are adopting the idea, and a growing number of research studies show that students who are more active in their learning perform better.

At first glance, you might think flipping the classroom is nothing more than outsourcing teaching to the students. In an era when information flows like water, it's almost impossible for any professor to stay on top of a field and deliver knowledge in an engaging way. The role of a faculty member is changing to one more akin to a coach than a revered figure at the head of the class. "A good coach figures out what makes a great athlete and what practice helps you achieve that," explains Carl E. Wieman, former associate director of the White House Office of Science and Technology Policy. "They motivate the learner to put out intense effort, and they provide expert feedback that's very timely."[1]

Unfortunately, not all professors are willing to change their approach to teaching. On every campus, some faculty members cling to tradition despite incentives to experiment. The problem is, colleges make it difficult for prospective students to sample classes. Most high school students visit college campuses during the summer or on weekends, when very few classes are in session. Instead, prospective students should try to visit during the regular semester, so they can stop by some of the classes they might end up taking to see how the teaching style of the professors fits their needs.

Matchmaking for Admissions

Personalized classes are one way that big data has the potential to shape the future of higher education. A farther-reaching application of the data is to use it to help students make decisions about their education long before they ever set foot on a college campus or in a classroom.

Despite the stakes involved, the college admissions process is incredibly inefficient, and in many ways, ineffective. Every year, elite universities recruit far and wide to expand their pool of applicants in the hope of finding that perfect student. Much of the time they choose correctly. Sometimes they miss. Either way, recruiting is a time-consuming, difficult, and expensive process each and every year.

For students, the process is even more fraught, whether they are going to a top-ranked college or a local school. Many students simply make bad decisions. As I mentioned in earlier chapters, one-third of students transfer between institutions at least once before they graduate, and half of students who enroll in college never get a degree. If Web sites such as eHarmony and Match.com can help two people fall in love based on a short questionnaire, we should be able to design a better method for matching students with colleges.

The practices of student recruitment have remained relatively consistent over the years even in a world reshaped by technology. Every year, colleges buy lists from testing companies of hundreds of thousands of student names who scored above a certain threshold on the SAT or the ACT and then start marketing to them. If one thing has changed, it is how early that marketing now begins. Nearly half of colleges start sending materials to prospective students during their sophomore year. Almost 10 percent begin contacting students in eighth grade or earlier.[2]

Colleges devote well into the six figures and more a year to acquire those lists, dispatch admissions officers around the country to high school guidance offices and college fairs, and send piles of mail to the homes of prospective students. Four-year public colleges spend more than $400 to secure an applicant, and four-year private schools more than $2,000.[3] The best schools need to toss a wide-enough net to increase the pool of applicants in order to craft that perfect class. Most colleges, however, are less concerned with the perfect class than with getting students to enroll. For them, admissions is their lifeblood, so drawing as many applicants as possible is a hedge against the complex game of predicting yield — that is, how many admitted students will actually matriculate.

For students and their families, the problem is that colleges know more about them — through the data provided on applications and transcripts — than students know about the institution where they might spend the next four years and spend upward of $200,000 on a degree. Steve Smith wants to make the relationship between the two more of an even playing field. "We want students as informed about the institution," he says, "as the institution is informed about students." Smith is cofounder of Naviance, a technology platform that helps students plan their careers, guide their college choices, and manage the application process. Smith created the tool with a partner in 2002, and sold it to Hobsons, an international education company in 2007. Today, nearly 5,500 schools in eighty-nine countries use the software.

Students start using Naviance as early as sixth grade when their information is added to the system, providing the foundation for a portrait that is constructed as students take personality quizzes to help focus their career goals and plan which courses to take. As students get close to college, the point at which many schools actually begin using Naviance, the software goes into overdrive. The most popular feature is a scatter graph, where students can judge their chances of gaining acceptance to specific colleges through a plot of anonymous applicants with similar grades and test scores who previously applied from the same high school.

"Naviance has helped students think more about the feasibility of a match to a particular school," said David Coates, a college counselor at Kenmore East High School near Buffalo, which uses the software. Indeed, Smith says the scatter graph encourages students who don't think they are college-going material to apply, inspires others to aim for better schools, and is a dose of reality for some who have their hearts set on the Ivy League but lack the needed academic credentials.

Even with Naviance, students still face a multitude of college choices. The software doesn't make a decision for them. Craig Powell wants to eliminate the angst-ridden process of admissions altogether by taking the idea of matching a step further. Powell is the founder of Connect-EDU, and his dream is that students will not apply to colleges in the future "because an algorithm will have already told them and the schools where they would fit best."[4]

When I met him at a forum on the future of higher education in Washington in 2011, he wasn't shy about his plan to make college admissions as we know it obsolete within the next decade or so. Powell is motivated by his own upbringing in a rural Missouri town, where, as in many public high schools, he received minimal advice from uninterested or overextended guidance counselors (on average, every high school guidance counselor advises four hundred students).[5]

Powell wants to start collecting data on students as early as the seventh grade. The decisions students in middle school make, he explains, can impact their college choices five years later, when it's too late to make changes. He's a big advocate for the need to pick the right courses throughout high school if you want to go to a top college. You can't do that if you don't take the foundational classes in middle school.

Powell regularly tells the story of a Detroit high school student who wanted to go to college but didn't know he'd failed to take a required math class in his sophomore year until two weeks before graduation. In many ways, ConnectEDU would be insurance against this kind of error or bad counseling by regularly monitoring data points from each student, alerting them if they are on or off track for certain colleges that might be a good fit for their career plans, geographic locations, or finances.

When I first discovered ConnectEDU several years ago at a higher-education conference where companies peddle their wares, the company's demonstration left me thinking about the lasting impact its algorithms might have on how colleges hunt for students in the future. Powell calls the current system a broken process. Kids in rural Missouri or inner-city Detroit might get a brochure from a faraway college that is a perfect fit, but if they never heard of the school or don't think they can afford the tuition, they probably won't consider the institution. Federal privacy laws prevent ConnectEDU from giving student names and addresses to colleges. But Powell can offer colleges something almost as valuable: anonymous demographic information on students who might interest them. When an admissions office is looking for a particular kind of student, it sends a Facebook-like friend request. If the student accepts, the college gets access to the student's profile, and the courting begins. And this can happen in the sophomore and junior year of high school, well before college applications are due.

Nudging Students to Carve a Better Path Through College

The transition from high school to college for many students is rough. The relative comfort of a compact high school is gone, replaced in many cases by a vast college campus. The friends since kindergarten are spread out elsewhere. For those who leave their hometowns for college, family is now at a distance. There is another thing that we don't often think about left behind in the transition: All the extensive data collected on a student from the application process remains sitting in a folder in the admissions office.

To the delight of many students, this means a fresh start. But what if the treasure trove of data housed by colleges could be stitched together with bits of information on students going all the way back to elementary school? With that information, we might be able to redirect students much earlier in their college careers to pick a more compatible major or register for the right classes.

A groundbreaking project at Austin Peay State University, about an hour northwest of Nashville, is doing just that. The provost, Tristan Denley, is a mathematician by training. On a trip to Europe to visit family in the summer of 2010, he read two books that would shape his thinking on how he could get more students to complete a degree at Austin Peay (only 32 percent of its 9,800 students graduate within six years). The first book was *Moneyball,* the precursor to the movie of the same title, about how the Oakland Athletics used player data to field an inexpensive, yet competitive baseball team. The other was *Nudge,* which argues people need to be gently encouraged to make better decisions in life.

As he read the books, Denley wondered if he could nudge students to choose courses that would lead to a degree, if they knew in advance how well they might perform. Denley figured he could predict grades by matching current students to similar students who previously took the classes. The university had years of grade data just sitting in databases waiting for alumni to request transcripts. "We do a great job of collecting data in higher ed, but then not using it," Denley said. When he returned to campus, he started putting his ideas to work. In the spring of 2011, backed by a grant from the Bill & Melinda Gates Foundation, Austin Peay unveiled a piece of software that recommends courses based on a student's predicted grade, and how those courses might satisfy degree requirements or general education credits (in case the student switches majors). The software then creates a list with star ratings showing how well suited the student is for a particular course. It's meant only as a guide. Students are still allowed to choose, although the software is incredibly accurate. In more than nine out of ten courses in which the software predicted students would get an A, B, or C, they actually received one of those grades. As a result, more students are taking recommended classes. Nearly half of the classes on student schedules in the fall of 2011 were from recommendations in the top ten.

When Denley first described the Degree Compass software to me, I was skeptical. After all, isn't part of going to college exploring the course catalog? This software funnels individuals into a particular line as if they're at the supermarket. Denley asked me about the last time I was on Amazon or Netflix. "Did you click on what was recommended to you?" he asked me. Sure, I said. "And I bet you didn't even know that book or movie existed," he told me. "That's exactly what happens here. In reality, it's empowering, not limiting."

Most people who give advice, whether doctors, lawyers, or college professors, are heavily influenced by the advice they have given in the past, he said. When he tested his software at the University of Texas at Austin, for instance, it recommended a hypothetical student take Arabic. A university adviser wondered why it didn't suggest Spanish. "I asked him why he would think that," Denley recalled. "He told me, 'Because most of the time I recommend Spanish. Most people take Spanish.'"

One problem with human advisers is that their knowledge of an inch-thick course catalog with hundreds or thousands of classes and dozens or perhaps even hundreds of majors is limited. They often know their field the best. When students need guidance on classes outside the major or even in other majors, advisers struggle and sometimes make bad recommendations. The student, of course, ends up suffering the consequences. One result is that students are forced to take extra classes. On average, students who earn an associate's degree graduate with 19 more credits than the 60 they need. For recipients of bachelor's degrees, it is 16 credits beyond the 120 needed.[6] That's fine if the student ends up graduating (although the degree still costs more than it should), but plenty of students end up dropping out because they got off track as a result of poor advice.

Arizona State — once again, the test bed for new education technologies — largely takes key decisions out of the hands of the human adviser with a system it designed called eAdvisor. The system tracks students during the critical first four semesters when they are most likely to drop out. It clearly outlines important courses, GPA requirements, and milestones that predict success, including encouraging students to take more difficult courses early on to see if they have what it takes to succeed in the major. If students wander off the pathway by failing to sign up for a class or not doing well in it, the software sends an off-track notification to the student and the adviser. If that happens for two consecutive semesters, students receive a warning message: *You have been off track two semesters in a row and need to seek advising to change your major. You must change your major by [insert date] or your next semester classes may be administratively dropped.*

The message seems detached and harsh to me. But the tough love seems to be working. Phillips, Arizona State's provost, said eAdvisor, along with adaptive learning technologies such as Knewton, have helped raise the university's retention rate — the percentage of freshmen who come back for their sophomore year — by seven points to 84 percent. I ask her the same question I posed to Denley — does a system like eAdvisor limit choice? "That's partly the point," she said. "You can't just explore. You need to move in some direction to a degree."

At Austin Peay State University, Tristan Denley has turned to his next project, applying the same concepts of Degree Compass to another key decision in college: choosing a major. By looking at historical grade trends, Denley plans to isolate the courses that indicate success in a particular major — "fingerprint courses," as he calls them. Then he will link those courses to the Degree Compass software, allowing students to see majors where others like them performed well. About one in five students come to Austin Peay without a major, and Denley suspects many more are undecided but have picked their current major because a relative suggested it. (I'll focus more on choosing majors in Chapter 8.)

To see how Denley's two ideas might work together, let's follow a hypothetical student at Austin Peay. We'll call her Jessica. She picked psychology as a major because she was a fan of the fictional Dr. Melfi, the psychiatrist on HBO's *The Sopranos* (students commonly pick majors based on popular television shows; forensics remains popular because of *CSI*, for instance). As Jessica registers for classes for the spring semester of her freshman year, she notes that one of the requirements is a statistics class. Jessica struggled through her first semester, so she fires up Degree Compass to get a sense of how a student like her might do in statistics. Not good. It displays one star. She scrolls down the list to see other classes this virtual adviser recommends for someone like her.

Jessica then turns to check out the suggested majors. She's doing well in her English Composition class this semester. Her SAT verbal score was also above average. The program displays some other majors, such as English, communication arts, and marketing, with links to the potential careers for each one. When she goes home for Thanksgiving break, she discusses the possibility of changing majors with her parents. In early December, she switches her major to communication arts, in time to register for spring classes. Jessica is still on schedule to graduate in four years.

Without a data robot analyzing Jessica's every move, she might have registered for statistics in the spring. If she failed, her above-average grades in the other classes probably would have carried her to the following fall. Perhaps she would have taken statistics again, but by then, Jessica would have been into the second year of her major. Changing majors at that point might have required an extra semester of classes and another student loan. It could have also resulted in her dropping out.

Data sharing will become a reality for college students everywhere in the future. An era of protecting student privacy at almost any cost may be coming to an end. Since 1974, when the federal government first enacted a sweeping student privacy law, college leaders have consistently backed further protections for students. In a day and age when young Americans share the minute details of their lives on Facebook, Twitter, and FourSquare, college students may not care when or how their personal information is accessed, or by whom. Perhaps they will take more of an interest when a data point they generated in sixth grade is used to channel them into a certain major in college, but by then it will probably be too late to close the floodgates.

Siemans, the analytics expert at Athabasca University, sees "few things on the horizon that will have a more dramatic impact on the future of higher education than data analytics." He often tells the story about a day in the not-too-distant future where students will have an array of data about themselves from various sources and will choose which pieces to open up to colleges. "The more students give, the more targeted their learning experience will be," Siemans predicts.

This much is certain: As the price of college climbs at the same time the economic cost of dropping out also rises, the marketplace will demand better tools to inform students about the choices available in higher education. In many cases, these tools, based on data inputs, will limit options. Will students and parents accept these restrictions in exchange for more reasonable prices and finishing on time? For generations, we have seen college as one of the last opportunities in life to explore interests and passions or simply curiosities. Those days might be over for most students. It simply costs too much not to follow the roadmap.

Justin Wolfers, the economist at the University of Pennsylvania, explains that a college education is what is called an "experience good," meaning you don't know what you're buying until after you experience it. Picking the right college, the right major, or the right classes is difficult because students and parents lack the basic tools to make bottom-line comparisons between options. The result is a process in which students make important decisions based on an haphazard route, informed largely by friends and family, slick marketing materials from colleges, and bad advice from uninformed advisers. In the absence of good data, colleges will continue to benefit from the admissions process while students face impossible decisions, and too many families won't discover their predicament until it's too late.

6

The Online Revolution

S AM ROMANO FIRST LEARNED about the class on a technology blog he follows: Two leaders in the field of artificial intelligence, Sebastian Thrun and Peter Norvig, planned to offer their graduate-level course from Stanford University online for free. It was the summer of 2011, and Romano was working as a software engineer for Lockheed Martin in Orlando. Like many other twenty-something tech geeks, he had his sights set on landing a job with Google. The search-engine giant receives a million job applications a year. Only one in 130 is offered a job.[1]

The odds were clearly stacked against Romano. He was three years out of Stetson University with a bachelor's degree in computer science. He knew a handful of Stetson alumni who worked at Google and might put in a good word for him. But Google's interviews were notoriously unpredictable. He needed something else on his résumé to stand out, and this artificial-intelligence class could be the difference. The two instructors had deep ties throughout Google. Norvig was the director of research at the tech giant. Thrun was a Google Fellow who helped develop a signature project for the company, a self-driving car. "Here was my chance to learn from the very people who helped develop the field," Romano said. "Unless you get into Stanford, you'll never have that opportunity." So he signed up for the class, and talked several of his coworkers into doing the same. Romano suggested that they could form their own face-to-face study group for the worldwide online course.

Across the country at Stanford University, Thrun and Norvig watched as their enrollment numbers for the course ticked up by the day. Ideas to dramatically upgrade the experience of online courses and make them free to the world had been gathering steam for several years among a small group of faculty members in Stanford's world-renowned computer science department. In 2008, Andrew Ng put ten of Stanford's most popular engineering courses online for free. Afterwards he would run into strangers in Silicon Valley who recognized him from one of those classes. "It made me realize the power of free online education," Ng said. A year later, inspired by a talk at a Google faculty summit about the impact of YouTube, Daphne Koller started to experiment with short video clips and embedded quizzes to improve online learning. She used the materials in place of her face-to-face class, where attendance became optional. Twice as many students showed up for class where they worked in small groups and held open-ended discussions. "It just didn't make sense to lecture week after week," Koller says.

For his part, Thrun was looking for new ways to organize the content of a course around student exercises and quizzes. A few months before he decided to put his class online, Thrun had seen Salman Khan speak at the TED conference of lectures and technology demonstrations. He thought about how Khan's concept could be applied to the courses he taught at Stanford. Sure, MIT, iTunesU, and others had been offering free courses online for years. His idea would incorporate the lessons learned from the Khan Academy — use short videos (rather than entire lectures) and add in exams and some sort of credential. Thrun mentioned the idea to Norvig and by the beginning of the summer they had set up shop in Thrun's guesthouse.

Norvig predicted they might get two thousand people to take the course. Within two days of opening registration, ten thousand students signed up. Ng and Koller, now working together, also opened up two classes to the world, machine learning and databases. The experiment suddenly caught the attention of Stanford administrators. After all, Stanford rejects nine in ten applicants and charges $39,000 a year in tuition alone to those it invites to its gold-plated campus in Palo Alto. The university's brand is built on exclusivity. Now, several of its instructors wanted to give that away to anyone with a broadband connection.

Over the next several weeks, Thrun and Ng sat through more than a dozen meetings with various administrators across campus. Their chief concern was that the credential would look like a traditional Stanford certificate without verifying the identity of the students in the massive course.

The professors agreed to offer a "statement of accomplishment" rather than a certificate and make it clear that students won't get Stanford credit. Registrations didn't slow down. The courses Ng and Koller put up attracted about 100,000 students each. In August, a front-page *New York Times* article about Thrun's help pushed enrollment above the hundred thousand mark.

Thrun's class started in October with 160,000 students from 190 countries. In Florida, Romano's four-person study group gathered nearly every morning around their cubicles, skipping their usual coffee run to talk about the latest problem sets before their daily department meeting. These precious few minutes were often the only time the group could find to get together. This self-paced class was built for busy students like them. There were only two specific time requirements: Students needed to complete assignments in the week they were given and they had a seventy-two-hour window to finish the midterm and final. Everything else related to the class was on the students' schedule.

The ten-week course was divided into topical areas. A new collection of lectures was posted each week and remained online for the semester. In a makeshift studio in the basement of the Palo Alto guesthouse, Thrun and Norvig recorded short talks that provided the opening shots for each module. Their hands were the real stars, however. Most of the videos featured tight shots of a hand holding a pen as they sketched out diagrams and calculations on a pad. Taking a page from the Khan Academy and the TED talks, the videos ranged from one to five minutes long and were interjected with questions that allowed students to put answers right into the browser. That was a key improvement over earlier experiments with delivering college courses to massive numbers of students. When you download a talk from MIT's Walter Lewin on Apple's iTunesU, you're not getting much more than a video of the classroom lecture on the science of everyday phenomena. Improvements in Web technology, and more important, broadband access, now allowed a sharper, more interactive experience. Even so, a few students complained. "In a world of slick presentations and animated diagrams," one student blogged, "this looks a little homespun."

It was now the end of October. Until this point, Romano had been on cruise control, acing the homework assignments posted each week. With a goatee and glasses, he fits the stereotype of a computer programmer: He first started writing computer code in high school and breezed through college in three years. But here in week four of the course, he hit a bump, with a score of eighty-one on a logic and planning assignment. He went back to watch the videos again to see what he missed the first time around. In this class he could watch the lectures as many times as he needed to. If this were one of his classes in college, the professor would move on to the next topic. There would be no way to pause and rewind.

Right before Thanksgiving, more than thirty thousand students took the midterm exam. Romano scored a ninety-eight. Soon afterward, he received an e-mail message from Thrun asking for his résumé. The professor asked the same of his other top students, about a thousand in all, promising to pass the résumés on to tech companies in Silicon Valley.

By Christmas the course was over, and a few weeks later the 23,000 students who finished the class got their "statement of accomplishment." A newspaper columnist writing about the course referred to the statement as a "certificate," and within hours Stanford officials called to correct the record. They called it a "letter."[2] They were still obviously worried about this experiment carrying the university's brand name. Almost 250 students, none from Stanford, earned perfect grades in the class.

Romano snagged his first interview with Google the next month and was eventually offered a job in Pittsburgh. Around the same time, Thrun surprised the audience at a digital conference in Munich by telling them he wasn't going back to teaching at Stanford and would instead focus on a start-up company called Udacity, which would offer low-cost online courses. For Thrun, his basement experiment proved that teaching practices at traditional universities were evolving too slowly to be effective. "Professors today," Thrun said, "teach exactly the same way they taught a thousand years ago."

An Elite Education for Free

In 2008, two faculty members teaching a class on learning theory to twenty-five students at the University of Manitoba decided to invite the rest of the world to join them online. The class ended up attracting 2,300 people. A new format was born and so was a new term: massive open online course, or MOOC for short. The pioneers of the idea hoped to democratize learning and do for teaching what the Massachusetts Institute of Technology did for course content nearly a decade earlier when the school posted online lectures and assignments from 2,100 of its face-to-face courses.

Trun and the other Stanford professors were hardly the first to teach classes to thousands of students online or to give away course content for free. But the attention their Stanford courses garnered sent competing institutions scrambling to figure out if they were missing out on the next big thing in higher education. In the short span of six months, a spate of elite universities announced their own efforts to start massive open online courses. The University of Michigan, the University of Pennsylvania, Stanford, and Princeton joined together to offer classes through a new company called Coursera, backed by $22 million in venture capital and led by Ng and Koller. A few weeks later Harvard University partnered with MIT pledging $60 million to an effort dubbed edX. By the summer, a dozen others, including the University of Virginia, Johns Hopkins University, the University of Washington, Duke University, and the California Institute of Technology, joined Coursera.

The money that MIT and Harvard alone invested in edX is equal to twice the annual budget of the typical four-year college in the United States, all for courses that, for now, won't bring in a penny in tuition revenue. For that kind of money, you would think that these wealthy, respected universities had discovered the magic bullet solution to the future of higher education. But none of them have a plan for making money. Instead, they are following a tried and true path to success in Silicon Valley: Build the product, get people to use it, then worry about a business plan. "Our VCs [venture capitalists] keep telling us that if you build a Web site that is changing the lives of millions of people, then the money will follow," Koller says.[3]

The idea that massive courses will produce a revenue stream that rivals tuition or endowment returns at these elite universities — and in turn, reduce prices for students — is highly unlikely, at least for the foreseeable future. One hurdle is that many of the course founders want to keep them free or open. They are less motivated by money and more passionate about spreading knowledge around the world. Thrun was moved by Khan at the TED talk in part because as a graduate student at the University of Bonn in Germany in the late 1980s he often retreated to the library to seek out additional information that he found lacking in his classes. He craved access to the experts that today's students have at their fingertips.[4]

In some ways, the debate over open courses in higher education mirrors the one the newspaper industry encountered in the late 1990s, when most publications began giving away their content for free online but continued to charge for the print product. Within the decade, as online readership skyrocketed and print readership declined, newspapers realized they had a problem: Their content was more popular than ever but they were hemorrhaging the revenue needed to hire reporters and editors to actually produce the information. The question is whether higher education is following the same path. After all, these open courses are not free to produce.

Even so, the format has the potential to reshape how we think about higher education. For a start, let's imagine how the courses might create a new admissions path to the top schools. The open courses enable elite universities to discover talented students participating in classes equivalent to the ones offered on their campuses, and completing assignments made by their professors. It's an easier and cheaper way to find that diamond-in-the-rough student from a village in Turkey. And it's a safer bet that these students will ultimately succeed, given they're already doing the work. This alternative admissions route could feed a new school created at the university where these students could enroll, in person or virtually, for a high-quality education; perhaps taking classes there for the first two years before moving into the traditional university to finish their degree. Or maybe the new school within the university would take them through graduation. There are plenty of options, many of which would allow these elite schools to expand enrollment at the same time they attempt to maintain their quality and air of exclusivity. Open education has an opportunity to change how we produce the elite in our society.

At the other end of the college pipeline, Udacity and Cousera are positioning their companies to become matchmakers between students looking for jobs and companies searching for talent. Think of how Thrun matched Silicon Valley companies with his best students by asking for their résumés. Tech recruiters usually get a finder's fee equal to 10 to 30 percent of an employee's first-year salary. Not only do these classes have large pools of potential employees, but they also have detailed information on how well the students performed on various assignments. Udacity has already partnered with six companies to offer classes on skills that are difficult to hire for, including building 3-D graphics and designing apps for the Android platform.

Open courses could also shift the higher-education pricing model to one more akin to that of airlines. Traditional colleges charge by the semester: a one size-fits-all approach. The open courses offer the potential for a different pricing scheme: an à la carte menu. Signing up for the massive course is free, but students might be charged for other services, including the credential at the end. Coursera now offers a verified certificate for select courses for $30 to $100 a course. I took a class from Coursera, and soon afterward, received an e-mail message about study groups and social meet-ups planned for the next round of courses. Right now it's free to join those face-to-face meetings, but I could imagine older students like myself, who are no longer in a college setting, willing to pay for the chance to meet others in their courses or for an opportunity to meet the professor. The course companies could organize an annual face-to-face gathering where students participate in seminars with the professors and take assessment tests to prove they have done the work online themselves. Coursera organized a picnic in San Francisco in the summer of 2012 for students who took its classes the previous year. More than a thousand people showed up.

These ideas, however, fail to address the central problem with the open courses right now: They don't award real academic credit, the gold standard that undergirds a degree. I doubt this will remain an issue for much longer. As the number of colleges signing up with MOOC providers rises, so will interest in offering credit for the courses. In early

2013, the American Council on Education, a higher-education association that has for decades certified training courses offered outside of traditional colleges, reviewed several of the free online courses and recommended that other colleges accept credit for five of them.

Attaching credits to the massive courses could prove most helpful to adult students who might be a few credits short of a degree. One in five Americans between the ages of twenty-five and sixty-four attended college but never earned a credential. One reason so many Americans hold credits, but not degrees, is that half of the students who enter college drop out before they earn a credential. Students fail to graduate for a variety of reasons, but the fundamental problem is that nearly forty percent of freshmen arrive unprepared for college-level work and must enroll in remedial reading, writing, or math courses. Some 75 percent of colleges offer at least one remedial course. All this adds to the cost of higher education. The Minnesota State Colleges and Universities system spends a quarter of its budget on remedial education every year, for courses that don't count toward graduation but are necessary to move on. Imagine the cost savings if the thirty-one universities in the Minnesota system could serve even a portion of those students who need remedial work with free open courses provided by other institutions.

None of these potential uses of the massive open courses are a panacea to the myriad of problems facing higher education. Nor can they fix the troubles facing any one college. But the self-paced classes with constant feedback offer a substitute for some of what universities do, and they offer students high-quality options to choose from. It's a choice that even students at top-notch schools like Stanford want to have.

Dispersing the Lecture Hall

When Thrun and Norvig put their class online in the fall of 2011, they continued to offer the traditional face-to-face version on Stanford's campus. Some 200 undergraduate and graduate students signed up for CS221: Introduction to Artificial Intelligence. But within a few weeks a curious trend emerged, Thrun said: The number of students showing up to class on a regular basis dwindled to about thirty. The same students Stanford administrators worried about alienating were back in their dorm rooms taking the free online course like so many others, and they scored a full letter grade higher on the midterm and final than their predecessors in previous years.

College students have always skipped classes. Now when they can easily download materials online, students take an even more blasé approach toward classes, especially introductory lecture courses. Nearly every school has gateway courses that essentially mimic similar classes on other campuses, right down to the textbooks they assign. These are plain vanilla courses with very few extras added by professors. I call them commodity courses. Take Contemporary Microeconomic Principles 103 at George Mason University, a public college in the suburbs of Washington, D.C. The section taught by Donald Boudreaux, an economics professor, stuffs 308 students into a tiered lecture hall every Wednesday evening for three hours. There is no homework, discussion groups, or required readings. It's all lecture. There are three exams over the course of a semester, all multiple choice. The cost to students: nearly $1,400 for Virginia residents and almost $3,600 for out-of-state students. "If you show up regularly, don't fall asleep, and you're not intoxicated you should be able to pull a B minus," Boudreaux told a reporter who observed the course over a semester for the *Chronicle of Higher Education*.[5]

These types of courses rarely engage students in learning. Indeed, some of the students who show up to the economics class at George Mason are more intensely engaged in movies on their laptops or texting on their smartphones than in the course itself. Which raises the question: Why bother to have traditional lecture classes? Do the math on the George Mason course and you'll see why colleges cling to them. This one course brings in more than $420,000 (and probably much more since some of the students are nonresidents of Virginia). The profit on that course, and others like it, subsidizes many of the money-losing classes and activities at George Mason.

Now picture more effective alternatives to this class. Students grab lectures online and spend the three hours of class time each week discussing the material, working through problems, or role playing. A more fundamental redesign of the course uses frequent online quizzes that don't count toward a grade but gauge student progress better than just three exams. A radical approach has George Mason joining other colleges to share the course, so the best professor at one of them teaches in a classroom outfitted with conference capabilities, and students on other campuses participate in real-time discussions. Such course-sharing is already taking place among a group of sixteen liberal-arts colleges in the South, including Davidson College, the University of Richmond, and Rhodes College. The process is seamless for students: no need to transfer credits or tuition payments between schools.

The true potential of course-sharing goes beyond just small groups of schools. Think of courses designed by the best teachers and researchers around the world that are then given to colleges. That's already happening at Carnegie Mellon University in Pittsburgh, where faculty members, learning scientists, and software engineers are working together to build online courses for the university's Open Learning Initiative.

Building Courses with Students in Mind

The group is gathered around a small conference table in the computing administration building on Carnegie Mellon's campus watching a bouncing ball on a laptop screen in front of them. The four-member team—two professors and two learning scientists—are designing a new section of an undergraduate chemistry course. For the last hour they have remained stuck on a tough concept to explain: understanding temperature and why different substances have different heat capacities.

Introductory chemistry is a course taught by thousands of instructors on college campuses across the country. Most of those professors outline their lectures by themselves and probably explain this temperature concept the same way it was taught to them thirty or forty years earlier. It's unlikely any of them spend an hour trying to figure out how to better explain, or test out new ways with students to get the point across.

At Carnegie Mellon, the learning scientists play the role of student, looking for the sweet spot in any concept that professors want real students to understand and then constructing the best ways to explain it. The Open Learning Initiative here has designed two dozen courses this way in statistics, biology, and other core subjects using the latest research on how people learn instead of relying solely on the intuition of professors. The result is virtual simulations, labs, and tutorials that provide immediate feedback to students and information to faculty members to help them spend their face-to-face time with students in the most productive way. With the financial backing of charitable foundations, Carnegie Mellon provides the courses free to more than a hundred colleges.

The Open Learning Initiative is the Cadillac of online courses. These classes take months to build and the teams are constantly searching for clues in the student data they collect and track in order to improve the product. I sit in on a meeting where faculty members and learning scientists are sorting through the data bread crumbs left by students in an engineering course. The seventy students in the class performed more than a thousand activities over the semester, and each one is tagged to specific skills the professor wants them to learn. In this meeting, the group is going through problems in the course that generated high error rates. They zero in on a multi-part problem where students perform subtasks that lead up to a more complex task. Something is wrong. Too many students seem to miss the point of one of the subtasks but succeed with the overall problem. The team pores over the data to figure out why and how to nudge more students to ask for the hints built into the course.

Candace Thille, director of the Open Learning Initiative, says the courses are not designed to replace traditional courses but to supplement them, enabling professors to focus their time on more high-value activities. "I think of this as a combination of a TA [teaching assistant] and a book," Thille says. "We spend a lot of faculty time on activities that a computer can do better."

The biggest benefit of such course sharing is that it delivers high-quality content at a low cost and provides relief to an ailment that has afflicted colleges for generations: Baumol's cost disease. First described by the economist William Baumol in the 1960s, the cost disease is a situation that exists in industries such as higher education and health care that are unable to increase productivity as easily as others, like manufacturing.[6] It takes General Motors fewer people and less time to produce a car today than it did in the 1980s. The company can hold down prices even as it raises salaries and profits increase. The average college classroom has sixteen students for each professor, about the same ratio as in the early 1980s. Schools have no choice but to raise prices in order to pay higher salaries.

The emergence of open courses from Carnegie Mellon to Coursera will spread online learning even further and faster than its swift and steep growth during the past two decades. In 2002, 1.6 million students were enrolled in at least one online course. By 2010, that number had soared to 6.1 million, about 31 percent of overall enrollment in higher education in the United States.[7] Nearly every type of college in the United States offers online courses, including 61 percent of liberal-arts colleges, which are known for their small classes and intimate environments.[8] Online learning has clearly moved from a fad to a fixture, and nowhere is that more apparent than at one of the largest universities in the country.

Online, In-Person, Part of Both Worlds

The University of Central Florida, located on the outskirts of Orlando, opened in 1968 as the Florida Technological University. With two thousand students at its start, its primary mission was to provide training to employees at NASA's Kennedy Space Center, thirty-five miles to the east. Over the next forty-five years, as the tourism and hi-tech industries fueled extraordinary development in the Orlando area, enrollment ballooned, and the school transformed itself from a commuter campus to a full-fledged research university, much like its better-known in-state rivals, the University of Florida and Florida State University.

By 2012, UCF had become the second largest public university in the entire country — just behind Arizona State — with 58,000 students, a modern 1,400-acre campus with 158 buildings, and more than ninety undergraduate majors. That year, nearly 6,300 students received bachelor's degrees at spring commencement. Among them was Jennifer Black. As she first told the *Chronicle of Higher Education*, the twenty-two-year-old Jacksonville native had a fairly typical undergraduate experience: She lived in a dorm, served as a resident assistant and orientation leader, worked part-time jobs at a nearby Marriott and Universal Studios, and kept up a busy schedule of dance performances.[9] When I caught up with Jennifer her last semester of college, she told me she was able to maintain her frenetic pace and graduate on time largely by taking a quarter of her classes either online or in what UCF calls a mixed-mode format, meaning the class met face-to-face once a week and the rest of the time online.

The idea that a student paying to live on campus — within spitting distance of hundreds of physical classrooms with human professors — would take so many of her classes online might seem odd. At Central Florida, Jennifer's experience is increasingly becoming the norm. Some six in ten students there take an online or mixed-mode course each year. About 2,700 students enroll in an online, mixed-mode, or face-to-face course at the same time in any given semester. With that many invisible classes a university runs the risk of fragmenting the cohesive character of a residential campus, but students at UCF seem to move easily among the different formats like any other part of their daily routine.

On a humid day, in late April during the last week of classes, the student union is buzzing with activity. A group of five students grab a quick lunch at Subway before settling at a table where they barely look at each other before switching on their laptops or iPads. Within minutes one of them is toggling between Facebook, Twitter, and the discussion board for her web-based child-development class. The union, open twenty-four hours a day during the week, is a second classroom for many students. As at most campuses, finding a parking spot is an almost impossible task here. That and Orlando traffic is one reason online classes are so popular with those who live off campus. When students come to campus for their face-to-face or mixed-mode classes, they often gather in the union, squeezing in a few extra minutes of work for an online course before they head off to a real classroom.

Jennifer often waits here for a shuttle back to her dorm. A hospitality major, she lives forty minutes away on a resort-style campus where the hospitality school is housed. In this final semester, she is taking two online courses, three face-to-face, and one mixed-mode course. She doesn't have a favorite format. To her, each offers advantages and disadvantages. Face-to-face courses force discipline because class times are set in stone. Online classes offer experience for working remotely. The mixed-mode format is perhaps the most challenging, she says, because professors typically assign work for the online segment as well as the in-class portion. Even so, the mixed-mode classes receive the highest student evaluations at Central Florida. For some classes, Jennifer doesn't have much of a choice in which mode to take. "I'm a dance minor," she says. "You need to be physically present for those classes."

Fitting dance classes around her schedule requires the flexibility that online and mixed-mode courses offer. She likes having those options, which allow her to add a certificate in leadership to her major and minor. In early May, Jennifer graduates with 149 credits, twenty-nine more than is required for a bachelor's degree. In the fall, she heads off to the University of South Carolina for a master's degree in higher education and student affairs. If Central Florida offered courses in only one format (face-to-face), Jennifer admits she would have never finished in four years without giving up some activities or eliminating a few classes. She's a prime example of what Central Florida leaders hope their experiment achieves—getting more students through faster (or at least on time) while limiting the need for additional brick-and-mortar classrooms.

The image of a college education on a moving walkway, where getting a student through as quickly as possible is paramount, is exactly what worries traditional faculty about online learning. Indeed, few other issues in higher education have sparked as much heated debate in recent years as those surrounding the quality and rigor of courses delivered digitally. Professors who have spent their whole lives teaching in a classroom think the face-to-face method is the established and verified mode of instruction and any other way depersonalizes education, is uncontrolled, and most of all, ineffective. This argument, however, is tainted by the fact that there are many flavors of online learning, of varying quality, and delivered by brand names as well as mom-and-pop shops. The growth of online learning has coincided with the rise of for-profit colleges, so the two have often been conflated in the media. The University of Phoenix, for instance, is commonly referred to as an online university when only a portion of its students study purely online.

Still, as the quality of for-profit colleges has come under scrutiny by federal regulators in recent years, so too has the value of online education in general.

In many ways, higher education is like any industry that has produced its product a particular way for a long time and is suspicious of anything new. This cynicism runs even deeper on college campuses because everyone is an expert in something. Despite their scholarly credentials, a vocal slice of professors and administrators remain skeptical of the research into the strength of online programs. This persists even as every new study of online learning arrives at essentially the same conclusion: Students who take all or part of their classes online perform better than those who take the same course through traditional instruction.

The Hybrid Model: Just as Good and Faster?

In the fall of 2011, undergraduates at six different public universities taking a face-to-face introductory statistics course were asked if they would participate in a study.[10] Some of them would stay in the class and others would be assigned to a hybrid version of the course designed by Carnegie Mellon's Open Learning Initiative. More than six hundred students took part in the research and were randomly assigned to either the blended course, which had an hour of face-to-face instruction each week and the rest online, or the traditional course, which met for three hours once a week or an hour and a half twice a week.

The group turned out to be a diverse set of learners. This was an important factor for researchers since the commonly held assumption is that those who perform best in online classes are self-motivated, high-achieving students. Half of the students in this study came from families with incomes less than $50,000 and half were the first in their families to go to college. Fewer than half were white, and the group was almost evenly split between students with grade point averages above and below a 3.0.

At the beginning of the semester, all the study participants took a test of statistical literacy. They took the same exam at the end of the semester along with a questionnaire. How faculty members taught the course varied from campus to campus. In general, the professors tended to lecture more often in the purely face-to-face sections (without the on-line component to pick up that task) and attendance was lower in the weekly meetings for the hybrid sections (where students appear only when they needed extra help). The bottom-line finding of the study was that students learned just as much in the hybrid format as they would have in the traditional course. What's more, they found that the hybrid students took about a quarter less time to learn just as effectively, a discovery that has the potential to significantly reduce costs for large introductory courses. "Online education is here to stay, and it's only going to get better," said Lawrence Bacow, former president of Tufts University, who serves on the board at Harvard University.[11]

We tend to romanticize what happens on college campuses, including the actual learning that occurs in traditional classrooms. Faculty in the past gathered students in a classroom to either lecture them or lead a discussion because there weren't many alternatives. Despite the various learning styles of students today and the new tools to reach them, some professors still teach the same way they did ten or twenty years ago. Some of the biggest skeptics of online learning are unfortunately those who have never taught a course online. They see it as the modern equivalent of the correspondence course, a second-rate alternative for students too far from a physical campus. William Bowen, a former president of Princeton University and one of the architects of the hybrid study, said, "the most important single result" of the research was that "it calls into question the position of the skeptic who says, 'I don't want to try this because it will hurt my students.'"[12]

Part III

THE FUTURE

7

The Student Swirl

S TART COLLEGE FOR $99!" This is not a late-night television infomercial, it's a web advertisement for a real online educator called StraighterLine. In a world with a dizzying array of college options and tuition discounts, this for-profit company with the funny name has a simple pitch: $99 for a month of classes, plus $39 for each course started, or the entire freshman year of college for $999.

The offer catches Jose Brown's eye. The fifty-seven-year-old retired Secret Service agent recently lost his job as a contract security officer near Washington, D.C. He is looking for similar positions to supplement his pension but keeps running into the same problem: They all require a bachelor's degree, and Brown doesn't have one. After graduating from high school, Brown deferred an offer from Graceland University in Iowa in order to support his mother. A secure job with the federal government soon followed, one that, like many in the 1970s, did not require a degree. So he never went to Graceland or anywhere else.

As Brown approached retirement in 2008, he noticed that many of his contemporaries were taking classes to set up post-retirement careers. He decided to join them. Now Brown is just six credits shy of a degree in police science from George Washington University. He landed in this program after several years of accumulating pieces of his bachelor's degree by skipping from one college to the next: Northern Virginia Community College, Montgomery College, and Strayer University.

All he needs is six math credits to complete his general-education requirements. "I haven't taken a math class in forty years, since high school," Brown says. Like a typical undergraduate of any age, he delayed taking the required courses. To get the six credits he needs, he considers going back to Montgomery College, near his home. But he discovers the two-year community college requires that he first complete remedial courses in math, which would delay his ultimate goal of a bachelor's degree and cost him even more money.

That's when Brown sees the ad for StraighterLine. At first, he thinks the deal is too good to be true: a diploma mill that doesn't offer degrees. He's been warned of places like this by advisers at other schools who told him to be sure the credits would transfer before he took classes anywhere else. So when he asks about StraighterLine at George Washington University, he's surprised by the answer. Sure, it will take the credits for his general-education courses.

It's April and at most colleges he would need to wait until the summer or fall to start a new class — and that's assuming it would be offered, available, and scheduled at a convenient time. StraighterLine courses are self-paced, meaning Brown could start immediately (and better yet, finish when he has completed the exams). He signs up for College Algebra. He buys the textbook published by McGraw-Hill and logs on to the Web site at night to download materials and watch videos. When he needs help with problems, he accesses the ten hours of online tutoring he gets with the course. Within four months he finishes both classes for under $500. When I catch up with him in August — when he would have started his first class at Montgomery College — Brown is in the process of transferring his StraighterLine credits to George Washington. He is about to be a college graduate.

StraighterLine is the brainchild of Burck Smith, a well-spoken, boyish-looking forty-two-year-old, Harvard government-school graduate who is ubiquitous on the circuit wherever higher education and innovation are discussed. He arrives at every gathering with a similar spiel about the future: Colleges today make huge profits on the backs of first-year students in introductory courses. If students drop out, they are left thousands of dollars in the hole, often with nothing to show for the debt. To Smith, his company offers a low-risk alternative. If students stop taking classes, they are out only a few hundred bucks. What irritates Smith is that traditional universities and for-profit colleges typically charge the same price for online courses as they do for face-to-face versions, even though the online format is much less expensive to produce. Higher education in his opinion sees online classes as profit centers, not opportunities to cut prices for students. That is where Smith's company comes in and why he is able to offer two dozen courses at a price closer to the true cost and still make a profit.

With such a model you would think that StraighterLine might have served hundreds of thousands of students by now, instead of just a few thousand. The problem is that the courses Smith is trying to replace are the lifeblood for the average college. At traditional schools, the excess cash they generate helps subsidize everything else, while at for-profit institutions the profit goes to the bottom line. Introductory courses have been compared to the newspaper classified ads that bankrolled newsrooms for generations and generated enormous profits. In this story, Smith and StraighterLine play the role of craigslist, the free online classified site that killed off a significant revenue source for newspapers.

Unlike newspapers, colleges have protection from StraighterLine in the form of accreditation. The currency in higher education is the credits students earn for each class they take. As I mentioned earlier, students cannot access federal financial aid without attending an accredited college. Accreditors give their stamp of approval only to entities that grant degrees, places that meet their artificial standards for the number of books in the library, full-time professors with a PhD, and so on. StraighterLine doesn't offer degrees, and it certainly doesn't have a library, so it cannot get accredited. Just imagine how fat classified ad sections would be today if home sellers had to advertise in a newspaper in order for the buyer to secure a mortgage.

For Burck Smith, StraighterLine's lack of accreditation is not a worry when it comes to federal aid for his students. After all, most students can pay a few hundred dollars out of their own pockets. Accreditation is only required if he wants to give course credit. Credits are *the* currency of higher education: They add up year after year to eventually buy a credential at graduation. Classes without credits are useless to students if what they desire is a degree. For StraighterLine to survive, Smith needs accredited colleges to count his company's courses for credit.

The credit transfer business in higher education is arbitrary at best. Credits given by a community college might be accepted by a state university across the state, but not one in the same town. This is why students who transfer often rack up more credits than they need to graduate, which costs them both precious time and money.

StraighterLine tries to ease credit transfer through contracts with colleges that agree to accept the online company's courses. In recent years, a handful of traditional colleges have ended those agreements, amid faculty complaints about the quality of StraighterLine's courses.[1] "Faculty will turn a blind eye to poor-quality courses on their own campuses," Smith tells me, "but go after our courses that are vetted more than most." Indeed, Smith's courses are designed by current and former professors and use the same McGraw-Hill materials supplied to hundreds of students in face-to-face classes across the country. Brown says his two StraighterLine courses were just as tough as any he took on a traditional campus. Smith sees another, more nefarious reason for schools refusing to count his courses. "Colleges have a real conflict," he says. "They don't want to offer credit for StraighterLine courses if they offer similar courses because that means lost revenue for them."

The question remains how much longer colleges can so firmly protect their turf, especially if they are preventing students like Jose Brown from easily moving around the higher-education system. Or keeping those like Inessa Volkonidina from completing a degree on time. Inessa went to StraighterLine after she learned she needed precalculus in order to graduate at Long Island University. This kind of technology gives students more choices than ever on how and where to get their education. As families increasingly struggle to find the best quality and value for their money, students will jump from college to college — or providers like StraighterLine — until they find the right fit or can stitch together a degree on a dime. In other words, students will be less brand loyal to one institution in the future. It is already happening.

One Student, Many Colleges

It is one of the enduring rituals of American higher education — three months after graduating from high school, eighteen-year-olds across the country begin the journey from adolescence to adulthood. They pack up the family sedan or SUV with milk crates, a fridge, laptop, and other possessions, and head off to college. Every few months they come home for short breaks, spend the summers working, and then four years later don a cap and gown and walk off with their diploma. This story makes a great Hollywood narrative; however, it is far from reality: Only two in ten undergraduates attend a residential four-year college full-time, and not all of them graduate on time. The movement through college these days is much more of a swirl than the straight line of earlier generations.

This new version of American higher education is rapidly unfolding on campuses like Valencia College in Orlando, Florida. Like many other two-year colleges nationwide, the institution shed the word "community" from its name in 2011 to reflect the growing size and diversity of its academic offerings. With fifty thousand students and seven hundred courses a semester, Valencia now awards four-year degrees in two academic disciplines. It also has a University of Central Florida outpost located right on one of its five campuses, so students can complete a bachelor's degree in a variety of majors from Central Florida without ever leaving Valencia.

Valencia's generically named "West Campus" is reached by taking a winding road off a busy stretch of highway. The modern collection of squat buildings sits on the side of a lake. This looks like a typical residential college campus minus two amenities: dorms and a leafy quad, which in this case is replaced by a sea of parking lots for Valencia's commuter population. Inside Building 9, a group of architecture students are studying and discussing tiny wooden models of buildings they constructed. The faculty chair of Valencia's architecture program, Allen Watters, explains to me that no formal classes are scheduled in this room, a strategy that enables "a collaborative studio culture" to develop, giving students valuable experience for the workplace. "I'm a complete convert to the community-college model," says Watters, who received his degrees from the University of Florida. "If students don't know quite what they want to do, it gives them a chance to try things out and get taught by actual professors."

On the studio door is a list of more than a dozen schools where the previous year's graduates transferred for their bachelor's degree: Auburn University, the University of Michigan, Columbia University, and the Savannah College of Art and Design. A popular pathway to a degree is through a partnership that Valencia has forged with two other public universities in Florida. It permits architecture students to complete their bachelor's at the University of Central Florida and their master's at the University of Florida without leaving Orlando. Total price for the three degrees from three different institutions: $58,000. That's the list price at some private undergraduate colleges for just one year.

Jose Jaimes is two weeks away from finishing the architecture program at the University of Central Florida, although he has never set foot on its campus for a class. Around noon on the last day of the spring semester on the West Campus, Jaimes grabs lunch in Building 11, a new glass-encased facility with forty classrooms, computer labs, and study rooms that Valencia shares with University of Central Florida. Jaimes is a poster child for today's student who swirls through college. Over a sandwich with a few other students, he describes the route that brought him here. After graduating from an Orlando high school, he went off to the University of Florida's main campus in Gainesville, about a hundred miles away. He studied mechanical and aerospace engineering, a major he chose in part because his parents are both engineers. After two years, he was homesick and returned to Orlando. It was too late to enroll at the University of Central Florida, so he ended up at Valencia taking another year of engineering classes. Then, he says, "I saw a friend with a model, and I fell in love with architecture." He switched majors at Valencia, completed his associate's degree, and moved into the bachelor's program at Central Florida. Now he's off to the NewSchool of Architecture and Design in San Diego for his master's.

Jaimes' circuitous route to a four-year degree is a familiar one at Valencia. Four in five students transfer to the University of Central Florida. In fact, anyone who graduates from Valencia is automatically accepted to Central Florida. Such guaranteed transfer paths are becoming more and more common among public colleges. Even without them, students are carving out their own unique trail to a credential. One in three students today transfers from one college to another before earning a degree. About a quarter of them transfer more than once, and the same percentage cross state lines when they do. Students switching colleges, of course, is not a new phenomenon. What is new is that their behavior no longer follows conventional wisdom. While those who transfer are typically in their second year of college, about 22 percent make the move as late as their fourth or fifth year. And, contrary to popular wisdom, students today are more likely to move from a four-year college to a two-year one rather than the other way around.[2]

Why would students on the path to a four-year degree stop and turn around? The reasons for these so-called reverse transfers are not always clear, but academics and finances certainly play a role. For students underprepared for a four-year college, courses at a community college provide a good refresher in a lower risk environment. With an average price around $3,000 a year, community colleges remain a much cheaper alternative to a public four-year college, where tuition rates average more than $8,000 annually, a cost not including room and board. The difference in price is why students from even affluent families are increasingly choosing community colleges over four-year schools from the start. A survey by Sallie Mae, the student loan company, found that 23 percent of students from households earning $100,000 or more attended community colleges in 2011–12, up from 12 percent three years earlier.

Of course, moving from school to school to save money or bolster academics is prudent only if students achieve their original goal: obtaining a credential. In one study, about half the students who reverse-transferred and never returned to a four-year campus ended up dropping out of college altogether. Students who create their own path to a degree through multiple colleges require a bit of luck, too. In California, where public colleges enroll one of nine college students in the United States, students are finding even the best-laid plans often go astray. Because state budget cuts have sliced almost $2.5 billion from the three public college systems since 2008, more and more students there are finding obstacles blocking their pathways to a degree. Edgar Guzman, a student at Long Beach City College, told the *Chronicle of Higher Education* that he regularly has trouble getting into classes, delaying his dream of transferring to California State University at Long Beach. He remembers showing up to one full math class on the first day of the semester hoping to join it, only to find a standing-room-only crowd. The professor asked those who were not registered to go out into the hall. "More than half of the people in the room left," Guzman said. The professor told them "OK, only two of you will possibly be able to add the class. The rest of you, sorry, it's not going to happen."[3]

For Guzman, the overcrowded classes at Long Beach City College mean he is stuck working the drive-thru at the Chick-fil-A in Long Beach, while he completes his associate's degree ever so slowly. Many students in the swirl lack the time or the money to wait around to take their next step toward a credential. "Students just want to know what's the quickest way to get their degree," says Fontella Jones, an academic adviser at Valencia. That is why one revolutionary idea to measure learning in an entirely new way promises to cut costs and offer degrees with more demonstrable value in the future.

Measuring Learning Based on Time Spent in a Chair

Higher education in the United States is measured in units of time: credits, semesters, academic years. The foundation of this system is the credit hour, a concept defined officially by the federal government as one hour of direct faculty instruction and two hours of work outside of class each week during the semester. The rules allow for alternatives, including internships and lab work, but all are based on the standard of time spent in a chair.

This method of measurement, of course, fails to assess what is actually learned in those seats in any meaningful way. It is why Burck Smith cringes when professors at (pick any) college claim their courses are better than his. They have no way to gauge quality except to say that their students spend more time, on average, sitting in a classroom. When employers see a job candidate with a bachelor's degree they are assured of only one thing: that the person had the self-discipline to complete 120 credit hours to qualify for the degree. It is why rankings play an outsized role in higher education. For employers and the public, a diploma from a top school is a signal that the graduate had to at least survive a rigorous game to get past Go.

A credit system based on seat time was adequate when there were few alternatives to classroom learning, when most college students were eighteen- to twenty-two-year-olds who had plenty of time on their hands, when the price tag of a degree was a lot smaller, and when we trusted the rigor of courses offered on most campuses. None of those principles holds true today. Yet traditional nonprofit colleges educate students, for the most part, the same way they did twenty or thirty years ago. But one institution that did not even exist until the late 1990s — Western Governors University — is slowly gaining traction with an innovative approach to measure learning and award credentials. The idea behind this institution is simple and practical: Degrees should be based on how much students know, not how much time they spend in a classroom.

This competency-based model allows students like Sheryl Schuh to demonstrate mastery of a subject through a series of assessment tests, instead of following a prescribed set of courses. If the forty-five-year-old mother of three girls understands the material, she moves on without waiting until the end of the typical fifteen-week semester she would find at most colleges. On the other hand, when she struggles with a concept, she is free to spend as much time as she needs to grasp the subject, unhindered from the traditional academic calendar that puts a clock on the class. Schuh's shortest class, Reasoning and Problem Solving, lasted just two weeks; her longest class, Tax and Financial Accounting, ran fourteen. By skipping what she knows and focusing on what she needs to learn, Schuh saves on tuition, too. She pays just under $3,000 a semester for as many courses she can complete in a six-month period. The average student at Western Governors completes a bachelor's degree in about two and half years for a price tag in the neighborhood of $15,000. That's about half the time it takes the typical student to get a bachelor's degree and half the price of the average public college.

Schuh will finish her bachelor's degree in accounting in just under two years. When she decided to go back to school after leaving the Air Force and raising her children, the available options were either too expensive or too rigid with their schedules. That's when her husband suggested Western Governors. "They explained the model to me, but it's not until you take a class that you understand why it makes so much sense," Schuh says. "My first classes were management classes. I spent fourteen years in the military. I know how to manage. Anywhere else I'd sit there paying tuition to listen to a professor."

For adult students like Schuh, who are most interested in just getting the degree, Western Governors offers a no-frills experience. It is, of course, online only. It focuses its fifty degrees in just four disciplines: education, business, information technology, and health professions.

The university has no full-time instructors, at least in the way most of higher education defines that job. It has an army of course mentors who work closely with students throughout their degree program to design a schedule and access the learning materials they need. Students take high-stakes assessment tests throughout, at first to figure out what they know coming in and then later to prove their competence to move on. Another group of course evaluators grades those assignments. As Ken Sorber, a vice president at Western Governors, explains, the process separates the person teaching a student—who might have a vested interest in that student doing well—from the person evaluating the performance. Another advantage of separating the two is that Western Governors is able to provide detailed feedback on assignments within days, not the weeks it sometimes takes professors at more traditional schools to grade tests and papers (during which time struggling students lose precious time to improve). Even so, the competency-based model strikes me as less legitimate than a high-quality classroom experience where the serendipity of the experience may result in learning that is never defined by some universal learning plan. I ask Schuh about this, and she tells me about the tax class she struggled with. "I couldn't pass that assessment and move on until I got a B," she says. "So I studied more, I read more, I worked through more problems. Anywhere else, I would have been happy enough with a C and moved on. Here, I couldn't quit. I'd call that rigorous."

Like many new ideas in higher education, Western Governors University grew out of frustration with the status quo. In 1995, nearly twenty governors from Western states gathered for a meeting and agreed it was easier to form a new college than try to reform their existing ones.[4] Western Governors University now boasts 25,000 students and is growing at a breakneck pace of 40 percent a year. Its teacher-education program is the largest supplier of math and science teachers in urban schools. Since 2010, three states—Indiana, Texas, and Washington—have created official spin-offs, allowing residents to access state financial aid programs to pay for tuition. Despite these successes, the idea of competency-based education is often met with skepticism within academic circles. Few colleges want to risk defying the financial and academic model that has long defined higher education.

If there is one old-line university willing to take a gamble, it is Southern New Hampshire University. Although it has a name that makes it sound like a public college, Southern New Hampshire is one of hundreds of small private institutions in the crowded New England college market. When Paul LeBlanc arrived there as president in 2003, he looked around the campus just a few miles outside of Manchester on the banks of the Merrimack River and realized that it was destined to decline right along with the downward projections for high school graduates in the state. "I studied the cards we were dealt and looked for the best ones," he says. In one corner of campus, he found his ace in the hole: a small online operation. Over the next several years, by moving it off campus and hiring talent from the corporate world, he watched as the university grew into the largest online provider in New England with more than 21,000 students and $118 million in revenue and a total budget of more than $200 million.

To illustrate just how fast the venture expanded, three years earlier it had seven thousand students and $39 million in tuition revenue. This makeover of the online operation is one reason the university was the only higher-education institution named to *Fast Company*'s list of the World's 50 Most Innovative Companies in 2012 and why colleges across the country are constantly knocking on LeBlanc's door for advice.

At six-foot-four with a booming voice, the fifty-four-year-old LeBlanc doesn't strike you at first as someone out to shake up the higher-education establishment. He is a product of traditional higher education, and his two daughters even more so. They both went to Brown University, one of them a Rhodes Scholar. There is something else in his background that might explain the passion he holds for expanding access to a higher education. In the rarefied, educated world of college presidents, LeBlanc's life story is unusual. He is truly a first-generation college student. Neither of his parents went to college, and he was the only one of their five children to graduate from college.

For LeBlanc—a long-time friend of the father of the disruption movement, Clay Christensen—online education is no longer the big innovative breakthrough in higher education. It has entered the mainstream. While many of his counterparts are still trying to get a handle on online learning, LeBlanc is already worried about the next disruption. Working closely with an Innovation lab he established "to figure out how to put us out of business," he has sketched out the beginnings of the future for a new degree program on a whiteboard in his office. On the day I visit, it's a mess of different colors, arrows, and boxes, but one number circled in red in one corner catches my eye: $2,500. "That's our goal for this new degree program," he says of what would be the *annual* tuition rate. As his team builds the degree program, whenever it adds something that pushes the price over that number, it has to subtract something else. At most universities, the final price of a new degree would not be determined until *after* the program was designed.

What Southern New Hampshire is planning to offer is a competency-based associate's degree modeled in part after that of Western Governors. What's different is that it is built within the confines of an existing traditional university, and Southern New Hampshire has fashioned partnerships with several local employers that help design the curriculum and provide students to the programs. "We haven't had anyone say yet, 'Where are the courses?'" LeBlanc says. "Employers understand competencies. They have told us they can't find people with basic skills, who can write, communicate, or use a computer. This gives them some reassurance that the students can actually do what they say they can do." The program, awarded a $1 million grant from the Bill & Melinda Gates Foundation, is aimed at working adults who never earned a college degree and feel uncomfortable on a college campus or in a traditional online course. Like his online program that now advertises in markets ranging from Milwaukee to Oklahoma City, LeBlanc is not limiting his university's ambitions to his tiny state. He has already traveled to Memphis to meet FedEx officials to see how its workers might be part of the new competency-based degree.

LeBlanc maintains that the low-priced competency-based model will not replace the high-priced standard undergraduate experience Southern New Hampshire provides to 2,500 students, at an annual price tag approaching $30,000. Nor will it replace Southern New Hampshire's fast-growing online program, or a three-year degree program that is designed largely around internships outside of the classroom. A university, LeBlanc explains to me, has "many jobs to do" from conducting research for society, to maturing eighteen-year-olds, to providing education to various populations. While most higher-education institutions continue to follow one model to do those varied jobs, one size no longer fits all students.

Getting Credit for What You Already Know

If you think Jose Brown or Sheryl Schuh took unconventional pathways to a degree through StraighterLine or Western Governors, meet Mike Russo, who received college credits for his life experiences. The square-jawed fifty-five-year-old is part of a radical rethinking of college that abandons the age-old idea that learning happens in structured ways, whether face-to-face with an instructor or, in recent years, in virtual classrooms.

Russo graduated from high school in 1975, with plans to work for a year in construction before enrolling in college. As he puts it, "life then got in the way." Within two years he was married with two kids, and soon after, divorced. Rather than go to college as a single father, he continued working, eventually landing on the production line at an Owens Corning insulation factory outside Albany, New York. He joined the union, and over the next two and a half decades moved up through various leadership roles, first in the local chapter, then in the international union. By 2006, he was ready for a new challenge. He thought it was time to finally get his bachelor's degree.

Russo had been taking classes on and off at local colleges since the mid-1990s. But he was well short of the 120 credits he needed for his bachelor's. The last thing he wanted to do, however, was sit through dozens of classes regurgitating information he would probably know as well as the instructor. During his career, Russo was often the lead negotiator for national labor contracts and taught training seminars on arbitration. He was a trained mediator. Russo simply lacked the piece of paper to prove it all. "My family all has college degrees, successful people all around me have college degrees," Russo said. "You never know what life is going to bring you. I wanted to be sure I had a degree, too."

To reach that goal, he needed credit for his work. That led Russo to Empire State College, part of the State University of New York. Created in 1971, the institution was at the vanguard of an education movement where students plan their specific degree programs in a dozen broad areas and are assessed on what they have learned through their own experiences. It was designed for adult students exactly like Mike Russo. Colleges can provide credits for what someone has learned outside the classroom through various means: scores on standardized tests such as the College Level Examination Program, evaluations performed by a national association of corporate or military training, or portfolios of work put together by students.

Russo completed nearly two dozen portfolios. In one for Advanced Arbitration, he described how his many union leadership roles "provided me the opportunity to personally process grievances through all of the steps, including arbitration. This has allowed me to thoroughly understand and prepare the case for the actual arbitration and to understand what should be done from the very early stages of the process in order to be successful." After each portfolio was completed, a professor, an expert in the subject matter, read it. Russo then had a series of meetings with the evaluator, who recommended the number of credits he should earn. The seventeen-page paper for Advanced Arbitration earned him eight credits. In all, he received eighty credits for his prior-learning portfolios, about two-thirds of what he needed for his degree. Shortly before Russo graduated, he landed a new job: as head of government relations and regulatory affairs for a global semiconductor manufacturer. The position description, Russo notes, required a bachelor's degree.

Students who receive credits for prior learning are more than twice as likely to graduate than those who do not earn such credits.[5] As schools face more students returning with credits but no degree, they are increasingly adopting some form of prior-learning assessment, but the practice produces plenty of skepticism in the academe. "Folks are really up in arms that you can learn anything outside of the hallowed halls of traditional higher education," explains Amy Laitinen, of the New America Foundation and a former Department of Education official. "If even traditional higher ed examines itself, it will realize that's a little bit hypocritical because we already give credit for prior learning in certain isolated circumstances. So for students who have passed AP [Advanced Placement] exams — the 3.7 million students who passed AP exams last year — many schools will accept them for transfer credit." Laitinen blames the mistrust of credits for prior learning on the elitism of American higher education. Traditional colleges are "disdainful of adults" who might need a credential for the workplace, she said, but "they're okay" with eighteen-year-olds who pass AP exams and disproportionately come from well-prepared backgrounds.

Despite their novelty, prior-learning assessments are based on the premise that traditional credentials matter to employers. Otherwise, skilled workers could bypass higher-education institutions altogether and display their life experiences through other means, for instance on their LinkedIn or Facebook profiles, by showing portfolios of their work, or earning free badges on the Web. "At the end of the day, you've got to have something that employers really believe in," Microsoft's founder Bill Gates, who himself lacks a college degree, told the *Chronicle of Higher Education*. "And today what they believe in by and large are degrees."[6]

Not all students who seek discrete learning opportunities necessarily want a credential. Some people need to learn a new skill in order to launch a business (think Web design) or upgrade their experience (master Excel, for instance). Others already hold degrees and are looking to exercise their brain or discover a new hobby in their free time. It used to be that these students had little choice but to go to a traditional college to find classes, whether it was a state university's extension service offering courses at a local high school or night classes at a community college.

Today the definition of education has expanded, and with it, so too has the market of providers. There are free sources, of course, such as the Khan Academy, and even YouTube, where you can learn to fix a leak in a pipe or change the oil in a car right from your mobile phone. There are other Web-based schools that focus on just one subject. You can learn how to write computer code at Codecademy or take guitar lessons on James Taylor's Web site. Surprisingly, even in our hyper-connected online world, several of these new providers are finding their niche by supplying old-fashioned face-to-face instruction. Take General Assembly as an example. This start-up attempts to re-create the feeling of a college campus by combining shared space and instruction. It provides physical locations in New York and London to entrepreneurs who need a place to house their businesses. While many cities offer shared space for start-ups, General Assembly's twist is that it also delivers classes, workshops, and lectures in the offices on everything from public speaking to writing a business plan. In some ways, the model represents a return to education's roots: people learning from those around them. That's also the idea behind Skillshare, which organizes people who want to teach classes on subjects as diverse as baking muffins to photography with those who want to attend them.

General Assembly was among the tech start-ups that made pitches to investors at Arizona State's Education Innovation Summit. One question that came up repeatedly with companies that distribute content was whether they plan to offer college credits. Not one of them said they would. Maybe they learned from Burck Smith's experience with StraighterLine that operating on the fringes of higher education is better than taking on its sacred cows. Jake Schwartz, one of the founders of General Assembly, said that his goal is to duplicate the best pieces of college, not replace the overall experience. "We see the liberal arts as the core," the Yale and Penn grad said. "We complement the liberal arts."

Other ed-tech entrepreneurs mock the credit system as a relic of an industry on the decline. Their plan is to break the tyranny of the degree, and at the same time, the credit-based system underlying it. What is missing from their plan, at least for now, is what will replace that market. Because these entrepreneurs are immersed in the culture of Silicon Valley, their models are based on educating and hiring primarily technical workers who have specific skills. It is relatively easy to provide online courses in computer coding and then assess that learning through tests. It is much more difficult to do that for intuitive disciplines, like English, or softer skill sets, like critical thinking and communication. "If we break up certification into packages, badges, and classes, who is going to verify the entire package?" asks Josh Jarrett of the Gates Foundation.

One such verifier could have been Western Governors University, which was part of the original vision for the institution. Students would have brought credits from multiple providers or life experience, and Western Governors would have certified them with a degree. The problem, according to Kevin Kinser, who has written an exhaustive history of Western Governors, was that students wanted a degree from a university with its own curriculum, not one that acted as a launderer of credits and experiences.

Perhaps the concept of Western Governors was an idea ahead of its time, before the influx of online education services and the beginning of the student swirl through college. The early Western Governors experience also shows that even in the midst of innovation, there remains a place for some standard features of the college experience, especially for motivated but immature eighteen-year-olds who are ill-equipped to jump into the workforce and not suited for the alternatives. Campuses across the country are not going to suddenly go dark in the next decade. The residential experience turns adolescents into young adults — living with different people, participating in activities and athletics, and being responsible for one's self — and gets them ready for life. It provides students with access to mentors who shape these formative years and face-to-face networks that provide the seeds for start-up companies and big ideas. Mark Zuckerberg, the founder of Facebook, might have dropped out of Harvard University, but if you saw the movie, *The Social Network*, you might recall that Facebook might never have been if not for the residential experience Zuckerberg had while he was at Harvard. Now the challenge is how to figure out the value of the traditional undergraduate experience amid rising prices and in a marketplace crowded with options.

8

Degrees of Value

I S IT WORTH THE MONEY?

It's a question we ask about every major purchase we make. A house. A car. And increasingly, a college education.

Every number used to assess the economic value of higher education makes clear that it does pay — college graduates far outearn those with a high-school diploma. Few people question that a bachelor's degree has financial value, even when the back-of-the-envelope estimates diverge wildly. The difference in lifetime earnings between college and high-school graduates ranges anywhere from $279,883 to $570,000, and up to nearly $1 million in one study.[1]

This wage premium has long been the best selling point for colleges. The marketing pitch went something like this: Don't worry how much you spend on our degree; we all know that getting a college credential is worth it.

Of course, not all colleges are created equal. It has been nearly impossible for consumers to get information about how much a graduate from a *particular* university with a *specific* major earns. That data would probably be the best measure of the financial return on investment in higher education, but, as with so many other tools that would allow consumers to make bottom-line comparisons, colleges are loath to share such information (even if they have it). In the absence of data, it is easier for colleges to sell the dream of higher education at any cost.

But the price of tuition is too high these days for institutions to simply tell prospective students and parents to put their trust in the value of that college's degree. Hard numbers are needed — not to channel students into specific high-paying degree programs, but to help inform their choices. Academics remain uneasy — and in some cases downright hostile — to the idea of placing a monetary value on the campus experience, even though the higher-education industry has been touting its worth in economic terms for years. The College Board, the owner of the SAT, publishes a report every three years proclaiming the public and private benefits of higher education. Students, too, are ever more focused on the financial benefits of higher education. Freshmen now say the number one reason to attend college is to "get a better job," according to a major annual survey of incoming students. Before 2006, students told researchers that the number one reason was to "learn about things that interest me."[2]

Going to college, of course, is about more than the paycheck after graduation. There are significant benefits to both the individual and society that are not easily measured in dollars and cents (more on this in Chapter 10). Calculating the value of a degree from any college requires a complicated formula that differs for each student. In other words, there is no simple answer to the perennial question "Where should I go to college?" "There's no checklist. That's expecting too much," Richard Hesel said about the college search and selection process. Hesel is a principal with the Art & Science Group, a Baltimore-based admissions consulting firm that works with colleges. "For most kids and families, it's not going to be a rational process."

As a result, more college-bound students are hedging their bets. In the fall of 2010, three quarters of college applicants submitted three or more applications. A quarter of applicants sent in seven or more.[3] At the same time, the percentage of incoming students who say they are attending their top-choice school is declining.[4]

Why there and not here? That's the question admissions officers at colleges around the country ask every spring when they lose students to competing schools. Finding the answer to that question is a puzzle. Often the decisions of eighteen-year-olds cannot be explained. Students make selections based on a fuzzy concept called "fit"; families on an equally fuzzy concept called "value." Right now, neither camp knows until it is too late if they made the right choice. In an age when we are flooded with information, the process of picking a college seems to be getting more complicated, not easier.

In the previous chapters, I discussed some of the ways technology will transform the delivery of higher education in the future and how the path students take through college will have many more stops and starts along the way. Traditional higher education as we have come to know it — manicured campuses and bright-eyed eighteen-year-olds — will not disappear. This chapter and the next one are about that traditional system, and how we can better evaluate fit and value to determine whether a specific major or a degree from a particular college is worth it.

Picking a College Based on Earnings of Graduates

In the value chain of American higher education, community colleges often find themselves near the bottom. The conventional wisdom in a society that imagines college as a four-year, residential experience is that the associate's degree is worth less than a bachelor's degree.

This perception is weighing heavily on Tom Carey's mind. His life-long love affair with cars has led him to the automotive technology program at Northern Virginia Community College. Stretched over five campuses in the sprawling suburbs of the nation's capital, Northern Virginia Community College has grown alongside its surrounding neighborhoods and is now one of the largest community colleges in the country, with more than 75,000 students. Given its size, Northern Virginia might have the look of a four-year college, but to Tom Carey the campus feels too much like the local commuter school. He wonders about his high-school buddies who went off to college, and the college acceptance he turned down from Radford University in southwestern Virginia so he could "take it easy" at a two-year college.

With the end of Carey's first semester at Northern Virginia Community College fast approaching, the nagging feeling that he is missing out on the traditional four-year college experience just won't go away. Carey decides he needs a change. He transfers to Radford with a little more than a year left at Northern Virginia. Without an academic counterpoint at Radford in automotive technology, he picks business as his new major. He quickly settles into college life, especially the partying. Virginia Tech is nearby; so is the city of Roanoke. The academic fit at Radford, however, is not right either. Carey likes to work with his hands, and he is sitting idle in his business classes.

After two years at Radford, Carey decides he has had enough. He heads back to Northern Virginia Community College and secures work as a technician with a local Cadillac dealer that has a partnership with the institution. He graduates two years later, and keeps the dealership job. It's a smooth transition. His friends from Radford, meanwhile, are struggling to find good-paying jobs. "I always thought the right thing to do was pursue the four-year degree — there was definitely pressure to do that," Carey says. It's a little after 5 p.m. on a weekday afternoon, and he just got off work. "I soon found out [you should] do what makes you happy. Schooling didn't make me happy. I had no interest in whatever degree I was getting at Radford. Automotive technology was my best bet."

It turns out that it was his best bet from an economic standpoint, too. Over the long run, college graduates with bachelor's degrees typically earn more than those with a two-year degree. In the years right after college, though, the two degrees are near equals in terms of payoff. This is certainly true for Carey. The average first-year wage of graduates from his automotive program at Northern Virginia Community College who end up working in the state is $37,312. The average for Radford's business degree is $34,938. That small difference grows considerably once you take into account the lower price tag of Northern Virginia and the fact that its students enter the workforce two years earlier. Of course, Carey transferred twice, erasing some of those savings, but his ambivalence about Radford meant that he was at risk of dropping out without anything to show for his efforts (only 57 percent of Radford students graduate within six years). I show Carey the two salary figures and ask him if the numbers would have been helpful in his college search. "Money always talks," he says. "I would have thought twice about transferring to Radford."

Such precise salary figures, however, were not available when Carey looked at colleges. These numbers come from a public database recently released by Virginia (esm.collegemeasures.org/esm/virginia/) that lists the average salaries for the graduates of hundreds of academic programs across sixty-seven institutions in the state. Lawmakers passed legislation requiring the tool, which they hope will provide politicians and families more detailed information on exactly what they're buying in a college degree. As I browsed the database, I found myself quickly engrossed in the numbers and discovered how easy it is to focus solely on the financial payoff of a degree.

Take the University of Virginia. By almost every measure, it is among the top public universities in the country. In the rankings of first-year salaries of bachelor's-degree recipients who work in Virginia, however, the flagship institution comes out below fourteen other universities, including Washington and Lee, George Mason, Virginia Tech, and the University of Richmond. The average salaries of graduates of the forty-two four-year colleges in the state range from a high of $70,700 at the Jefferson College of Health Sciences to a low of $26,300 at Hollins University. Salaries also vary greatly among the most popular academic programs, from $30,100 for a degree in biology/biological sciences to $52,800 for a registered-nursing degree.

Some of the most interesting — and perhaps most useful — information comes from examining the first-year wages of graduates from the most popular academic programs. Graduates from two of those majors, psychology and biology, tend to cluster between the mid-20s and mid-30s in their salaries, no matter where they went to school. But there are wide variations among those who have business degrees. A graduate in business from Virginia State University makes $31,500, while someone with the same degree from George Mason University makes nearly $50,000. At the state's twenty-five community colleges, graduates with an associate degree in career and technical fields (such as registered nursing and criminal justice) make more than those with a degree in fields more geared toward transferring to a four-year college (such as general studies and social sciences).

This is useful information for prospective students. As you might imagine, this data also leaves many Virginia colleges apprehensive. Institutions that score low on the salary measures agonize over whether it will drive potential students away. Even those colleges that score high worry that the data might lead students and families to place too much emphasis on post-graduate salary when picking a college or a major. "This is a worthy first effort," Peter Sterns, the provost of George Ma-

THE FUTURE / 127

son University, tells me. His school does well in the overall rankings on first-year salaries—fifth out of the forty-two four-year colleges. "My biggest concern is that hasty judgments could result. First-year results are really important, but in the long haul it's a combination of larger income patterns and work satisfactions that should be used to measure."

Virginia is not alone in attempting to put a numerical value on the college degree. Arkansas and Tennessee have created similar databases, and a handful of other states are planning their own consumer-friendly tools. Getting to the calculation is actually quite simple. Two sets of figures are needed. One is from the unemployment-insurance program that every state runs. Employers who are part of that program must report the salaries of their employees every quarter. The second number is a unique ID for each student enrolled in an institution in the state. These findings do have their limitations. They include information only on students who graduate from colleges in the state and also work there (a shrinking group in a mobile society), and exclude the self-employed.

"It turns out not to be complicated to calculate," explains Mark Schneider, a vice president at the American Institutes for Research, which worked with the states to build the databases. Even with its limitations, why has it taken so long to establish the database? Technology? "It's not an IT problem, it's a political problem," says Schneider, who served as US commissioner of education statistics from 2005 to 2008. Colleges worry that the results might cast them in a negative light and reveal numbers they don't want families to know. Right now, higher education benefits from confusion in the market because schools can hide behind national averages on salaries and would-be students are more apt to trust a school's marketing materials in the absence of better information.

The federal government tried to develop a structure to provide better consumer information in the mid-2000s. Its idea to create a national unit-record tracking system to follow students throughout their college careers was buried by Congress after intense lobbying by private colleges. The system would have enabled not only the matching of college graduates with earnings data from the Social Security Administration, but would have also allowed the government to publish more accurate graduation rates (because transfer students would be counted, unlike now). The private colleges argued that the system would compromise the privacy of student data. "We have a battle between two competing goods, better data on one hand and privacy on the other," says Sarah Flanagan, a lobbyist for the private-college association in Washington, D.C.

Higher-education leaders who favored the concept tell me the concerns about student privacy are overblown. One theory why private colleges oppose an improved system is that it would probably elevate the standing of public colleges, particularly when it comes to their graduation rates. It would close the perceived quality gap between public and private schools and raise serious questions about the argument lower-tier private colleges make that they may cost more than public institutions but are worth the price.

Whether the state or federal governments step in or not, other rudimentary tools already exist for families to compare what graduates of different schools earn. Since 2008, PayScale, a popular Web site that gathers data on salaries for various professions, has released its own college rankings showing which colleges and majors pay the best, based on information provided by its users. At the top of the list for starting salaries is MIT at $69,700 (Princeton tops the list for highest salaries a decade after graduation, at $130,000). At the bottom for both starting salaries and pay ten years after graduation is Coker College in South Carolina ($27,600 and $43,400, respectively).

Remember, this is far from a scientific survey. It's a self-selected group of people who give their salary information to PayScale — and this is a figure many of us have inflated from time to time. In 2009, PayScale added another set of rankings, this time calculating the return-on-investment. It used a complicated formula that factored in both salaries and the cost of going to a particular college. Topping the most recent list: Harvey Mudd College, with a lifetime ROI of nearly $1.5 million, or 11.2 percent a year (note that the college's most popular major is engineering). At the bottom: the Savannah College of Art and Design with a negative ROI of $189,000.

Alumni of many schools that rank near the bottom have flooded the PayScale Web site with comments challenging the rankings. The value of one's degree is worth it only if enough others validate the choice. Katie Bardaro, PayScale's lead economist, said that salary potential is a factor that "has often been overlooked" in the college search process. "We believe it's irresponsible to not encourage students to think about their financial future when thinking about school and major choice," she said.

There is one downside to these salary tools I worry about—if students and parents rely too much on them, colleges will begin to take them more seriously. When they do, they will start to game the system (much like they do with the *U.S. News* rankings) by offering more high-paying majors and chasing certain kinds of students. Then a tool that is supposed to help students make an important decision will become simply one more incentive for institutions to focus solely on improving numbers in one particular area instead of enhancing quality across the board.

In the end, the salary figures from both Virginia and PayScale, while more detailed than anything we have seen in the past, are not terribly surprising. After all, we have known for years that if you want to make money, major in engineering, not English. Yet even armed with that information, students have not abandoned English or other low-paying majors. Sure, the more specific the tools become, the more families might think twice about sending Suzie to State U. to major in philosophy. Students who pick their major based solely on post-school salaries will in all likelihood, without a passion to motivate them, struggle in both school and career.

Do College Majors Matter?

Studying the relationship between higher education and the economy has been a life's work for Anthony Carnevale, director of the Center on Education and the Workforce at Georgetown University. From its cramped offices a few blocks from the historic Georgetown campus, the center has produced a series of high-profile reports about the value of college in the job market by analyzing the complex interaction between different degrees, career paths, and earnings. To Carnevale, an economist by training, college majors matter. He has concluded that what you study in college determines your earnings, your chances of landing on the unemployment line, and ultimately whether that education will pay off with a higher salary.

For college students most interested in going to school to get a better job, Carnevale's studies basically tell them to stay away from the classic liberal-arts degree. Using census data, he has found that the lifetime earnings of those who majored in computer science, engineering, and business are nearly 50 percent higher than those who have studied the humanities and the arts, a group of graduates also more likely to find themselves unemployed, according to Carnevale. The undergraduate major with the highest median salary is petroleum engineering at $120,000; the lowest is counseling-psychology at $29,000.

You probably won't find many petroleum engineering majors roaming college campuses. Indeed, the most popular majors — business, education, humanities, and the health professions — are all over the charts when it comes to earnings, evidence that few students base their career choices on money alone. The median salary for education majors is $42,000, the humanities $47,000, and business and health professions both $60,000. What's more, high salaries do not always correlate with job security and vice versa, Carnevale has found. The highest rates of unemployment for recent graduates are among architecture, arts, and humanities majors; the lowest are those with degrees in health and education.

Carnevale received his bachelor's degree at Colby College, a small liberal-arts institution in Maine. I ask him why the presidents of liberal-arts colleges who come through my office always tout the long-term value of their type of education, which promotes critical thinking over training for specific jobs. In an increasingly complex and changing world, this ability to be flexible and solve problems is what is needed, the presidents maintain. "You always hear that," Carnevale tells me, "but an engineering degree is the best problem-solving degree in the curriculum. The more specific and technical the degree, the better graduates do out of the gate and they make that move later in their career, which is, who gets to become the boss" — and make more money as a result.

It's not only liberal-arts presidents hyping their own education. Employers say they favor the skills students gain from the liberal arts, too (I'll discuss this in more detail in the next chapter.) Here lies the difficulty with using salaries in isolation to make any value judgment about a particular school or major: There are plenty of contradictions in the data. There are just too many variables. Remember, each of these studies reports median and average salaries. That means the lowest-paid workers from schools that rank near the top in the Virginia or PayScale surveys may earn less than the highest-paid alumni of schools ranked much lower.

The pay surveys also fail to account for the fact that the students who attend these schools come from varying academic backgrounds. The students who enroll at the University of Texas at Austin are different than the students who attend the University of Washington. The freshmen who major in English at Gettysburg College are different than those who major in the same subject at Williams College. Whether any of them would be better off financially if they had gone somewhere else or picked a different major is almost impossible to know. After all, you can't send the same exact student to two different colleges at the same time.

What would happen, however, if you could enroll similar students at two colleges, one more difficult to get into (say the University of Pennsylvania) than the other (say Penn State University)? Would the student who went to the University of Pennsylvania hold a significant advantage in earnings than the one who went to Penn State? Those questions are at the center of some of the most cited research on this topic of whether it matters to your future earnings where you go to college. The bottom line — it does matter, but in some cases a lot more than others:

Between the very top colleges, there is no difference. While the University of Pennsylvania would like to think it is much better than Penn State, at least when it comes to lifetime earnings of their graduates, the research shows no significant difference between the two institutions. In two studies, conducted a decade apart, Alan Kreuger and Stacy Berg Dale examined the incomes of more than 30,000 adults who had graduated from thirty colleges (including both the University of Pennsylvania and Penn State) nearly twenty years earlier.[5] In both research efforts, the two economists were able to match students of "seemingly comparable ability," based on their SAT scores and class rank, who were admitted to the same colleges but made different choices. Some went to the most selective colleges, while others chose to attend slightly less elite institutions. The study could compare earnings for the same student — at least in terms of academic ability — who went to colleges of differing quality. The finding in both studies was surprising: The earnings of the two groups were basically the same. As with most academic research, nothing is definitive. There are a few important exceptions to note in the work by Krueger and Dale. One is that a college's selectivity did matter in terms of future earnings for a few groups of students: black, Hispanic, low-income students, and those whose parents did not graduate from college. The two economists say those students are helped more than others by the skills and connections that they get from going to a very elite college. Another note on the research: They found a college's tuition price has an impact on future earnings. Students who went to more expensive schools earned more than those who went to cheaper alternatives. One theory for this is that high-priced colleges provide better resources. The research by Krueger and Dale has not been without critics who say the studies failed to evaluate a broad-enough range of schools in terms of selectivity. In other words, the thirty schools they looked at are all difficult to get into, some just more than others.

Students benefit from going to the most selective college they can get into. A study by Caroline Hoxby, a Stanford economist, separated hundreds of schools into eight groups based on selectivity.[6] She looked at men who entered these colleges in 1960, 1972, and 1982 (the earnings for men are more straightforward during this time period, she explains). A student who entered one of the colleges in the best group in 1982 (Amherst and Harvard would be in that category) could expect to make $2.9 million over his career, compared to a student who enrolled in a college in the eighth group, who would make about $1.75 million. What's more, the income gaps between the various groups have been growing since 1960. That's significant because less selective colleges are increasingly offering significant discounts (or free tuition) to talented students to lure them from choosing more selective colleges. Hoxby argues such discounts are bad deals for most students.

Barely getting into the public flagship is better than not getting in at all. In 2009, Mike Hoekstra, a professor at Texas A&M University, examined the salaries of young men who were barely admitted to an unnamed state flagship university to those just on the other side of the line who were ultimately rejected.[7] While the students were nearly identical in their academic profiles, the difference between getting in and not was significant for their financial futures. Those students who attended the state flagship had wages that were 20 percent higher.

All these studies focus on the lifetime earnings of graduates from specific colleges in an attempt to determine the value of graduating from one instead of the other. Perhaps a more important measure to consider is the one that allows someone to earn the salary of a college graduate in the first place—and that is completing a degree. On this point, a growing body of evidence indicates that selective colleges provide a better value. Too often, however, students fail to apply to the best colleges (even when qualified) or undervalue the importance of graduation rates when deciding where to go to school.

It's Not Just About Going to College, It's Also About Completing College

Sam Schmader and Cullen Edmunds represent the two sides of the value equation in the modern American higher-education system, where the payoff is in finishing college, not just starting.

Schmader was the typical high-achieving, college-bound kid at the Lawrenceville School near Princeton, New Jersey. In his senior year, he took two AP classes, a full load of college-prep courses, and volunteered at the Boys and Girls Club of Camden every week on top of an assortment of other activities.

He had several small liberal-arts colleges on his short list: Hamilton, Trinity, Gettysburg, Dennison, and Franklin & Marshall. On his second visit to Franklin & Marshall, a college with 2,300 students, he sat in on a class, Psychology 100. It was an introductory class, the type he would take as a freshman. Schmader was surprised by the level of discussion among the students, the give-and-take with the professor. This was not a lecture class. He was sold on the college and applied during its early admissions round. By Christmas of his senior year, he knew that he was going to the Lancaster, Pennsylvania, school.

But in March, Schmader realized he wasn't quite ready for college. The intensity of his rigorous high school had left him in need of a break. Schmader deferred enrollment at Franklin & Marshall for a year after he was accepted to AmeriCorps, the national-service program. The summer after high-school graduation, as his high-school friends set off to college, he headed to New Orleans, where he spent his gap year building houses in the hurricane-ravaged city for Habitat for Humanity. "It gave me a different perspective," Schmader said. "It taught me about what I missed in an academic setting. I knew that I wanted to go back to that."

At Franklin & Marshall, he was not required to choose a major until his sophomore year. "I came in thinking psychology, history, then maybe Spanish," he said. "I liked to explore, taking all kinds of classes. In the end, I had to choose a major. It happened to be government." He interned at a nonprofit that provided immigrants with legal services. His junior year, Schmader was one of only two students to serve on the search committee to pick a new president for the college.

Around the same time, Cullen Edmunds was getting ready to settle in for his first semester at Plymouth State University in the foothills of the White Mountains of New Hampshire. An avid snowboarder, Edmunds arrived at the state school sixty miles from his home after considering several other institutions with the required topography and weather to keep up with his hobby, including the University of Colorado, Colorado State, and the University of Vermont. But those institutions were out of state, and the tuition prices scared him away.

A few months into the fall semester at Plymouth State, Edmunds was already thinking about transferring to another school after he completed his general-education requirements. The classes rarely challenged him. The dorm life was boring. And the two majors he was interested in pursuing—physics and engineering—were not offered. "It felt like high school all over again," he said. "Every class I had was something I had in high school." His history course, Creating a Nation, was "a little more in-depth," he said, but the math course, Problem Solving in Algebra, was "easier than high-school math."

During the spring semester, he broke his collarbone while snowboarding. The resulting surgeries forced him to miss too many classes. He dropped out in March. Over the summer he decided he wasn't going back. "It's not worth the money," he said. "I eventually want a degree. I'll go back to school somewhere." Edmunds has fifteen college credits to his name. He hopes to move to Boston. For now, he's working at a Mobil gas station as a cashier. In retrospect, he wishes he had delayed going to college, worked for a few years to put away some money, and then chosen a school that better fit his needs. "The broken collarbone is what did me in," Edmunds said, "but Plymouth State wasn't working for me."

I meet up with Sam Schmader on the Franklin & Marshall campus on a sunny, warm spring Friday afternoon, just a few weeks before he is scheduled to graduate. He has lined up a short-term gig as a research assistant at Duke University. After that he hopes to land a policy position in Washington, DC, as he considers law school or graduate school. I ask him how his major in government and a minor in philosophy will help him when it comes to finding a job. "This is the sort of place where the core values of being a good employee are cultivated and held to the highest regard," he says. "People will recognize that as valuable in the workforce."

Schmader's experience — going to a four-year college and actually graduating in four years — is shared by only about half of students today. The majority of college freshmen are more likely to end up like Edmunds. Yet we know the real value of a college education is in the credential itself, not in simply collecting credits. "Employers don't advertise they want six years of college," says Schneider, the former commissioner of education statistics. "They want a degree."

Before Schmader or Edmunds ever set foot on their respective campuses, their chances of completing a degree on time were pretty much decided, even if they didn't know it. Only 57 percent of students at Plymouth State complete a degree in six years, compared to 87 percent at Franklin & Marshall. The two institutions are obviously very different places: Franklin & Marshall is a small, selective private college; Plymouth State is a larger public university that is much easier to get into. As a result, you might say it is unfair to compare the two because the academic background of their students differs so much. But students should have equal chances of graduating no matter where they go to college. If they don't have the same shot at getting a degree, they should take that fact into consideration before they pluck down thousands of dollars for their freshman year. Even with its higher out-of-state costs that initially scared him off, Edmunds would have been better off at the University of Vermont (which graduates 77 percent of its students in six years).

Until recently, few parents and students noticed, or cared much, that so many colleges were failing to graduate a significant portion of their student body in a reasonable amount of time. Finishing college in four years is like "leaving the party at 10:30 p.m.," according to one graduate.[8] As costs have continued to climb, a college's completion rate has become an increasingly important metric by which students and parents measure the value of a degree. Now when students fill out the online federal application for financial aid, the Department of Education displays the graduation rates of the colleges in which they express interest. There is evidence that families have paid significantly more attention to a school's graduation rate since that feature was added.

How much responsibility do colleges have for graduating students on time? Edmunds, for example, broke his collarbone and then dropped out. Isn't it his fault that he didn't return to Plymouth State, not the university's? Wouldn't Edmunds have also dropped out even if he had gone to Franklin & Marshall? In this debate over the value of a degree from a particular college, the question I keep returning to is this: Does the student make the institution or the institution make the student?

It's both, I have learned, although depending on your measure of success, one of them is more important than the other. When the primary measure of a degree's value is actually graduating, then getting the right match between a prospective student and a college is what matters most, William Bowen, the former president of Princeton University, says. In making that match, institutions are the more important player. Now, Princeton doesn't have a problem graduating its students (nor did it when Bowen was president in the 1970s and '80s), but at age seventy-eight and still very much engaged in the issues facing the future of higher education, Bowen has dedicated his research in recent years to learning the causes of why students drop out of college. Like so many others, Bowen, as an economist, is worried about the growing human-capital needs of the United States and our falling level of educational attainment compared to the rest of the world.

In a 2009 book called *Crossing the Finish Line,* Bowen and his co-authors found that the harder-to-get-in colleges that they studied had higher graduation rates for all types of students, even those the admissions office may have worried about admitting in the first place. The authors diagnose the problem of lagging graduation rates as partly what they call undermatching: students who choose not to attend the best college they can get into. There are all sorts of reasons why students pick less selective colleges. They might want to stay close to home or be near ski resorts (like Edmunds). They might want to go to the least expensive college (this is particularly true of poorer students). Or maybe they are worried they won't be able to keep up with their classmates.

Bowen and the other researchers studied a rich set of subjects: 60,000 seniors who attended more than 300 high schools in North Carolina in 1999. Not only did they have access to wide-ranging demographic data on those students, but they were able to link them to their college experiences. Of the 60,000, they determined about 6,200 students were eligible, based on grade-point average and SAT scores, to attend the best college they could have. They found that four in ten of those students chose *not* to attend one of those schools, either because they didn't apply or didn't enroll. What is interesting about their findings is exactly who decided not to go to the best college they could have: Only 27 percent of students from the wealthiest households undermatched, but 59 percent of those from the poorest households did. Among those students whose parents did not go to college, 64 percent of them went to the less selective college.

These are students who could have been admitted to Ohio State (where 78 percent of students graduate in six years), but instead they went to Youngstown State (37 percent) or the University of Akron (35 percent). Bowen tells me there might be a good reason for this. The criteria for picking a college often conflict with one another. In his mind there needs to be a good reason for deliberately choosing not to attend the best college you can get into. Too often the reason students make these questionable choices is some "combination of inertia, lack of information, lack of forward planning for college, and lack of encouragement."

Sometimes students rebuff the best college because they are getting a free ride somewhere else. A dozen states, including Georgia, Florida, Massachusetts, and West Virginia, offer full-tuition scholarships to smart students to stay in the state and attend public universities. Many of those students would probably be better off turning down the free money and going to better schools. Researchers at Harvard University's Kennedy School of Government looked at two groups of students in Massachusetts, one who scored just high enough to qualify for the state scholarship, and the other who barely missed the cutoff. They found that students who chose to attend in-state public colleges because of the scholarship reduced their chances of graduating on time by 40 percent.[9]

Like Bowen, the Harvard researchers define the value of a college in terms of getting a degree on time. Others in this chapter have defined the value of college in terms of lifetime earnings. Both measures serve as a proxy for real elements of quality, however. Despite all the money we spend on higher education, we still don't have a method for adequately measuring how well colleges do in turning adolescents into adults, and then providing a way to compare those results across colleges. It's not for a lack of trying.

The Ultimate Question: What Is Quality Higher Education?

In May 1994, I came to Washington, D.C., one of thousands of college students who descend on the nation's capital each summer, to intern with nonprofit organizations on Capitol Hill and national media outlets. My home for the next three months: *U.S. News & World Report*. Each weekday morning, along with half a dozen other interns who came from Princeton, Brown, Colby College, and the University of North Carolina at Chapel Hill, I reported to a small, windowless room in the basement of a sleek office building on N Street. From there, we would all stare at monochrome computer monitors as we made phone call after phone call to college campuses around the country. Our task was to track down missing numbers, or in other cases, double-check questionable figures for the massive data collection that composed the secret sauce for the magazine's annual college rankings guide. It was often a thankless task made better only by the camaraderie of twentysomethings, the stories we'd sometimes get to help out with for the magazine, and of course, the paycheck (when so many internships are unpaid). We often joked that with a few keystrokes we could perhaps reorder the rankings, putting any of our colleges in first place, knocking out the perennial favorite, Harvard.

The *U.S. News* rankings began in 1983 as just another one of those magazine "Best of" lists. That's when the editors first surveyed college presidents, asking them to list the nation's best universities and liberal-arts colleges. By the time I arrived as an intern, the magazine had moved into what I would call the domain of *Consumer Reports,* with attempts to rate the quality of a product by using quantitative measures supplied by colleges. Those included figures such as SAT scores, graduation rates, and faculty salaries, in addition to the survey of college leaders. Today, the rankings have grown in size and influence to become their own brand, even though the weekly print magazine from which they were born has ceased to exist.

How a magazine that is no longer published turned into the arbiter of quality in higher education for consumers continues to confound people in academia. For its part, *U.S. News* never sought that role. The rankings, says the magazine's editor, are "a journalistic device."[10] They are also a business. Other magazines have entered the fray by publishing their own college guides, yet no one has replaced, or even really competed with, the authority of *U.S. News.* This dominance endures in large part because colleges and universities have failed to develop their own trusted alternative. They cannot agree on what defines quality in a diverse American higher-education system. Until recently, they were never under pressure to put together any sort of mechanism for the public to compare the performance of colleges.

Enter Margaret Spellings. In the fall of 2005, the reform-minded education secretary in President George W. Bush's second term convened a Commission on the Future of Higher Education. The task for the nineteen-member panel was to develop a comprehensive national strategy for higher education. "It's time we turn this elephant around and upside down and take a look at it," she said.[11] From the start, academics were largely suspicious of the panel's work. They viewed it as an effort to extend the administration's No Child Left Behind law by turning a laser-like focus on testing to higher education. While the commission was largely made up of leaders from research universities and liberal-arts colleges, those within traditional higher education worried about the other members on the panel, who were from for-profit colleges and business heavyweights from IBM, Microsoft, and Boeing.

Eleven months later the commission gathered on a steamy August morning at the Department of Education building in Washington, DC. Their task was to vote on a final report. The document, though watered down from earlier draft versions, contained dozens of sweeping recommendations to measure learning, monitor quality, and overhaul the federal financial-aid system. One by one, the members went around the table voicing approval for the report. There was only one dissenter: David Ward, the president of the American Council on Education, the top representative of the higher-education establishment. In the end, James B. Hunt, the former governor of North Carolina, called the document "one of the most important reports in the educational and economic history of our country, if we act on it."

The moment marked perhaps the most significant attempt in recent history to address the quality question in higher education. It also captured the attention of colleges — and quickly. Fearing the government would impose requirements they didn't like, groups of colleges and universities ramped up efforts to release easier-to-use consumer information and measure what is learned in college. Some of it is simple window dressing. Web sites that purport to give useful information to prospective students often fail to include details on job placement or allow comparisons between public and private colleges. But more colleges are, for the first time, making serious attempts to answer the question "What am I buying with this degree?"

"We're trending here to a profile of college that looks like the annual physical of a patient, where you'll see some score well on some but not others," David Paris says. Paris is a vice president at the Association of American Colleges and Universities. He envisions recognizing colleges for doing certain things better by giving them a certification, much like new buildings get LEED-certified for their environmentally friendly design. At the same time, the Lumina Foundation for Education is backing a project in several states, including Indiana, Utah, and Texas, to define the expectations for graduates at every degree level of certain academic disciplines. Colleges are spelling out very specific guidelines about the knowledge, thinking, and skills that students should be able to demonstrate.

The ultimate — and most controversial — measure of quality is a standardized test. Think of it as the college version of the SAT. In early drafts of its report, the Spellings Commission had called for states to require public colleges to give tests to determine what students have learned. The final document only recommended it, but even so, more than a thousand colleges now use one of three competing tests to measure what students learn between their freshmen and senior years. "There is starting to be some acceptance," Margaret Spellings said recently, "fueled by public demand and anxiety about affordability."[12]

These efforts, however, fail to meet the simplicity and comparability of the *U.S. News* rankings. We all define the value of higher education in different ways. It's unlikely that we will have the perfect tool anytime soon, one that allows would-be students to measure lifetime earnings, graduation rates for students just like them, data on the employment of graduates, and information on how well a college has added to the base of knowledge and skills that students came to campus with. Even if such a tool were possible, it's doubtful colleges would cooperate with each other on a standard template allowing consumers to compare institutions in one place — unless they are forced to do it by the federal government. As a vice president at the national association that represents private colleges put it, his institutions "are not fans of standardization."[13]

Government subsidies account for close to 90 percent of revenues at some colleges, when you add up grants, loans, and research funds. Given that investment, the government has the right to demand that colleges cooperate with each other to provide better and easier-to-use information on value. "In the absence of a government subsidy, most colleges could not fill up their seats," said Ronald Ehrenberg, a higher-education economist and professor at Cornell University. We can do better than the patchwork systems that overwhelm and confuse families (just Google "college search" and you'll see what I mean). Students need to know what they will get in return in terms of skills, knowledge, and employment prospects if they pick College A over College B. Until that happens, families will continue to pick a college based on location, marketing, recommendations from friends, or a reputation determined by a magazine.

9

The Skills of the Future

IF THE COLLEGE EXPERIENCE is becoming like an à la carte menu that students can personalize by picking their own set of classes and providers, there are students similar to Tyler Sax who still want the buffet of options all in one spot.

The chance to explore at Georgetown University landed Sax in Computer Science I. He had just started his sophomore year and was dabbling in the intro class for computer science majors. Growing up in New Orleans, he had toyed around with different coding languages in his free time, but at Isidore Newman School, he never had the opportunity to take anything even close to a real computer course. His interest in politics ultimately drew him to the government major at Georgetown, the elite Jesuit university on the banks of the Potomac River not far from the White House. In his freshman year, Sax added economics as a second major.

As he got ready to register for his spring courses his sophomore year, he again felt the pull of computer science. "Turns out I really loved it," Sax said about the intro class. So he signed up for the next course and considered adding computer science as a minor. Halfway through the spring semester, he reached an epiphany. Forget the minor; computer science should be his major. "I thought it would serve me well in the long run," he said.

Still, he needed to figure out which of his three majors to drop. Sax came across a different solution in the course catalog: a new major in political economy, the perfect combination of politics and economics. At the end of his sophomore year, he changed his degree plan to a double major in political economy and computer science. "I saw an opportunity to come away with everything I wanted to do," said Sax, now in his senior year. "It's a plus in the job market. It makes me a more interesting candidate."

Sax is not alone among recent college students in hedging his bets in a tough economy. The number of double majors is on the rise on campuses nationwide, particularly at the most elite schools where supercharged students want to do it all. Nearly four out of ten students at Vanderbilt University in Nashville have two majors. At the University of California at Davis, the number of double majors has risen 50 percent in five years. Double majors at MIT have jumped twofold since 1993. "Demand is up not because schools are encouraging it, but because students are demanding it," Richard Pitt says. Pitt, a sociologist at Vanderbilt, has studied the rise of double majors on nine campuses as part of his research on identity.

On Georgetown's campus, nearly a quarter of students are like Sax and have two majors. Sax is typical of double majors at the colleges Pitt has studied. He arrived with a head start on credits and he chose two unrelated fields of study. Georgetown awarded Sax eighteen credits for his Advanced Placement work in high school, which enabled him to add a second major without overloading on classes or extending his stay on campus. Sax's unrelated majors will likely yield bigger gains in the job market than if he had picked two related majors, Pitt says. "It increases your breadth of knowledge."

One's major is the ultimate identifier on a college campus. Whenever you meet a student, inevitably the first question is "What's your major?" Having a major is one of the customs of higher education. With a few notable exceptions, nearly every college respects this ritual. There are only a few outliers. Sarah Lawrence College in New York doesn't have majors. St. John's College, with campuses in Maryland and New Mexico, has a "great books" curriculum that follows the major works of Western civilization. Then there are a handful of "work colleges," including Warren Wilson College and the College of the Ozarks, that combine manual skills with the study of the arts and sciences.

For the most part, every school has a similar list of majors, minors, and concentrations. In an era when depth and breadth seem to be the best hedge in a dynamic job market, few educators can easily explain why we have so many narrowly tailored majors, except to say this is how the faculty have chosen to organize themselves. It raises the questions—how much do majors actually matter in the end and how correlated are they to a student's ultimate career and success?

How to Pick a Major

Kids are asked from elementary school to high school: "What do you want to be when you grow up?"

If they followed through on their answers into adulthood, we would have a complete surfeit of teachers, firefighters, football players, dancers, doctors, and nurses. Very few of us can predict what we want to do at forty, let alone when we are fourteen. Americans switch jobs, on average, about every four years.[1] That means in a forty-year working life we may have ten jobs, and perhaps half as many different careers.

This instability shows in the way today's students talk about how they chose their majors. So much time, effort, and anxiety is spent picking the right college, but students are not as deliberative in picking their field of study.

In my research for this book, I met with groups of current students at a half dozen colleges, including Georgetown, Valencia College and University of Central Florida in Orlando, Arizona State University, Southern New Hampshire University, and Franklin & Marshall College. One question I asked them was how they selected their major. Some were focused on pursuing a specific profession (marketing, for instance) and wanted a degree that would give them a skill set to secure the right internships that eventually would lead to a full-time job. "It's all about building toward the job," said Rene DiPietro, a communications major at Southern New Hampshire. "You need the major to get the internships, the internships to get the job."

Other students said they were less concerned with picking the right major than with choosing the classes that would expose them to new ideas or help them connect issues across academic subjects. Most of all, they wanted to study what interested them.

"I had to pick something my last week of my senior year of high school to put on my college application," said Ian Samms, a student at Valencia. "So I said, 'What have I always liked to do?' I knew as a kid that I liked Legos and always liked to take things apart to see how they worked. I did research and put that into Google and engineering came up." Samms plans to major in mechanical engineering at the University of Central Florida, where he's already been accepted through the automatic transfer program it operates with Valencia.

"Coming out of high school, I had no idea what I wanted to do," said Paul Berry, an English major at Franklin & Marshall. Berry liked film and met the producer and writer Steven Bochco, who gave him this advice. "He said I didn't need to go to a big California school. If I came to F&M, he said I'd learn how to write well and learn how to learn anything, and that's valuable. I knew I could come here and live out my interests."

Nine in ten college students say it is important to find a major that is interesting "no matter how practical it is," according to a survey conducted by the University of California at Los Angeles. Almost as many say that the skills they gain in college will be useful on the job no matter what they major in.

Indeed, some students I interviewed said they never viewed their major as preparation for a specific job, given that the economy is in a constant state of flux. A few of the students at Georgetown who interned at banks, for instance, were struck by the fact that they saw English majors sitting next to finance majors doing the same job.

"As information changes constantly in a rapidly transforming world, skill sets won't matter as much," a philosophy and psychology major at Georgetown told me. A few international students who were part of the various groups said they specifically decided to study in the United States because they live in countries where students are tracked into specific majors and careers early on. "I loved studying everything, and I could do that here," said a Georgetown student from South Africa.

Majors are also seen as fungible — if you don't like your field of study, trade it in for another one or add a different major to the one you already have. By the end of their first year, a quarter of all freshmen change their mind about their field of study. Another half of first-year students say they plan to change majors, according to surveys by the UCLA researchers.

Some of the students I talked with described selecting what they thought was the perfect major, only to discover that it required too much math or science. The large number of students changing majors is partly a result of an early exodus from the hard sciences. About 60 percent of students planning to major in engineering, science, or pre-med end up picking other fields, or not getting a degree at all. "They come in thinking this is what they want to do, and they get in these large lecture classes for calculus or chemistry where faculty treat it as a weeding-out process," John Pryor, director of the Cooperative Institutional Research Program at UCLA, tells me.

The UCLA research dovetails with the overall trend in majors for the past five decades, a trend bemoaned by scholars as a "dramatic flight from the arts and sciences" to what is now termed the "practical arts."[2] The number of bachelor's degrees awarded in traditional arts and sciences fields (English, math, and biology, for example) has tumbled from almost half of the undergraduate credentials awarded in 1968 to 26 percent in 2010. The majority of credentials today are awarded in occupational or vocational areas such as business, education, and communications. The most popular undergraduate major is business.

With the perceived value of higher education increasingly tied to potential lifetime earnings, students face pressure at home and in high school to figure out what they want to do with the rest of their lives and then pick a major in college that will lead to a job. Students are not always responding to that pressure, which is why we see so many contradictions. Students choose vocational majors, yet tell researchers that they are not necessarily looking for practical fields of study. Another reason for the inconsistencies is that today's high-school and college students are largely "drifting," according to studies conducted by psychologist William Damon. Only one in five young people has a clear vision of what they want to accomplish in life.[3]

My roommate in college was one of those people. He had known since middle school what he wanted to do — become a television journalist. Now almost twenty years after we both graduated with journalism degrees, David Muir is an anchor and correspondent for *ABC World News*. Given the immense changes in how the news is reported and delivered since we graduated, I asked him what parts of our practical degree still serve him as he covers a presidential campaign in the

United States or races around the globe to report on the latest uprising in the Middle East. He said the classes where the emphasis was on using the technology of the era are useless now (after all, we used videotape and reel-to-reel audio then). "The greater lessons I carry with me today are the other classes—the critical thinking, questioning public policy, forming arguments, and the discussions that put what we learned in the broader context of where the world is heading," Muir said. "We're in such an attention-deficit culture now that there is a premium on people who can take a step back, dissect an issue, spend some time on it, and write about it."

Does the college major matter then? Not really, he said. He works with plenty of people who do not have journalism degrees. The commonality among them, he says, is that "we all majored in what we were interested in. The curiosity and the willingness to adapt are more important than what the degree is in."

These are many of the same qualities that employers say, in survey after survey, they want in future workers. Hiring managers complain that they often find today's college graduates lacking in interpersonal skills, problem solving, effective written and oral communication skills, the ability to work in teams, and critical and analytical thinking. Employers say that future workplaces need degree holders who can come up with novel solutions to problems and better sort through information to filter out the most critical pieces.

Which college majors best equip students with those skills? The question has touched off heated discussions between those who advocate for a practical major and others who think that the skills of a liberal-arts major are the best insurance in rapidly changing fields. Employers are almost evenly split on the issue. In one survey, 45 percent of hiring managers prefer that students acquire an education that specifically prepares them for the workplace; 55 percent favor a broad-based education.[4]

"Ideally, you want to do both," Richard Arum says. Arum is the co-author of *Academically Adrift,* the book discussed in Chapter 2, that found nearly half of students failed to improve their critical-thinking skills in the first two years of college. Arum says the field of study matters less than how much you work in the major. For instance, math and science majors don't write or read much for their classes, but they show gains in critical thinking because they spend the most hours studying. "It doesn't matter what these students focus on," Arum says, "as long as they focus on it in a rigorous way."

Subjects Don't Matter, Cognitive Abilities Do

Roger Schank, a cognitive scientist and artificial intelligence theorist, has the passion of a preacher when you get him started about what needs to be reformed in education. He has taught at Yale and Northwestern universities and now runs Socratic Arts, a company which builds learning tools for businesses and schools. When I first met him at the launch of Georgia Tech's Center for 21st Century Universities (a lab for experimenting with new higher-education models), Schank asked me if I knew the quadratic equation. Of course not, I said, that's why I majored in journalism — no serious math needed. He said it's a question he asks nearly everyone he meets. No one can give him the answer, including the former chairman of the College Board, Gaston Caperton, even though the "SAT makes you memorize all these useless facts," Schank says.

Schank is beginning to seethe now as he tells me that the entire structure of universities is designed incorrectly. The institutions are built around the research interests of the faculty and what they want to teach, not how students need to learn. If he ran a university, he would eliminate departments, majors, even courses. Subjects don't matter, he said, cognitive abilities do.

In his book *Teaching Minds,* Schank explains that when he worked in artificial intelligence he realized that teaching the computer more facts did not make the machine smart or do what he needed it to do. The same thing with students. Feeding them more facts might make them pass a test, but it won't help them diagnose a problem or make an accurate prediction. "If we wish to teach people," Schank writes, "we want to understand what we have to do in order to make them better able to think."[5]

Instead of traditional majors, Schank proposes dividing the four years of college into two parts. The first two years would be dedicated to teaching what he calls the "twelve cognitive processes that underlie learning" (such things as prediction, modeling, planning, negotiation, teamwork) and the last two years to instruction in specific subjects. He is not the first academic to suggest that universities abolish departments. Mark Taylor, a religion professor at Columbia University, proposes that colleges create problem-focused departments in place of the ones they have today. "It is possible to imagine a broad range of topics around which such zones of inquiry could be organized: Mind, Body, Law, Information, Networks, Language, Space, Time, Media, Money, Life and Water."[6]

Perhaps one day more colleges will do away with departments and majors. Until then, on most campuses students will need to pick a field of study. In some industries, majors matter to the job (take engineering, as an example). But overall, I have found by talking to employers and educators that what they want most in their workers is the ability to learn how to learn. In other words, the capability to find the answers to the questions of tomorrow that we cannot envision asking today.

The economy is changing at warp speed. The ten jobs most in demand in 2010 did not exist in 2004. Rather than recommend majors of the future — which may well be on their way to obsolescence by the time you read this book — I highlight below four activities that help develop the skills necessary to succeed in the workforce of tomorrow. If students focus on these activities, the majors won't matter as much.

Seek Passionate Faculty Mentors

Passion and curiosity are what drove most of the students I interviewed to choose the majors they did, but several undergraduates at Georgetown University suggested another reason, their faculty. "I look at the top courses on RateMyProfessors and want to sign up for those," one student at Georgetown said. "I want to be challenged. I want professors who care more about their students and less about their research." She is probably unusual among her classmates in terms of seeking out rigorous courses, but nearly all of the Georgetown students identified — by name — professors who already had an impact on their undergraduate career. The mentorship relationship between the professor and student is one big advantage traditional colleges hold over online providers, where students might never have meaningful conversations with their instructors. Yet in recent years, traditional colleges have been slowly diminishing this benefit by hiring more part-time professors who cannot spend as much time interacting with students outside the classroom.

Finding passionate, engaged professors is critically important in the first year of college, when it is easy to remain anonymous in large lecture classes. George Kuh, an emeritus professor at Indiana University, tells me that getting to know at least one faculty member well in that year improves the chances that students will get more from their college experience (including a degree). Kuh has written extensively on "high-impact practices" in higher education — routines that, by building on the foundation students bring to college, will lead to their ultimate success. He maintains that students are not engaged in enough of these activities, which include interactions with professors. About two out of five freshmen say that they have "never discussed ideas from readings or classes with faculty members outside of class." Another three out of five freshmen say they never worked with professors on activities other than coursework.

These findings come from the National Survey of Student Engagement. Tens of thousands of students in their freshmen and senior years at hundreds of colleges take the fifteen-minute survey every year. It asks questions related to the experience in college: how much they collaborate with other students, participate in activities outside the classroom, and how hard they work at any of those pursuits, including studying. The questions are designed around the high-impact practices Kuh talks about.

The survey provides precisely the type of information that would be helpful to families when it comes to selecting a college. Good luck in locating the results. The findings for individual colleges are not released publicly, although some institutions do share their results in various ways.

Even so, the survey itself and the questions it asks give a road map to students trying to figure out the value of a particular college. You can even download a handbook with questions to ask on a college tour, such as: How many students work on research projects with faculty? Do students receive prompt feedback on academic performance? How often do students talk with advisers or faculty members about their career plans?

The most engaged students on campus, Kuh says, are those who take part in "deep approaches to their learning," meaning they are active participants in their intellectual pursuits rather than students who simply take notes in a class. An important measure of active learning is "time on task," Kuh says. In other words, as Arum suggested, rigor makes a difference. Two of the other activities that help develop the skills of the future also require deep, active learning — undergraduate research and study abroad.

Dive Deep into a Research Project

"I have a feeling that I'm not just a student," Heidi Klise says. "I'm someone who has added to my area of study."

Klise is describing a research project she has just completed. It's an historical narrative of the 15th Army Air Corps, which operated in relative obscurity during World War II. Based in Italy, the squadron carried out several dozen bombing raids in Eastern Europe. Klise's ninety-one-year-old grandfather was a member of the unit and served as a primary source for her project. She also received a grant to spend several days at an Air Force museum in Georgia where she combed through the archives of letters, journals, and other documents. "I was able to delve into the time period and bring it alive in my writing," Klise says.

Klise is not a graduate student in history. She just received her bachelor's degree from the College of Wooster in Ohio. Her paper is part of an undergraduate research project that every student at Wooster must complete before graduation. The research is carried out over the course of the senior year. Students meet one-on-one every week for an hour with their faculty adviser, who helps to focus the research, ask questions, and provide feedback on drafts. Near the end of the spring semester, students defend their thesis in front of a committee. "It was great to connect with the professor in this way," Klise says. "All the talking was about my research. It was all about the student's research, not about the professor."

Klise's faculty adviser was Hayden Schilling. He has been teaching at Wooster for nearly fifty years. The research experience, he says, comes to define the undergraduate years for so many students. "This is a rite of passage," Schilling says. "It's intense. They learn a lot about themselves, about what they can do and what they can't do. And I think many of them are surprised by what they learn."

Faculty members at Wooster begin preparing students for the experience with extensive writing and research assignments as early as their first year. The end result, the thesis itself, "is a piece of evidence that students can take to employers or graduate schools to show that they can write, reason, and be successful," Schilling says.

Undergraduates conducting research is not a new phenomenon. Its value has long been recognized in the sciences, where students have been able to work with professors and graduate students on teams in the lab and have their findings published. What is new is that the idea has spread to nearly every academic field. Nearly a third of seniors produce some sort of capstone project. Some three thousand students present their projects at the annual gathering of the National Conference on Undergraduate Research, up from just a few hundred at its first meeting in 1987.

Studies over the years have found that undergraduate research stimulates critical thinking, gives students a better understanding of what they learned from a lecture, allows them to work in situations with uncertain results, and provides a sense of accomplishment. "There seems to be a tremendous amount of growth," says David Lopatto, a psychology professor at Grinnell College, who has conducted studies on undergraduate research. "Students report they can work more independently. They feel they can tolerate obstacles to their work better than they used to. They feel ready for challenge."[7]

Go on a Transformative Global Experience

Ronnie Wimberley had never been on a plane until he went to Egypt for three and a half weeks in the spring of 2012. A freshman at Duke University, he was part of a team of students interviewing Iraqi refugees for a class. When they returned, the students wrote articles based on their interviews and performed narratives of the refugee life stories in short three-minute monologues. The experience abroad encouraged Wimberley to spend part of the following summer in Geneva, where he took two courses in economics and business.

When you go abroad, "you learn the depth and breadth of what it means to have a different culture," Wimberly said. "You take things in on a human level rather than the theoretical level of a class."

More than 270,000 Americans study overseas each year, nearly triple the number of two decades ago, but still a tiny fraction of all American undergraduates. Study abroad used to be seen as something wealthy kids did in Europe to take it easy for a semester. Now there is growing recognition that overseas study in college helps in the global job market, which is apparent from the countries in which students choose to study. Fourteen of the top twenty-five destinations are outside Europe, with the biggest gains in students going to India, Brazil, Israel, and New Zealand.[8] Those who study abroad often see it as a life-changing experience. In one survey of alumni, it was the most significant aspect of their undergraduate years, ranking higher than college friendships and courses.[9]

Lack of money is the biggest hurdle keeping students from studying abroad. At Duke, about half of the undergraduates go overseas by the time they graduate, thanks in large part to the university's financial support. The first trip abroad for Lauren Hendricks was paid for by Duke. The public policy major spent the summer after her freshman year in South Africa. In Cape Town she conducted research for a nonprofit on a new national health insurance plan. A year later, she took a semester of classes in Italy. The most enlightening part of that time for her was gaining a broader perspective on global issues. "I saw the problem from an Italian or European Union vantage point and suddenly the issue looked completely different," she said. "A part of my brain lit up, and I realized how much nations were connected to each other and how complex policies on an international scale could become."

Be Creative. Take Risks. Learn How to Fail.

American public schools, colleges, and universities are very good at teaching for the test, and students are now comfortable learning in that way. Jonathan Cole, a former provost at Columbia University and a professor in the law school there, says even his best students can't recall the facts of cases they learned in constitutional law courses in which they received A's. He blames this partly on an admissions process that is too tied to test scores and results in "one-dimensional students." He thinks the smartest people on campuses should be working in admissions so they can pick more interesting students.

Many academics believe students have lost the ability to be creative — to learn through doing, to learn through failing, to learn through just having fun. "I remember kindergarten where you actually got to do things, not like today," Alan Kay lamented on a panel discussion at Georgia Tech. "Now that's graduate school." Kay is a computer scientist who leads the Viewpoints Research Institute, a nonprofit to improve "powerful ideas education."

The failures of our education system are beginning to reach the workplace. Amid worries that workers are becoming less innovative, some companies are rewarding their employees for mistakes or questionable risks in order to encourage original thinking.[10] In this hyperconnected world, where companies have access to the best talent anywhere, being book smart alone doesn't cut it. If colleges want to justify their value in the future, they need to establish learning environments where students can be creative, try things out, and, on occasion, fail without being penalized.

This was the message that Daniel H. Pink delivered to several hundred college leaders at a higher-education conference a few years ago. Pink is the best-selling author of *A Whole New Mind*. His central argument to the college administrators in the room was this: Both the economy and society are moving away from the logical, linear, computerlike attributes of the left brain to a conceptual age when the big-picture capabilities of the right brain will be increasingly important.

At first, some in the audience saw the message as a sermon against math-and-science education. That was not his intention, said Pink. Indeed, the "idea that math and science are routine disciplines is one of the most dangerous things going on in this country today," he said. "The idea that math and science are turning kids into vending machines for right answers is really dangerous." He showed a picture of a group of medical students from Mount Sinai School of Medicine visiting an art museum. It was not a field trip, but rather part of their diagnostic training. "Certain kinds of diagnoses defy routine, and there is so much medical information today for one to learn that delivering the right answers sometimes means asking the right questions," Pink said. "The best physicians have the observation skills of a painter or sculptor."

Pink told the group about the six abilities he thinks matter most in the new economy. The one that struck me is what he called "symphony." He described it as "the killer app." People usually think of successful leaders as being extremely focused. "The opposite ability — the ability to step back, see the big picture, and connect the dots — is more important." In a study done by Daniel Goleman the stars of a dozen organizations were given a battery of tests. Goleman found that one cognitive ability set them apart from everyone else — pattern recognition. Those stars had the big-picture thinking that enabled them to pick out meaningful trends from a mass of information and think strategically.

Colleges and universities need to help students develop such abilities. Otherwise, graduates will be skilled only in routine work. That may help them on an assessment test, but when that routine work is automated and outsourced, it won't help much in the job market.

The skills needed for success in the twenty-first century may sound like a throwback to the classic liberal-arts course of study of arithmetic, geometry, grammar, logic, and rhetoric. Indeed, as the United States moves away from a broad educational approach into narrow, practical majors, many Asian countries are moving precisely in the opposite direction out of fear that they are producing nothing more than a nation of test takers. As a reporter, I hear over and over again that students and colleges need to have more balanced degrees, with both broad knowledge and in-depth study in a particular area. Employers say that is what they want, but their hiring practices might be working against that goal.

Business Leaders Value the Liberal Arts

For much of the 2000s, Samuel Palmisano and A. G. Lafley led two of the biggest names in American business, IBM and Procter & Gamble. Both men joined their companies at the start of their careers and climbed through the ranks. By the time they were named chief executive officers, the two iconic companies were in need of makeovers. Under Lafley, Proctor & Gamble became a more innovative company and more than doubled its sales; at IBM, Palmisano jettisoned the company's personal computer line of business, focused on selling services to businesses and governments, and its profits swelled. The two men have something else in common as well — they graduated from college with degrees in the liberal arts.

Palmisano and Lafley both credit their undergraduate education for their accomplishments. Now retired, they often talk about the inherent strengths the liberal arts bring to a workplace where creativity, problem solving, flexibility, and teamwork are paramount. With the liberal arts "you get to exercise your whole brain," says Lafley, who graduated with a history degree from Hamilton College. "Inductively reasoning in the science courses, deductively reasoning in some of the philosophy and humanities courses, abductively reasoning in design. You understand inquiry. You understand advocacy."[11]

Palmisano maintains that college graduates need a "deep skill" in some academic subject, but that depth in one area needs to be supplemented with other knowledge. "Whatever you're deep in, you need to balance with the other side of it," says Palmisano, who majored in behavioral social sciences at Johns Hopkins University. "So if you're deep in math and science or engineering, you've got to balance it with the humanities, because you have to work in these multicultural global environments in the broadest sense of diversity. All religions. All cultures. All languages. You know in this place [IBM] we deal with 170 countries, so you have to demonstrate that you have that ability to listen and understand and be sensitive to cultural issues as well as deep and smart in some discipline. But if you're not deep and smart in some discipline, you're going to have a hard time competing."[12]

It is easy for Palmisano and Lafley to advocate hiring people with liberal-arts degrees. IBM and Proctor & Gamble are well known for their training programs. Take smart college graduates, put them through an apprenticeship, and it doesn't really matter what they majored in. Most companies are not like IBM and Proctor & Gamble. Corporate training has largely disappeared, along with the recruiters whose job was to locate the best candidates for those programs, argues Peter Cappelli.

Cappelli is a professor at the University of Pennsylvania's Wharton School and author of *Why Good People Can't Get Jobs*. While corporate CEOs might say they favor applicants with a broad education at the foundation, leaders are largely removed from the hiring process. The people on the front lines of hiring these days are lower-level managers who want the job filled with someone who can do the work immediately. "This plays on their prejudices of the hiring manager," he says. "If they think they need someone with a master's degree, they'll ask for that. If they think it will take too long to train a liberal-arts graduate, they will toss those applications aside. All without evidence of what's really needed to do the job."

Recruiters also receive their initial pool of candidates through a screening process that has largely been taken out of human hands by automated software that scans applications and résumés for certain keywords. "They are trying to mimic the best of human decision making," Cappelli says. The problem, he adds, is that "computerized systems are not very flexible. They don't have judgment. They can't imagine the job skills or experiences you don't program into them."

Imagine each of the system's requirements as a hurdle, Cappelli says. If a degree is required, applicants who don't have that credential are thrown out, even if they have other certifications or experiences. These systems especially favor specific, practical majors, the kind often programmed in as keywords. "If you're a student, now you have to play this game to figure out how to get through these systems so you make that initial cut," Cappelli says. "It's a game of risk management."

Until recently, colleges have not felt much need to help launch the careers of new graduates. Many follow the same tired playbook year after year — a career office tucked away in a corner of the campus, employer fairs, visits from corporate recruiters, and then, six months or so after commencement, a survey of graduates, few of whom respond (yet that doesn't stop colleges from publicizing the amazingly high percentages of their graduates with jobs, including, though they may not make this evident, those working the coffee line at Starbucks).

With the economy stuck in neutral and college prices continuing to rise, prospective students and their parents are looking more closely at how a college will ease the transition into the working world. After years of talking about rosy job-placement rates during campus tours, colleges need to either drum up better numbers or do more to help the career prospects of their recent graduates in this tough economy.

"Too many students are struggling to launch after college," says Eric C. Wiseman, chairman and chief executive of the VF Corporation, the apparel conglomerate.[13] He maintains that everyone at a college — from those in career services to faculty members — needs to take ownership of the product they are creating, an educated student.

You might think that the leaders on this front would be the colleges that spent the last decade adding majors in every new professional field as a way to pump up enrollment. After all, they were responding to market demand for what are essentially vocational majors. But some strikingly innovative approaches to help graduates find work are coming from a sector that has long felt uncomfortable with the concept of preparing their students for jobs: liberal-arts colleges.

Take Franklin & Marshall College. The relatively new president there, Dan Porterfield, maintains that career development needs to be part of a "holistic learning approach" that better prepares students for their postgraduate lives and, most important, extends their education into those first few years after graduation. He refers to this period as a college's ten-year "zone of impact," which includes the year before college, the four years of undergraduate studies, and five years after college. "The twenties are a period of massive development," he says. "Our job doesn't end at graduation." To that end, he has created a new senior position at the college, responsible for creating programs in life skills, such as managing debt, and soft skills, such as conflict resolution, for both undergraduates and new alumni.

At Davidson College, in North Carolina, Carol E. Quillen, the president, was surprised when she met with a small group of successful alumni in New York to hear that they would hire a Davidson graduate three years out of college, but not a year out. The alumni said that new graduates needed more exposure to the real world of work, to "try out the talents we claim to be cultivating before they are on the job market." Following the model of Teach for America, the college is creating a one-year, postgraduate experience where students will work in nonprofit organizations, either closely with the leader or on a strategic project, in order to further develop their skills. The positions will be paid with the college subsidizing some of the costs.

St. Olaf College, in Minnesota, publishes what is perhaps the most comprehensive public listing of employment and salary figures for its recent graduates. Not only does the database answer one facet of the return-on-investment question discussed in the last chapter, but it helps students understand the types of careers they can pursue with a degree in, say, English or economics. Franklin & Marshall has a similar goal with a dinner it holds each year for sophomores, when they typically declare their major and are paired with working alumni who hold the same degree.

What these efforts indicate is that, for most students, the field of study is less important than how they acquire knowledge — and the best way is through deep commitment and time on task to one subject, combined with broad exposure to knowledge across the board. Like the credential itself, the high price of college has made the major a means to an end for students. For many, college increasingly is regarded as a long list to check off — classes to take, experiences to acquire, and a major to declare. Gaining underlying skills and knowledge is often an afterthought. Pitt, the Vanderbilt researcher, has found that students who combined a science major with a non-science one often described the non-science major as the fun one and the science major as the practical field chosen because of parental pressure.

Going to college and choosing a field of study should be a conscious, deliberate decision. Students need to know why they are going and why they are pursuing a certain major beyond "it's just expected of me." If not, the alternatives to traditional colleges, at least for a year or two for some eighteen-year-olds, might be a better option, as the final chapter will explore.

10

Why College?

HE FOUNDERS OF THREE of the most valuable technology companies in the world are all missing the same credential: Not one of them graduated from college.

Facebook's Mark Zuckerberg, Microsoft's Bill Gates, and Apple's Steve Jobs are often held up as examples of college dropouts who succeeded without a degree. Missing from those tales, of course, is how all of them did attend college and what role their time on campus played in their eventual accomplishments. The story of the wildly successful college dropout is a compelling one, though in reality the chances of such success are about as good as those of a high-school athlete hoping to make it big in the NFL or NBA.

The argument against going to college reached a crescendo in the spring of 2011, and has continued ever since. Over several months in 2011, it was nearly impossible to pick up a newspaper or magazine, browse a Web site, or turn on the television news without seeing stories questioning whether some high-school graduates might be better off skipping college altogether.

The coverage was prompted in large part by Peter Thiel. He is the billionaire cofounder of PayPal, who announced in March 2011 that he would pay twenty students $100,000 each to leave college and pursue their business dreams. "In our society the default assumption is that everybody has to go to college," says Thiel, who has compared the price escalation in higher education to the housing and tech bubbles. "I think there's a surprising openness to the idea that something's gone badly wrong and needs to be fixed."[1] Then in April, a new book hit stores, *How to Be the Luckiest Person Alive,* written by James Altucher. It included a chapter titled "8 Alternatives to College."

Altucher was a guest with me the following month on the nationally syndicated *Diane Rehm Show* on National Public Radio. When he led off the conversation by calling the need for a college degree "mythology," I knew it was going to be a long hour. Although Altucher himself went to Cornell, he told listeners that "any young person who is ambitious, intelligent, or achievement-oriented" would be better off just starting a career immediately and having a five-year head start. Left unsaid was how one might start a career that requires a degree (such as a physician). Or how the high-school graduates who need the intellectual and personal development that college provides would get it.

His argument didn't make sense to me. He encouraged kids, instead, to invest the tuition money, arguing they would realize a bigger payoff in the end. All the statistics on lifetime earnings and employment suggest a need for more education, not less. I went back to the office and wrote a blog post defending traditional colleges and the need for their style of education after high school.

Then I started reporting for this book.

Over the course of the next year, I met students who were struggling with their studies or their finances, and sometimes both. I met others who didn't know why they were in college, other than their parents wanted them there. I began to investigate alternative paths to a credential. I talked to students who took a year off after high school before going to college. I met adults who had delayed going to college for several years. I reflected on the dozens of campuses that I have visited over fifteen years as a higher-education journalist and realized that the idea of graduating from a four-year college is so firmly ingrained in our culture that many of us have trouble envisioning anything else.

I began to think that perhaps the current mode of what college is does not fit everyone, nor should it.

Don't get me wrong. I believe additional education after high school is absolutely critical. I still consider a two- or four-year college campus one of the best places to obtain that education. The problem is that a significant number of students today are poorly matched with the colleges they eventually attend. We lack high-quality educational substitutes for those who are ill-suited to traditional colleges and universities at eighteen. It seems we send some kids off to college because there is nowhere else to put them. The campus is a convenient, albeit expensive, warehouse.

"We're trying to push all students through this very narrow pipeline without any thought or regard as to what they want to do, where their interests are, where they'll be successful," says Janet Bray, executive director of the Association for Career and Technical Education. "If they don't know what they want to do and they have no skills at the end of that degree, they're in debt in many other ways. They're overeducated. They have a four-year degree when a one- or two-year program certificate would get them a job much faster. We all have people in our family who graduated from college who don't have a clue what they want to do."

The truth is, by clinging to the belief that education after high school can be found only at a four-year college campus, we exclude large portions of the American population from sharing in the nation's economic successes. In 1970, seven in every ten workers with a high school diploma or less were in the middle class; today, fewer than four in ten remain there. More and more jobs demand training beyond high school. By 2020, two out of every three jobs will require some sort of higher education.[2]

We need an expanded notion of what constitutes an education after high school. That definition should include on-the-job training and apprenticeships, coupled with learning across a range of subjects, as well as experiences before college that improve the often difficult transition from highly structured high schools to freewheeling college campuses.

Take Pedro Maldonado as an example of someone taking an alternative pathway to a college degree. Growing up in New York City, he was enrolled in the workforce program in high school and had decided he wasn't going to college at all. Then Maldonado was connected with Dennis Littky, who runs a network of seventy-two high schools around the country where the curriculum is tailored to a student's needs and interests and then applied in community internships. Littky, who disdains what he told me is the "factory model of traditional American education," was expanding the model to colleges. He had already signed up Roger Williams University in his hometown of Providence, Rhode Island. Soon after, Southern New Hampshire University adopted the model.

That's where I found Maldonado, although he spends more time off campus working in the real world than he does in a classroom. The semester I visited him in Manchester, New Hampshire, he was an intern at the State Department of Education, helping to write research papers and coordinate a student summit as an assistant to the deputy commissioner. "I'm taking my passion and doing something with it," he said. At the end of the three-year program, he'll get a bachelor's degree and probably have a clearer sense than most graduates of what he wants to do. "I'll be ready for a career because this whole program is meant to narrow my interests and inform my choices."

In extending our definition of higher education, more attention needs to be given to what Tony Carnevale, the Georgetown economist, calls "middle jobs." These are positions that do not require a bachelor's degree, but pay middle-class wages. Nearly half of the jobs in the United States today that put people in the middle class are these middle jobs. Corporate executives worry more about filling these positions than they do about finding employees for high-end careers in engineering, design, and technology. "We can secure all the grads we need from elite schools," Thomas Bowler, a senior vice president at United Technologies, says. "That's not a challenge. It's the other half of the workforce that I worry about."

As a result, some companies are taking it upon themselves to educate their own workers, bypassing the higher education system completely. In rural Macon, Missouri, a company called Onshore Outsourcing trains employees to provide technology services—ranging from software development to application support—to Fortune 500 companies that normally would send the jobs offshore to India or China. About 80 percent of the company's 150 employees are people who didn't go to college because they weren't encouraged to or couldn't afford it. Chuck Ruggiero, Onshore's president, says, "we're looking for that underemployed worker." The average salary at Onshore is $30,000, a solid wage in a part of Missouri where good jobs are few and far between. The process to get hired, however, is demanding. From an initial applicant pool that could number upward of two hundred, the group is narrowed to about thirty through a series of interviews and a test. About fifteen people get into an eight- to twelve-week boot camp of classes designed around problem-solving activities, not lectures. "The idea is to put them on an island and throw them a problem to solve," Ruggiero says. "After all, that's the way the real world works."

Bill Arends wanted to work in that real world, writing computer programs. After graduating from high school, he enrolled in Moberly Area Community College, a half hour to the south of Macon. Two semesters later, the twenty-eight-year-old dropped out. His transcript was filled with A's, but he was bored in his classes. "I've been doing this in my basement since I was eleven," he says. "They weren't inspiring me." One of his instructors worked at Onshore and suggested he apply. He impressed the interview team so much he was allowed to skip the boot camp and start right away. Now he works on cybersecurity for a power company that is one of Onshore's clients.

Arends plans to earn a college degree at some point so he can advance in his career, but for now he has achieved his goal of getting a job in computer programming. "My firm belief was that I couldn't work in the field without a bachelor's degree," he says. "It finally helped to show someone that I could just do the work without a degree." Ruggiero, Onshore's president, admits that his training is not meant to replace college. He wants his employees to eventually go to college, in part because "some clients want college-educated workers." In fact, the company is negotiating with one college to award credit for Onshore training so students can use the experience toward a degree.

In some ways, the Onshore model is reminiscent of the apprenticeship. Such on-the-job training has virtually disappeared in the United States as companies have left it to colleges and universities to supply an educated workforce. For the twelve million manufacturing jobs now in the United States, there are only 18,000 apprentices. Apprenticeships would take some of the pressure off the squeezed community-college systems in many states, reduce the loan burden for students, and help employers who complain about the lack of skilled labor. For students, they provide a structured environment where they work alongside adults of all ages, see the results daily of their labors, and learn responsibility. Many European countries have highly structured apprenticeship programs, and as a result, report fewer problems than the United

States in transitioning students from school to the workplace. Before the worldwide economic crisis hit, more than 80 percent of young Germans found jobs within six months of completing their education, compared to only about half of young Americans.[3]

In the United States, college is considered the de facto maturing experience for adolescents who have no interest in joining the military. Colleges weren't designed with that task in mind, however. One reason that college costs have risen is that institutions feel pressure from parents and the government to continually add services to help students mature. In many parts of the world, the maturing experience is provided before college by mandatory national or military service. In Great Britain, students take a gap year to travel or work. Harvard has encouraged its students for years to take time off before starting their freshman year. By doing so, students "come to college with new visions of their academic plans, their extracurricular pursuits, the intangibles they hoped to gain in college, and the many career possibilities they observed in their year away," the dean of admissions at Harvard wrote in a widely quoted essay in the *New York Times*.

Taking a year off before college, however, has long been seen as an excuse for rich kids to backpack through Europe. A few structured alternatives exist, namely AmeriCorps (recall Sam Schmader from Chapter 8), but there are still not enough options to appease parents concerned that their child may never go to college.

Evan Burfield was at one of the top public high schools in the country, Thomas Jefferson High School for Science and Technology in Northern Virginia, when he decided a month before his graduation in 1995 to defer a generous scholarship offer to be on the rowing team at Tulane University. "I graduated high school with 400 of the smartest kids and 399 of them went to college, but some of them didn't know why," Burfield says.

Instead, Burfield wandered through a few odd jobs that summer before joining with a parent of a fellow student to start a software company that attracted a million-dollar angel investment within a year. He applied to Dartmouth on a dare from a friend there, and was accepted, but deferred again as other business opportunities followed. Finally in 2002, seven years after he graduated from high school, he was ready for college. "There is something to be said in your formative years for taking a step back and examining your life and the world around you. I was ready for that," he says. He went off to Oxford, where he earned a degree in philosophy, politics, and economics.

These days Burfield continues to stick close to his entrepreneurial roots. He created another technology company and is chairman of StartupDC, a regional branch of a national effort that provides resources and funds to those who start businesses. Burfield also mentors young entrepreneurs at his former high school. He has already helped shepherd a start-up company there. I asked him if the students who created that company should delay college like he did. Although it worked for him, he doesn't immediately recommend delaying college to others. Plenty of eighteen-year-olds may not be ready for college, but they're not ready to simply roam, either.

"Instead of subsidizing college for all, what if we created a national service program to take some unruly eighteen-year-olds and get real stuff done?" Burfield asks me. We're having lunch across from his office, known as The Fort. It is home to a dozen tech start-ups, which share office space, mentors, and money. As we talk, we begin to sketch out what such a program might look like — think of it as a post-high-school version of Teach for America or Venture for America. Both of those programs take top college graduates and place them for short-term stints in schools and start-up companies. Using this model after high school could help ease the transition to college. It would be the structured gap year students in the United States now lack. "The reason college graduates don't know what it's like to work is because they study twenty hours a week and they have their life in college managed for them," Burfield says. "They are getting a warped perspective of what life is like."

Segregation by Education

Sitting in Washington, D.C., we probably have a warped perspective, too, not only of the role higher education plays in an individual's success but its impact on nearly everything in a community, from city services to the selection of retail shops and restaurants. As Burfield and I eat lunch, we're surrounded by people with college degrees. Even the cab drivers here have degrees. The nation's capital is the most educated metro area in the United States. More than half of the adult residents in Washington have college degrees. It is among a small group of US cities that, in the last four decades, have built their economy around knowledge and have prospered as a result. In cities where fewer than 15 percent of adults had a college degree, the average unemployment rate in 2012 was three points higher than in cities where more than 30 percent of adults were college-educated.

This means that every May, following commencement at colleges tucked in every corner of the country, newly minted graduates take off for many of the same places—cities such as New York, San Francisco, Boston, Raleigh, Denver, and Seattle, among a handful of others. The futurist Richard Florida calls this concentration of college graduates the "means migration." In 1970, nearly all the metro areas in the United States were within five points of the national average of adults with a college degree. Today, only about half are.

Take my hometown of Wilkes-Barre, Pennsylvania. In 1970, only 5.7 percent of adults in the Wilkes-Barre/Scranton region had a college degree, making it the least educated of the top one hundred metro areas in the United States. Even the cities at the bottom, however, were still within seven points of the national average at the time. Middle-class jobs without a college degree were abundant. Today, the good news for Wilkes-Barre is that it no longer ranks at the very bottom when it comes to college credentials. More than 20 percent of adult residents there have four-year degrees, a 17 percent rise since 1970. Despite its gains, however, the metro area is now ten points below the national average in terms of college degrees, and the spread between it and the cities at the very top is even wider than in 1970. In other words, even as places like Wilkes-Barre, along with dozens of cities, gain college graduates, they are falling further behind places that are soaking them up at a faster pace.[4]

This concentration of highly educated and highly skilled people in a small number of metro areas feeds on itself, says Florida, accelerating the pace of growth of the top metro areas and boosting ancillary benefits, such as higher wages. Income inequality is not just growing between the rich and the poor (as popularized by the Occupy Wall Street movement), it is also dividing along geographic lines. All of it is tied to a college education.

For much of the twentieth century, the supply of college-educated workers in the United States exceeded demand and boosted salaries for those with a degree and even those without. Since 1980, demand has outstripped supply, particularly among men, leading to the rising inequality. The Harvard economists Lawrence Katz and Claudia Goldin argue in their book, *The Race Between Education and Technology,* that if the proportion of college graduates since 1980 had kept pace with earlier decades, the wage inequality between the college-educated and those with a high-school diploma would not be as wide as it is today. A rising tide would indeed lift all boats.

Perhaps even more worrying is that the education gap is a vicious cycle. The odds of going to college, and going to a college that is hard to get into, are closely linked to income. Children from families who earn more than $90,000 have a one-in-two chance of getting a bachelor's degree by age twenty-four. That falls to a one-in-four chance for those from families earning between $60,000 and $90,000, and a one-in-seventeen chance for those earning under $35,000. Students from high-income families are also four times more likely than those from low-income families to attend a selective college (which we know from Chapter 8 could boost one's lifetime earnings).[5] Education begins much earlier in life, in preschool and elementary schools, and the quality there is highly dependent on income. The so-called peer effects also have an impact on this segregated map: Kids surrounded by other kids going to college are more likely to go to college.

This growing divide should matter to all of us, no matter where we live, because it impacts the quality of life for the entire country, and in the end, how we spend our limited dollars — investing in the future or throwing money at fixing problems that stem from a lack of education from poor health to drug abuse. While we often express the value of a college degree in dollars and cents, what is often lost in such calculations are the added benefits of higher education, both to the individual and to society as a whole. Summing up thousands of studies conducted on the impact of a college degree over a twenty-five-year-period, Michael Mumper, a political scientist at Ohio University, found that "college served as a turning point in the lives of almost everyone. It was a time and place where they learned how to better fit into the world and create a meaning for their life."[6]

Indeed, in a survey of college graduates taken by the Pew Research Center, nearly three quarters said their college education was very useful in helping them grow intellectually and mature as a person. The same survey found that college graduates, and especially those with advanced degrees, find their work more satisfying and interesting than do those with a high-school diploma.[7] By almost every measure, college graduates lead healthier and longer lives, have better working conditions, have healthier children who perform better in school, have more of an interest in art and reading, speak and write more clearly, have a greater acceptance of differences in people, and are more civically active. These attributes are passed down to successive generations as well.

Over the past fifty years, few states have been able to harness the power of higher education to drive growth and improve the quality of life for its residents quite like California. The state set its course in 1960, by adopting a Master Plan for Higher Education that landed it on the cover of *Time* magazine. The plan spelled out who should be guaranteed access to which state institutions and placed the state's fast-growing but unorganized web of public colleges into three well-defined tiers: the top high-school graduates and research functions went to the University of California, the middle graduates to the California State University System, and the rest to the state's community colleges. It was a plan admired and emulated by many other states, and one that held true to its origins until recent budget troubles in the state put it under incredible strain. Still, California's public higher-education system remains the best in the country, and it has more public research universities than any other state. It is no accident that many of the advances of the late twentieth and early twenty-first century have emanated from California.

In trying to place a value on a college education we focus almost exclusively on the cost versus benefit to the individual. After all, the student is the one ultimately paying the bill. But we also know that society profits greatly from a better-educated populace. In framing the debate about college in purely economic terms, we ignore the value of college as the place where students transform themselves — by meeting others with different backgrounds and beliefs, by exploring new subjects, and by making mistakes and learning from them, all with the end result that the student leaves the institution with an education, not just a job. It is why Evan Burfield eventually went to college even after he achieved economic success — to make better sense of the world around him.

The nation's best colleges and universities will continue to provide this type of higher education for students eager to find themselves. Those institutions with billions of dollars in the bank can afford to press on in their own way, even if they are going against the tide of change. One underlying issue in the current debates over the future of college that troubles me is that many of the people pushing the idea of alternative education (or skipping college altogether) graduated from some of the most prestigious institutions. I always wonder, and usually ask, if they think the experience they are proposing is as good as what they received. The question typically makes them uncomfortable, and the answers are usually nuanced. In the end, those building alternatives to traditional higher education are not trying to put Harvard or Michigan State out of business, but instead are attempting to disrupt the business model of hundreds of low-quality colleges spread throughout the country. Whatever alternatives emerge from those experiments, whether it's a degree from the online, self-paced Western Governors University or a certificate of completion from edX, the new online massive school formed by Harvard and MIT, these new options should be good enough for them or their own son or daughter.

CONCLUSION

From the runway of Phoenix's Sky Harbor International Airport, an office building rises in the distant desert, emblazoned with the name and logo that has become a ubiquitous sign in office parks across the country, the University of Phoenix.

In the mid-1970s, John Sperling, a former professor at San Jose State University, came here to create what would become the largest higher-education institution in the United States, with 600,000 students and more than two hundred campuses at its peak. Sperling started the for-profit university with $26,000, eventually becoming a billionaire on that modest investment.[1]

A decade ago, for-profit colleges, led by Phoenix, were heralded as the future of higher education for their efficiencies in delivering courses. Despite gaining about 10 percent of the market, the for-profit college financial model has not cut costs to students, and their aggressive admissions practices have come under widespread scrutiny by government regulators.

Now another future of higher education is rising in Phoenix. Just a few miles in the other direction from the airport is Arizona State University. With 72,000 students, Arizona State is the biggest university by enrollment in the country. Take a walk around the Tempe campus and you'll get a sense of the pressures bearing down on colleges and universities and see a glimpse of what the college of tomorrow might look like.

One Future at Arizona State

On a sunny, cloudless day in late October, the sidewalks of Arizona State's campus are packed with students rushing off to their next class or hanging out with friends. At quick glance, this looks like any other American university campus. Spend a few more hours here, sitting outside the student union or checking out some of the classrooms and labs, and you'll begin to notice significant differences.

A third of Arizona State's undergraduates are members of minority groups, one in three are the first in their family to go to college, and 40 percent of them get Pell Grants, federal grants that go to families making less than $50,000 annually. This is the future student body. Nationally, by the beginning of the next decade, nonwhite students will make up almost half of all public high-school graduates.

Every year, 26,000 new students arrive at Arizona State, four out of every ten of them transferring from other institutions, more than any other public university in the country. Some 3,500 of them come from the local community colleges, mostly through a program that guarantees admission into a specific program at a reduced rate.

Construction cranes dominate the desert landscape at Arizona State. On one corner of campus, an outdated dorm is getting a makeover by a private developer. All student housing here is now built by private developers and leased to the university, allowing the institution to keep such debt off its books and getting it out of the way of those who know how best to build and run what are essentially apartment buildings.

To help revitalize downtown Phoenix, the university built a campus there with the help of government dollars and moved entire schools, including communications and nursing. A light-rail line connects the two campuses. In Tempe, the newest academic buildings are dedicated to one primary mission: research. It is the one function of a university that can't be easily replicated by fragmented, simplified services on the Internet. With students increasingly opting to get their education delivered to them when, where, and how they want it, fewer physical classrooms will be needed in the future, so fewer of those are on the drawing boards. Already, nearly half of students who take face-to-face classes here on campus also take at least one online class each semester.

"We move forward by using every innovative technique that we could put in place to achieve our goals," says Michael Crow, Arizona State's president. He rejects the notion — shared by many of his counterparts — that quality in higher education is measured by the resources institutions spend, not by what they produce with that money. "Somehow they think that quality cannot be achieved through injections of technology, so that our objective of providing a world-class education at the lowest possible cost is, in their mind, a fool's errand."

Ultimately, it is the students of tomorrow who will drive colleges to re-imagine the future of higher education. These students of the future are in elementary and middle school today. Born around the turn of the century, they have always known a world with the Internet, smart-phones, and wireless connections. They are often referred to as digital natives. They pick up electronic devices and know intuitively to swipe instead of type on a keyboard. They feel comfortable in a social world that lives online. They text friends who are sitting only a few feet away.

In school, they remain largely uninterested in learning through tra-ditional teaching methods. Two out of three high-school students say they are bored in class every day, according to a report by Indiana Uni-versity.[2] Then they go home and fire up Khan Academy to view online lessons from Salman to better understand concepts they didn't get in school.

"We go to classes because we have to, but the learning is happen-ing after class and online," says Sean McElrath, a senior at Thomas Jef-ferson High School for Science and Technology, a public high school in Northern Virginia with competitive admissions. During his junior year, McElrath noticed that his classmates were using Facebook at night to discuss homework and help each other with problems. He and a few friends created a Facebook-like Web site to make that peer-to-peer learning easier to navigate. Now he is sharing the site with stu-dents at other high schools through a company called Hallway that he cofounded with the help of Evan Burfield, whom we met in Chapter 10.

"Today's students think and process information fundamentally dif-ferently from their predecessors," maintains Marc Prensky, a former teacher and author who coined the term "digital native."[3] By the time students reach their early twenties, they have spent some 10,000 hours playing video games, on average, sent and received 200,000 e-mail mes-sages and instant messages, but have allotted just 5,000 hours to read-ing books.[4]

Adults often complain that these trends signify a move away from learning. Peter Cookson Jr. of Teachers College of Columbia University observes that the digital world is "alive with ideas, communication and new ways of problem solving," which allow the youngest of students to learn "with greater speed and more deeply."[5] John Seely Brown, a computing pioneer who researches learning, believes students read differently now, navigating and discovering materials not laid out by any traditional rules of order. Navigation, he argues, is the literacy of the twenty-first century.[6]

The students who will be showing up on college campuses in the next ten years will want to absorb and apply knowledge on their terms. They will extend the customer mentality of the Lost Decade and decide when, where, and how they learn and what it means to have a degree. The question is not *whether* colleges will embrace alterations to their current nineteenth-century model, but *when* it will happen. A few hundred colleges have the status and money to remain resistant to the forces bearing down on higher education right now. But the colleges and universities that the vast majority of Americans attend will need to change if they want to survive and thrive.

Five Ways Higher Education Will Change in the Future

For the first time since the Great Depression, the incomes of middle-class families have dropped every year for more than a decade, nearly the entirety of the twenty-first century so far.

The American dream is built on a foundation of fairness and opportunity, wrapped in optimism. We believe one can be born into a poor family and through hard work rise to the top. We also hope that each successive generation will have a better standard of living than the one before it. These ideals are under pressure like never before.

Few entities in the country can relieve those pressures quite like college and universities can. Higher education is key to the United States emerging from the current economic doldrums and building a strong, innovative, and growing economy for the long run.

The best of American higher education remains a world leader. When I traveled with college leaders in recent years to Saudi Arabia and India, I was struck by how officials in both countries admired American universities. Saudi Arabia, by partnering with colleges here and sending thousands of students to the United States each year, wants to essentially buy the system; India wants to copy it by building its own collection of colleges. Both countries, along with China, remain behind the United States but are catching up at a rapid clip.

When I talk to people about the future of higher education, the inevitable question is always "Will online education replace physical campuses?" People want to know if Harvard, which was established in 1636, will still be around in ten years. Talk about the future of higher education reminds me sometimes of *The Jetsons,* with flying cars, homes hovering in space, robot maids, and holograms. The college of the future will certainly be different than the one of today, but robots will not replace professors in the classroom anytime soon. Harvard will remain Harvard.

But Harvard enrolls just over one tenth of one percent of college students in the United States. The colleges and universities enrolling most Americans will be radically different places in ten years. The experience for today's students is already becoming unlike that of students even a decade ago, and the pace of change will only accelerate in the coming years. Here are a few key ways that colleges will look different in the next decade:

A Personalized Education

College and university leaders often brag about the diversity of American higher education with its public and private colleges, small rural and large urban campuses, two-year and four-year institutions. Despite the rhetoric, higher education in the United States has largely adopted a one-size-fits-all model. Most campuses follow a semester calendar that starts in the fall; students register for classes at times dictated by faculty members; students need to spend a specific amount of time in a seat to get credit; and faculty members teach the same material at the same speed to all the students in a classroom. Some institutions have ideas about how to do things in other ways, but higher education is a heavily regulated and subsidized industry. Rules often make it impossible to do things differently. The traditional way of doing things is finally evolving, however, as accreditors are under pressure to consider new models, and states and the federal government rethink how they finance students and institutions in an age of tight budgets.

After meeting and talking with dozens of students, I have learned that the democratization of higher education—which has opened the doors of college to more Americans—has meant that the educational and emotional needs of students differ more than ever before. Some students are ready for college at eighteen; others are not. Some students can speed ahead in a class; others need a few extra weeks to master a concept. The idea of personalizing the educational experience for each student right down to the next question on a test is so potentially powerful because it holds the promise of keeping students focused on concepts that give them the most difficulty, while breezing through the problems that they find easy.

To some, the concept of a computer directing students to particular courses or pairing them with appropriate classmates for discussions might seem Orwellian. Such innovations will put the serendipitous nature of college at risk, where students discover new passions or become aware of their strengths and weaknesses by exploring courses, majors, and extracurricular activities. While students learn from their mistakes, those mistakes should come after they weigh choices grounded in solid information and receive advice from adults with more experience. The problem is that too many students lack access to the right information and mentors to make informed decisions.

The most important decision young people will make in their early lives is where to go to college or whether to go at all. If four out of five students are drifting in life, they need more assistance in making this choice than overwhelmed parents and an overworked guidance counselor can provide. Samantha Dietz, whom we met in the beginning of this book, went to one of the top high schools in New Jersey. Yet she based her college choice solely on money, choosing the school that gave her the most financial aid, even though it had a much lower graduation rate than the other colleges she considered. If Dietz had been able to find this consumer data, it would have helped inform her choice, but unfortunately it's hidden, not available in one place, nor easy to use. If she had had access to tools like Naviance or ConnectEDU, she might have been better matched to a college and could have significantly reduced her chances of dropping out. When we shop for a car, the government requires certain information be on the window sticker. When we purchase a house, every potential buyer is given a list of disclosures. Colleges should provide similar point-of-purchase information prominently on the front page of their Web sites, rather than posting marketing propaganda that leads students like Kelsey Griffith to take on more than $100,000 in debt because a school tells her to get over the sticker shock.

Hybrid Classes

For close to two decades, online education has been proposed as the solution to rising college costs. Online enrollments have dramatically increased, but the price of a college degree has gone up as well. Online education serves a significant market need for place-bound, time-pressed students—mostly working adults—but it will not replace brick-and-mortar classrooms anytime soon. Already, there is evidence that the demand to study solely online has flattened, and the public remains unconvinced that online education measures up to traditional classrooms.

But that does not mean that online education is a passing fad. While online education won't make campuses extinct in the near future, it will play a growing role at traditional schools by giving students more options to take classes outside of their home institution, accelerating the pace to completing a degree, or serving as a supplement to a face-to-face course. In other words, I see more colleges becoming like the University of Central Florida, where each year 60 percent of students take an online or hybrid course, or nearby Rollins College, which is part of a group of sixteen colleges in several states where a professor on one campus teaches a course shared through video conferencing with the others.

The biggest impact, however, will be the creation of many more hybrid courses. Students in the college pipeline are already accustomed to flipped classrooms, where they view traditional lectures online and spend precious face-to-face class time working with an instructor on specific problems. Research also shows that students are much more likely to be active participants in hybrid courses. Recall the massive open online course offered by the two Stanford professors. The same class, when it was taught on the Stanford campus that fall, attracted two hundred students at the beginning of the semester, but by the end only two dozen were attending because most had migrated to the online version. These free courses developed by elite institutions that serve tens of thousands of students at a time will likely become the content provider for the core courses that every college offers. By using online materials to power these face-to-face intro courses, colleges can accommodate more students with the same number of instructors or spend their limited resources on top professors teaching the courses best presented in a physical classroom. This is the only way to expand higher education to serve more students without its ever-rising price tag ballooning even more.

The study of the hybrid introductory statistics course at six public universities, which I described in Chapter 6, found that students learned just as much in the hybrid format as they did in the traditional course, and they took about three quarters of the time to achieve that same result. A hybrid future is already a reality on some campuses. The National Center for Academic Transformation, a nonprofit group, has redesigned courses at more than two hundred colleges, cutting costs by an average of 37 percent by using instructional software to reduce burdens on professors, employing frequent low-stakes online quizzes to gauge student progress, and providing alternative staffing like undergraduate peer mentors.

Unbundling the Degree

When I was growing up there was one telephone company. It provided you with a wall-mounted phone, local calling, and long distance. It was one product at essentially one price. It was what is known as a bundled product. The deregulation of the telephone industry in 1984 began a decades-long push to what we have today: a web of companies and products that consumers pick and choose from to put together their own telephone service. The same is true in almost every industry. Airlines still provide the basic services they did twenty years ago, but if you want to check a bag or have a meal, it will cost you extra. If you don't want either, you'll save a few bucks. With iTunes you don't need to buy an entire album the way you once did at a record store. Now you just buy the singles you want to create your own playlist.

Colleges and universities are one of the few entities left that provide a bundled service, from the classes to the dining halls to computer centers to career advice. One hurdle for students in unbundling the college experience is that courses are not always portable. That is, colleges can deny credit for students looking to transfer from another provider.

We learned in Chapter 7 that students are more mobile than ever before — with a third of all students transferring from one college to another before they graduate. It's only a matter of time before colleges are forced to offer an unbundled product to at least a portion of the student body that wants to consume higher education in that way.

This option certainly won't suit all students. I imagine these pathways will still be structured in some way, and students will be guided with better comparative information about colleges and advisers to lead them on the journey.

Fluid Timelines

The typical college classroom is used only 40 percent of the time. Classrooms largely sit empty on weekends and summers, and increasingly on Fridays as more classes are packed into the other four weekdays. When consultants from Bain & Company were designing the Dallas campus of the University of North Texas, they projected that 60 percent of the overall cost savings at the new university would come just from using the space better — with a year-round calendar and students starting classes at times other than only in the fall and spring.

Personalizing and unbundling the college experience allows us to rethink long-held assumptions about higher education: Why does college last four years? Why wait until students graduate high school to start college? Why are semesters fifteen weeks long?

Adaptive learning technologies adjust to the speed at which an individual student learns, enabling fast learners to move on to the next course and slow learners to take the extra time they might need. A semester restricts both groups right now. Personalization dismantles the academic calendar — students can start a course whenever they want and complete it at their own speed. Permitting students to move on before the end of the semester means that they could potentially take extra courses that might interest them, add another major, or complete a degree more quickly.

Students could also start college earlier. The senior year of high school for many students is often a waste of time. Several states, including North Carolina, California, and Texas, have created early college schools, enabling students to earn college credits, or in some cases, an associate's degree, before graduating from high school. Such programs ease the transition to college or provide peace of mind to parents worried that their kids will never earn a college degree if they take time off between high school and college.

After researching this book and interviewing countless educators, students, and parents, I have become convinced that we need more structured programs that give students an option to take a gap year before college. Perhaps a fraction of every generation meanders through college, but the cost of higher education means that today's students who drop out of school because they are unsure why they were there in the first place are stuck sometimes with thousands of dollars of debt and nothing to show for it. The self-discovery phase of college could easily be provided by a national-service experience that could also help students pay for their education at some point down the road.

College Moneywise

Student loans will not disappear, despite calls by Occupy Wall Street protesters to have the federal government finance public colleges entirely and write off all student debt. The higher-education establishment in Washington spends most of its time trying to protect the status quo on student-aid programs, all the while arguing for more money to help pay higher tuition prices. But if we're headed for an age of austerity in the federal government, then the student-aid system is due for an overhaul that gets better results for the money being spent.

How might a new system for financing college work in the future?

For one, colleges could more frequently limit loan eligibility. Right now, colleges are allowed to cap a student's loan eligibility only on a case-by-case basis. They can't, for example, limit how much students may borrow by major, even though we know that earnings by major vary greatly. This policy encourages excessive borrowing and permits some students to cash out at low-cost institutions where they borrow well above the price of tuition.

Tuition prices and financial aid in the future could be based on potential earnings. We know there are plenty of cross-subsidies at a college. Cash-rich academic programs pay for low-demand, high-cost programs. Such subsidies exist because most colleges charge a single price no matter the academic program. It's a similar story on student aid. Wealthy students subsidize financially needy students. On some campuses, programs where seats are difficult to fill have higher tuition-discount rates, another subsidy paid for by students in popular programs who don't get as much aid. Such a system takes into account students' current financial situation but doesn't consider their future earnings. A financially needy English major is treated the same as a low-income finance major, although it's likely that the latter will earn a lot more over a lifetime. What if the English major were given fewer loans and more scholarships than the finance major? Such a system might also encourage students to consider majors that they were interested in pursuing despite worries about paying back student loans. There are, of course, consequences to such a change. One downside is that it could discourage students from majoring in high-demand fields that pay well simply because they would need to take on more loans.

Another key reform in the future could allow graduates to pay back their loans as a percentage of their income. The United States has a small income-contingent repayment system compared to Great Britain or Australia. Most students pay back their loans over a ten-year period right after graduation — when they are most likely to make the least amount of money. With an income-contingent repayment system, students would pay a percentage of their income to pay off their debt, and employers would withhold the payments as they now do with taxes. After a specified time period of twenty years or so, what remained on the loan would be forgiven.

Finally, we need to do more to encourage saving for college. When the Pew Research Center asked parents in a survey if they expected their children to go to college, they overwhelmingly said yes. But when asked if they had started saving for college, the answers varied widely. In the long run, it's less expensive to save for college than to borrow. Some cities and states provide seed money when parents open a new 529 college-savings plan before a child's first birthday. Other places provide matching grants to low-income families. Mark Kantrowitz, publisher of FinAid, a Web site offering student-aid advice and tools, believes there are way too many savings plans for college and retirement. He advocates replacing all of them with two plans for saving for certain "life-cycle expenses" (retirement, college, medical, etc.). One plan would use before-tax dollars and one would use after-tax dollars. The annual contribution limits should be increased. So if your child doesn't go to college, you would have more money for retirement, instead of having to navigate a maze of programs.

The Student of the Future

In the end, it's best to imagine what one vision of higher education will look like in a decade or so through the eyes of a student.

Let's name him Aiden. He graduates from high school with a year of college already under his belt because of an early-college program he was enrolled in. For his sophomore year, Aiden lives at home, and for the first quarter works full-time at a pharmaceutical company as part of a cooperative-education program, which earns him money and college credit. For the remainder of the year, he takes four courses at two different local colleges with their best instructors and then fills out his course schedule with free online courses offered through Coursera and taught by faculty members at the University of Michigan and the University of Pennsylvania. At the end of those courses, Aiden travels to Penn's campus in Philadelphia for a week, where he lives with other online students, attends lectures and small group sessions taught by the professors he met online, and takes a series of written and oral exams to test his knowledge of the material. When the week is over, for a small fee, he's given credit for the free courses. In his junior year, Aiden works another co-op job, which helps him pay for college, and, of course, amass more credits. He finishes the year at another college that offers a low-residency option, where he takes online courses and resides on campus for two intense weeks of one-on-one meetings with professors, seminars, and social gatherings. Aiden's senior year is more traditional. He goes off to Michigan State University, which accepts his credits from various providers and supplies him with seminar-style capstone courses and hands on research opportunities. In May he graduates with a degree from the institution.

Even as we imagine what higher education will look like in the third decade of the new millennium, we must carefully balance the demands of the future with the strengths of the current systems that make US colleges and universities the envy of the world. Although I remain enthusiastic about the possibilities, I worry at times about what might be lost in an unbound, personalized experience for students. Will they discover subjects they never knew existed? If a computer is telling them where to sit for class discussions, will they make those random connections that lead to lifelong friends? Will they be able to develop friendships and find mentors if they move from provider to provider? However, I'm optimistic about what is to be gained: a more efficient system that better matches students and institutions and gets more students emerging on the other end with an actual degree.

FUTURE FORWARD

Throughout this book, you will find examples of colleges, and by extension their students, that are well-positioned for the future. The college of the future doesn't exist yet, but if you want a preview of what one version will look like, go to **Arizona State University, Southern New Hampshire University,** and the **University of Central Florida.**

In addition to the innovative campuses of **Valencia College** and **F&M College,** which you have already read about, I've also gathered a short list of forward-thinking universities to keep an eye on. The list of schools here is not intended to be a ranking nor is it meant to be comprehensive. These are just a sampling of colleges that have adopted strategies and programs that will help prove the value of their degree in the years ahead.

If there is one takeaway for me from these summaries it is this: College students desperately need real-world experience that will help them connect the concepts they learn in class to the everyday problems encountered in any occupation. Here are some colleges trying to do exactly that in a variety of ways.

Ball State University (Indiana)
SEEING THE PRACTICAL IN LEARNING

As President Jo Ann M. Gora of Ball State University sees it, an important component of a college education is learning how to do something with such professional skill that you can sell it to an employer beyond the university campus even before you graduate. At Ball State they call that process Immersive Learning. "We want students to partner with clients and solve real-world problems," says Gora, who has headed the Muncie, Indiana, institution since 2004. The Immersive Learning program was already on campus when Gora arrived, but she kicked it into high gear. Over the past five years, more than 16,000 students have participated in some thousand projects. "Immersive Learning not only helps students develop a stronger résumé," she observes, "but it also gives them networks after they graduate."

The program lasts for a semester, during which students can initiate a dizzying variety of enterprises from redesigning hospital gowns for cancer patients to creating computer programs that make history more appealing to elementary-school students.

A few years ago Ball State professor Beth Turcotte asked theater major Ben Clark, then a sophomore, to write a musical for a potential client, a professional producer. Clark wrote the music and most of the lyrics and with the help of fifteen other students created *Circus in Winter,* a play based on a novel about life in a small Indiana town at the end of the nineteenth century. It was performed at Ball State, "but it has also had a big life after school," says Clark. *Circus* became part of the Kennedy Center American College Theater Festival, was staged in Champagne, Illinois, and has won eight awards. The next step, Clark hopes, is a New York production.

Probably the most extraordinary effort of 2012 was that of forty students majoring in such disciplines as journalism, public relations, and graphic arts who ventured to London for several weeks to cover the summer Olympics. "It was a lot of fun but also a lot of work," says Kait Buck, a senior who headed a four-member public relations squad. The Ball State team used social media to get in touch with athletes, mostly those with Team USA, and arranged to write feature stories and prepare videos about them. Meanwhile, Buck's group contacted newspapers and television stations whose staffers in London were focused on the events rather than the personalities and offered to supplement coverage with engaging profiles. Ball State sold stories to the *Huffington Post, USA Today,* and Indiana TV stations, among others. The *Chicago Tribune* bought graphics.

"Immersive Learning is optional," Gora says. "It's not required. But we guarantee the students the opportunity if they want it."

City University of New York
A NEW-AGE COMMUNITY COLLEGE

The dropout rate among community-college students is deplorable. Nationally, of all the students who enter two-year institutions only 20 percent graduate, even after three years. Some experts have concluded that a major cause of failure is that the students are not given enough time to bond, either with the school or with their classmates. "They never really feel part of the place, so they turn around and leave," says Scott E. Evenbeck, president of an experimental new community college that the City University of New York (CUNY) has created to remedy the problem.

The new community college, so new that it doesn't have a formal name yet, admitted its first three hundred students in the fall of 2012 on a campus in the heart of Manhattan. They are predominantly recent high-school graduates from New York City, admitted on a first-come, first-served basis. All come from low-income families in which the parents have not gone to college. The students' first assignment — a mandatory one — is to attend with all their classmates a two-and-a-half week program designed to bridge the gap between high school and college. "First-generation students have a lot of trepidation about whether they really belong in college," Evenbeck says. "Through the bridge program they see that there are people like them in the college and that they like their company."

All students take the same courses, at least in their first year. "Options don't work well for first-generation students," Evenbeck says. "They are faced with a lot of confusing choices." At the heart of the first-year program is the city seminar in which students learn about New York in an interdisciplinary way. They read from sociology and history and other disciplines and then go out into neighborhoods and study them. What's the business mix in this neighborhood? How many delicatessens? How many dry-cleaning shops? They take a close and accurate count. "Math always seems abstract to them," notes Evenbeck. "This uses math in a real way."

The school year is apportioned in stretches of twelve weeks followed by a break and then six weeks followed by a break, a schedule that is repeated to prevent long vacations during which student interest in school might flag. In their second year students will have more choices. Most will major in the liberal arts; business will be the next most popular major, followed by human services, information technology, and urban studies. There will be no remedial courses if students are unprepared for college-level work.

"When students go into remediation they never leave it," Evenbeck says. "And among students who are in the bottom tier of remedial programs the graduation rate is less than 1 percent." Whatever remedial help they need will be integrated into their regular courses. Evenbeck is not so naïve as to think that the new college's program is going to keep everyone in school. His goal is a graduation rate of 35 percent. That would be enviable indeed.

Cornell University (New York)
THE UNIVERSITY OF THE FUTURE IN THE BIG APPLE

The mission of Cornell University's school-in-the-making—the New York City Tech Campus—will be a deep and integrated focus on making a difference in the world, says Dean Dan Huttenlocher. Historically, higher education "has left it to others to carry ideas through to commercial engagement," he observes. "Research starts at the university and then goes through a long development process that may take years."

A fundamental shift is taking place, Huttenlocher says. Innovation is happening at lightning speed and the flow of information now runs both ways from the university to the commercial world and back again. "A lot of data on human behavior doesn't originate with universities," he adds, "but with organizations like Google and Facebook that have enormous sets of data on how people interact with one another."

As a result, Cornell NYC Tech is establishing itself at the heart of one of the world's great commercial capitals, a center of the financial, health, and publishing industries. For the first few years, Tech will have office space in Manhattan, but by 2017 it plans to move into its permanent home on the East River's Roosevelt Island, where initially it will house about 250 students and eighty faculty members. When Tech reaches its full size in 2043, the student body is expected to be ten times as large.

There will be no undergraduates. All students will be candidates for master's or doctoral degrees in such areas as computer science, electrical and computer engineering, and information science and engineering. Each student will have not only an academic adviser but a mentor in the business community as well. Cornell has partnered on the venture with Technion—Israel Institute of Technology, the renowned public research university in Haifa that has three Nobel laureates on its staff.

How will Tech's students interact with the commercial community of New York? Dean Huttenlocher suggests one possibility. New York boasts some of the world's leading university hospitals and thousands of physicians. Like doctors and hospitals everywhere, they have a major problem in persuading patients to stick to their schedules of medications and other regimens. Technicians have devised electronic alert systems to remind patients to stick to a treatment schedule, but so far no system has been particularly successful. NYC Tech students can develop experimental software alert systems of their own, and large numbers of doctors can test them on recalcitrant patients. "New York is a place where there are a lot of passionate early users, including physicians," Huttenlocher says. "They will interact with students who don't think that anything is impossible."

The curriculum is likely to change rapidly as markets change with the needs of the city and the world. "We expect to attract students who are willing to put up with a fair amount of chaos," Huttenlocher says.

Drexel University (Pennsylvania)
THE CITY AS CLASSROOM

When John Fry was executive vice president at the University of Pennsylvania in the 1990s, he oversaw the multimillion-dollar revitalization of its West Philadelphia neighborhood, including the establishment of a charter school that the university helped run. A decade later, as president of Franklin & Marshall College he engineered the redevelopment of a massive manufacturing plant near campus—two hundred buildings on forty-seven acres — for athletic fields and a nursing college for the local hospital.

Now Fry is back in Philadelphia as president of Drexel University, and the neighborhood around Drexel (and Penn) is again on his mind. He has grand plans to remake the urban campus with a mix of academic, residential, and commercial buildings to create a sense of community. Drexel's vision extends thirty years into the future, but Fry has an impressive track record at two institutions of making dreams reality.

But rather than just act as another developer, Drexel is leveraging its students and research capabilities to help the local neighborhood improve itself. The university is establishing an urban extension center, taking a page from state land-grant institutions that in the early twentieth century built a system of extension offices around the state to provide local farmers with research-based solutions to their problems (and since then expanded their mission to local economic development). The Drexel center allows the local community to access the institution's academic expertise directly rather than be seen as an oasis and Ivory Tower in the middle of a troubled neighborhood. "It's the right way to have a real contribution to the community but also give students a chance to solve wicked problems," says Lucy Kerman, vice provost for university and community partnerships.

Already, students are engaged in projects around the perimeter of campus that are focused on "solving problems," Kerman says. Such "service learning," where students have direct experience solving issues in the community they are studying, is a high-impact teaching and learning practice that has been shown to benefit students. Rather than travel abroad to get a service-learning experience — as is the case at many colleges — Drexel students walk a few blocks.

One such project combined the expertise of engineering and architecture students who redesigned the space outside a senior citizen housing center. The students met at the center on a regular basis as part of class, and working with the residents, they learned their needs and were able to design and build structures that worked for them, including accessible benches and a curved walkway for those residents who need assistance. "The students see that learning is not abstract," Kerman says, "and we're able to help the community at the same time."

Georgia State University
MAKING COLLEGE MORE AFFORDABLE

Like much of the rest of higher education last decade, Georgia State University joined the amenities arms race when it came to student housing, building apartment-like residence halls with kitchens and private bedrooms and bathrooms. "The premise was that students wanted more and better," said Timothy Renick, the university's chief enrollment officer.

But the nicer facilities came with much higher price tags for financially strapped students, and because students often ate in their apartment kitchens, the living spaces didn't promote the feeling of community or healthy eating. So Georgia State decided to experiment with a return to the past, and in 2009, opened a new residence hall that was reminiscent of those from a generation ago: double rooms basically twice the size of a twin bed, common bathrooms, and a dining hall. "We built the least expensive rooms we could come up with," Renick said.

Students signed up in droves. Since it was built, the freshman hall has filled up before other residences as students can get a room there plus a meal plan that is equal to just the cost of the apartment-like residence halls.

A cheaper housing option is just one strategy Georgia State is employing to fill the unmet financial need students have after they pay for tuition using grants and loans. The money saved on housing helps lower a student's bill, freeing up money for other needs. University officials have found that the more unmet need a student has, the lower their grade-point average. "Financial strain has an impact on academic performance," Renick said.

That's why in recent years, the university has dedicated a pot of money to helping students pay the final few dollars they sometimes owe on their tuition bills even after classes start. When students don't pay those bills, they are forced to withdraw from their courses and are at risk of never returning. Sometimes the unpaid bills are as small as a few hundred dollars.

As soon as the deadline for payment passes, university officials scour their records to see which students owe small amounts of money, are close to graduation, and have good grades. They immediately contact them and offer small grants. In the fall of 2012, the university awarded $600,000 to 700 students, making the average grant less than $1,000. Sometimes just a little money goes a long way in keeping students in school.

Goucher College (Maryland)
A REQUIREMENT TO EXPERIENCE THE WORLD

Since 2006, Goucher College has been a pioneer in requiring students to study abroad. The mandate was put in place by the college's president, Sanford J. Ungar, partly as a way of distinguishing the school from competitors, but more important because he believes experiencing the world is essential to a young person's education. "There is so much to learn out there," Ungar says, "and we Americans aren't learning it." He cites the discouraging statistic that only about 1 percent of all American college students study abroad.

At Goucher, all 1,500 students do. No exceptions. For the most part they go overseas in their junior year, either studying for a semester or two at a foreign institution, or spending an intensive three weeks in a foreign country, focused on a particular issue, such as business in Shanghai or environmental science in the Galapagos; those short trips are preceded by a seven-week preparation course on the Goucher campus. Tuition payments to Goucher are sent to foreign institutions on the students' behalf for the time they are there. In addition, each student receives a $1,200 stipend from Goucher to help cover transportation and other additional costs.

Ungar asks students to bring back an example of something foreigners do better than Americans. Their answers include things like urban transportation and eldercare. Not all Goucher students are enthusiastic at first. "Study abroad was the most terrifying thing I'd ever heard of," says Allison Rich, a senior who grew up in nearby Baltimore. "You want me to come to college, get used to it, and then ship me off to someplace else." But Rich came to love her time as a Spanish student in Costa Rica. She lived with a warm, helpful family. "New things got a lot less scary," she says.

Leih Boyden, a peace studies major, spent the fall semester of 2011 in Rwanda, still showing the wounds of the genocide of 1994. "I learned a ton about conflict theories that you can't understand until you visit a place like Rwanda," says Boyden, who was part of a group of students who interviewed survivors. "People still live in fear. They don't trust one another. The air is harder to breathe there." Boyden concentrated on trying to understand the government's attempts to take care of physically or mentally handicapped children, noting that there was only one Rwandan official in the entire country paying attention to children with special needs.

Ungar has no doubts that Goucher is on the right path to helping students understand a world of complex problems as well as opportunities. "I ask the kids whether they regretted going abroad," Ungar says. "No one has ever replied yes."

Lynn University (Florida)
UNDERGRADUATES EXPLORING BIG QUESTIONS

"What employers are looking for these days are people with critical thinking and writing skills," says Gregg Cox, vice president for academic affairs at Lynn University, "and that's where students are weak." Lynn, a private university in Boca Raton, Florida, where most of the two thousand or so undergraduates are enrolled in programs such as management, hospitality, communications, and business, has developed a novel curriculum to impart those sought-after skills.

The curriculum, now about four years old, is called Dialogues of Learning, an examination of the big questions that have both fascinated and troubled humans since the beginning of civilization. Over the course of their undergraduate years all students are required to take twelve seminars in the three thematic areas that make up the dialogues: Self and Society, Belief and Reason, and Justice and Civic Life.

The names of the seminars are often catchy and even flippant, which clearly makes them appealing to a college audience. The demands of the seminars are rigorous nonetheless. In a course called "Murder, She Wrote," students dissect a murder trial in West Palm Beach. Instead of simply bantering about sensational details of the crime they are re-quired to research thoroughly such issues as how the homicide suspect was treated by the prosecution, analyze and critique the prosecution's behavior, and, most importantly, write well and cogently about the trial.

Irrespective of their majors, all students are exposed to a broad range of liberal-arts milestones. For example, the Self and Society Dialogue for underclassmen includes thirty-two selections ranging from the an-cient world to the modern, such works as Plato's "Allegory of the Cave" and Emerson's essay "Self-Reliance." "The dialogues give you a good perspective on life," says Tammy Reyes, a recent graduate who ma-jored in journalism. "You realize that the problems in the world have been around since the beginning." One of her favorite readings was "In Praise of Folly," the classic but often neglected work by sixteenth-century Dutch humanist and scholar Desiderius Erasmus.

Lynn also requires that its graduates acquire a fundamental under-standing of the sciences. "They don't necessarily have to know the parts of the cell," says Cox, "but they do have to understand the principles of scientific method." And the science is in large part centered on is-sues that are likely to engage the students in the world outside the class-room, such as global warming and other environmental issues. Simi-larly, courses in quantitative reasoning focus not on the abstract, such as algebra, but on the everyday and practical. "My quantitative reason-ing course helped me understand the real cost of the car loan I took out when I bought my car," says Stephen Proano-Amaya, a junior.

Northeastern University (Massachusetts)
A SIGNATURE CO-OP PROGRAM GOES GLOBAL

The college graduates of tomorrow will go to work in an American economy increasingly entwined in the world economy. That much is acknowledged by everyone. Many schools encourage study abroad; others help students find internships abroad. Northeastern University in Boston has gone a step further.

It has created a program in which students spend as much as half a year working in actual jobs overseas with real salaries. In Northeastern's cooperative-education program students have worked in an eye-popping range of settings, from corporate offices in European and Asian capitals to exotic sites for government agencies and nonprofits. A biochemistry major wound up in the Antarctic winter looking into the impact of rising ocean temperatures on the development of fish embryos.

"Ours is an unparalleled program," says Vice Provost Bruce Ronkin. "These assignments are very different from unpaid internships in which students might spend just a couple of months. These are real jobs and can last for six months."

Unlike internships, which are personally useful to the students who participate in them but don't have any prescribed communal purpose, in the Northeastern co-op program students must bring their experiences back to the classroom, where they can be invaluable. "For example," Ronkin says, "I teach a course in the music industry in which we talk about contracts. Fine. But when you have a fellow student in your class who has been working for a record label in London and has actually sat in on contract negotiations, he can give a perspective that I cannot."

A majority of Northeastern undergraduates sign up for the co-op program, but most of them choose jobs in the United States. Many students are not comfortable operating on their own in unfamiliar places, where their American looks and manners make them stick out. Nor is it easy for Northeastern to find job openings for undergraduates everywhere, especially overseas.

For those lucky enough to get a job outside the United States the rewards can be great. Not only is it a grounded global experience, in contrast, say, to a tourist's drive-by, it can be an advanced corporate experience as well. In some cases corporate hierarchies are less rigid overseas, especially where there are fewer personnel.

Christopher Turney, a Northeastern student from Cheshire, Connecticut, won an assignment working for IBM in Bangalore, India, as an aide to the operations manager. "IBM is constantly expanding in India," Turney says. "In a new installation something might go wrong with the wiring, for example. Every issue had to go through the operations manager and I was his point man. I got to be in on all of the leadership meetings." Turney got an early insight into the unpredictable way the corporate world often works, something that even the brightest junior executive might take years to discover.

Portland State University (Oregon)
AT THE CENTER OF URBAN RENEWAL

Portland State University is one of the fastest growing campuses in the country. In the first decade of the new millennium, its enrollment grew nearly 50 percent to some 30,000 students. Rather than pay for all that growth through debt like many other institutions, and eventually pass it on to students in the form of higher tuition and fees, Portland State has been a national leader in joining with public and private partners to expand its campus. At the same time, it has pushed forward with an ambitious agenda to become more environmentally sustainable.

"Universities are anchor institutions in cities," says Portland State's president, Wim Wiewel. "They are stewards of place."

In recent years, it has received grants to build sustainability education programs, formed a partnership with a local utility provider to develop sustainable transportation projects and a renewable-energy research laboratory, and it's building one of the greenest buildings in the country. A $90 million residence hall was largely financed by a private company.

The university's latest project is the development of a 160-acre area around campus. University leaders persuaded government leaders to create an urban renewal area, which diverts taxes that normally go the county, city, and schools in order to pay for development. Some $170 million will be diverted over a thirty-year period, with $50 million going to Portland State. "It was the result of years of doing good for the city," Wiewel says. "But it also gives our students additional opportunities to be connected to the city around them."

As part of the project, the county will build a new headquarters for its human services offices and the university plans to locate its social-work programs there. The two entities will undertake joint research and evaluation projects on issues important to the county, with the university promising to kick in the funds if outside support cannot be secured.

Students will be a key part in undertaking that research. Wiewel says such partnerships give students a feel for the real world and connect their education to everyday problems. "It's why our degree is seen as a good value," Wiewel says.

St. Mary's College (California)
TAKING ADVANTAGE OF TIME OFF

January is a quiet month on most campuses, but not at St. Mary's College, a liberal-arts school in Moraga, California, about twenty miles east of San Francisco. There, a program called Jan Term makes the first month of the year an intense and demanding academic experience focused on a single course.

"The only requirement is that the course does not fulfill any requirement for the student's major," says Jan Term director Sue Fallis. "This is the time they explore anything but what they are specializing in." The biology student takes a swing at writing poetry. Or the English major digs into a course on crime scene investigations taught by a chemistry professor, understandably one of the most popular offerings on campus.

Most courses are taught on campus and require two and a half hours a day of classes as well as field trips. Jan Term is a requirement and students are graded, but the good news is that they get to choose among 120 imaginative offerings. For example, Robert Bulman, an associate professor of sociology, invented a course that he eventually turned into a book: *Hollywood Goes to High School*. "I had my students look at how Hollywood depicts high schools in films," Bulman says. "Their papers had a lot of insight, discovering patterns and trends. I was tickled that they were having fun, and then I began to envy them." Over the summer Bulman started to do his own research, analyzed more than a hundred movies, and eventually wrote his book. (One conclusion: In middle-class suburban schools, the hero is generally a white student; in poor, nonwhite schools, the hero is generally a white teacher).

Nearly 10 percent of St. Mary's 2,800 students spend January overseas. Associate Dean Shawny Anderson took a group of thirteen students to a village in Haiti following the devastating earthquake of 2010.

"We tried to be collaborative and did whatever the people wanted," Anderson says. "We built a house for eleven people, but we recognized what the village really needed was waterworks." The villagers were not enthusiastic, pointing out that they got plenty of water from the river. Then cholera broke out and the villagers came to realize that they needed clean water. The St. Mary's team built a system that captured rainwater and installed a solar-powered water purification tower donated by a parent of one of the students.

For a forthcoming January term, St. Mary's was planning to send groups of a dozen or so students to Indonesia to study coral reefs and culture; to an orphanage in Rwanda; to Cuba to study history and ecology. Not all travelers leave the United States. One group was scheduled to go to Park City, Utah, under the guidance of a filmmaker to observe the Sundance Festival; another planned to go to Hawaii to examine natural and cultural history. It must be a struggle for St. Mary's to make the other months interesting.

Susquehanna University (Pennsylvania)
A NEW CURRICULUM TO ENGAGE STUDENTS

Many students see a core curriculum as a checklist of courses to get out of the way so they can focus on their major. When Susquehanna began redesigning its curriculum in 2005, it wanted to create something that wasn't "just a set of requirements bolted on top," says Carl Moses, the university's provost. Thus the name: central curriculum. "It emphasizes that this is central to everything."

The curriculum accounts for about 40 percent of a student's undergraduate studies at Susquehanna. While that might seem to be a significant chunk of time, Moses explains that many major requirements also count toward the central curriculum. The redesign was prompted in part by results from the National Survey of Student Engagement that found the academic experience wasn't as rigorous as faculty members thought it should be and that students were not having enough one-on-one interactions with professors. The new curriculum is part classic liberal arts, combined with skill development, and what's called a "cross-cultural experience." Every student must complete an experience either in the United States, or more likely abroad, for a minimum of two weeks and take a reflective course when they return to campus.

The redesign was also strongly influenced by ten high-impact teaching and learning practices that have been shown to benefit students. Of the practices, Moses says all students at Susquehanna get six of them and many get three more. The way Moses tells the story of the central curriculum is that "you'll leave here knowing some skills, some intellectual stuff, develop an understanding of yourself, and your responsibilities to others."

Explaining the benefits of the central curriculum to prospective students might be tough, but once on campus, students get it. Ariana Stowe is a senior and often finds herself in classes with students of different years and majors because of the requirements of the central curriculum. "Based on where they are in the curriculum, they bring something different to the class," says Stowe, a member of the women's basketball team who spent six weeks in Costa Rica working with youth sports campus as part of her cross-cultural experience. "It makes the classes much more interesting."

Tulane University (Louisiana)
A HURRICANE REQUIRES A NEW EXPERIENCE

No undergraduate education is complete before a student has spent time helping someone in need. That is the belief of Tulane University, where students are required to take two courses in service to the community, primarily to the institution's home city, New Orleans. "When we first started this it was part of a recovery program coming out of Hurricane Katrina," explains Provost Michael Bernstein. "It was all hands on deck."

The storm that battered the city in 2005 devastated Tulane as well, flooding large swatches of the campus. With the campus repaired, the university shifted student attention to improving the lives of New Orleans residents, who rank low nationally on such vital measures as health and education and high on crime. While helping those down on their luck, Tulane students mature and improve their cultural competency skills, says Bernstein, which is likely to help them in their careers.

"Students learn how to interact with people who are different from them, come from a different culture," observes Bernstein. "And in the modern world workplace, that's what they will have to be able to do."

The hours spent in public service have to be connected to the student's current classwork. Jolia Raymond enrolled in a music class and at the same time became a tutor to elementary school students in an elite marching band. To stay in the band they had to keep their grades up. "Few kids in the New Orleans school system get one-on-one help," notes Raymond. "This was an unusual and important experience for them."

Amanda Brackman entered Tulane with the intention of majoring in theater, so her first project was working at a nursing home, where she and other students put together a play and dance performance based on the lives of nine people before, during, and after Katrina. Nursing home residents took part in the performances as well. "This program had a really high impact on the residents," Brackman says. "They were so thankful to have people visit them, especially as a lot of their families had relocated to other cities."

A student's first project is relatively simple, the second more demanding. In her second effort Brackman, who had changed her major to anthropology, took an internship in Tulane's Cowen Institute, working on innovations in education. Brackman helped research a complex project to measure an elementary school child's progress not by how he was performing compared to his peers but how he was advancing compared to his own previous benchmarks.

How much difference has Tulane's public service requirement made? It will take years to tell how much it has helped the community and, of course, other institutions have come to New Orleans' aid as well. The program has been good for Tulane. "I think there is a buzz among high-school students about what we are doing," says Bernstein.

University of Iowa
MAKING CAMPUS JOBS A LEARNING EXPERIENCE

For most students campus jobs are simply burdens, necessary toil that brings in money to support their academic careers. The jobs subtract from their learning time or their leisure time, at least as the students view them.

The University of Iowa views those jobs as an important addition to an education. Others have recognized that campus activities like fraternities and even dance marathons help students learn how to work with others. "But we neglect a large body of students who spend a lot of time in campus jobs — working in food services, as receptionists, lifeguards, whatever," says Sarah Hansen, the university's director of assessment and strategic initiatives.

What students can learn on their jobs and integrate with their academic work is how to communicate, how to work with people who are different, how to be flexible, how to resolve conflicts. Job supervisors are asked to meet with student workers twice a semester and ask them to ponder four questions: How is this job fitting in with your academics? What are you learning here that's helping you in school? What are you learning in class that can apply here at work? Can you give me a couple of examples of things you've learned here that you think you'll use in your chosen profession?

"Some students think that all they are doing is making sandwiches," Hansen says. "The reality is that they have learned how to work with Sue or whomever, who is very difficult. They have learned that jobs have given them places where they are expected to show up. They've learned how to write e-mails without smiley faces on them."

As undergraduates both Caitlyn Crawford and Haylie Miller, health majors, worked as paid employees for Health Iowa, an organization that promotes intelligent behavior on issues like alcohol, nutrition, and sex. "In class I learned how to implement a program on alcohol abuse," says Crawford. "But when I was on campus working and actually conducting a survey on alcohol behavior I learned that you have to deal with people making mistakes, misinterpreting instructions, and so on."

Miller worked on a program to help students control risky drinking behavior. Health Iowa sent out e-mails to all sophomores, asking them such questions as whether they customarily consume five or more drinks at a sitting. Those who replied "yes" to such questions were invited to come in for counseling. Miller was one of the counselors. One might guess that she would have found it easier counseling females than males. Not so. "The men were more laid back, more willing to talk about their drinking habits," says Miller. "The women were more defensive, perhaps because society is more accepting of men drinking than women."

University of Minnesota at Rochester
A LINK TO THE MAYO CLINIC

How do you provide undergraduates with a world-class health and science education without spending hundreds of millions of dollars on laboratories and elite professors?

The University of Minnesota cleverly solved this problem by building a branch campus in Rochester, right next door to the Mayo Clinic, one of the world's great medical institutions. "We are able to use Mayo's intellectual talent, to get its doctors to lecture here and meet the students," says UMR Chancellor Stephen Lehmkuhle. Students have access to Mayo's labs and such extraordinary facilities as a huge medical simulation center complete with robotic surgical mannequins.

The partnership also works well for Mayo. The clinic must attract technicians who can be certified for such esoteric specialties as cardiotocography (recording fetal heartbeat and uterine contractions during pregnancy), but increasingly such technicians are required to have bachelor's degrees. Mayo has no undergraduate program of its own. UMR graduates can fill those positions.

UMR is tightly focused on providing health and science students a springboard for their careers, Lehmkuhle says. As a result, all academic courses are likely to have a scientific or medical twist.

Jessica Gascoigne recalls an English class in which she and classmates read a short story, "The Yellow Wallpaper." The narrator was a nineteenth-century woman suffering from an undefined mental illness. The class discussion revolved not so much around the literary merits of the story as the diagnosis of what ailed the narrator. "Her contemporaries thought she was just nervous and needed more sleep," Gascoigne says, "but in class we brought up the possibility that she suffered from anxiety and what would be the modern treatment."

A history class dissected the male bias that traditionally dominated medicine and taught that in conception the assertive sperm attacks the passive egg. But current evidence suggests that the egg is an equal partner, drawing the sperm to itself.

Even beyond the Rochester campus UMR links its students to Mayo. Senior Ellie Linscheid aspires to be a physician's assistant, a profession that would allow her to perform many of the same services as a physician, such as conducting general check-ups and writing some prescriptions. She accompanied a Mayo physician to a small rural town in Honduras, where they ran a four-day clinic and screened 1,200 patients.

"I speak Spanish so I did a lot of translating for the doctor," she says, "but I was also able to take 'vitals', such as blood pressure, weight, and other measurements." In addition, she had to ponder real-life problems that textbooks don't always address. "In the U.S. you can advise patients to drink a lot of water," she observes, "but in Honduras there is no clean water."

As Lehmkuhle looks into the future of medical education, he sees the enormous challenges presented by the immense and dynamic health industry. "We are being asked to prepare students for jobs that don't yet exist," he says, "to solve problems we don't know yet with technologies that have not yet been invented." Living next door to Mayo won't resolve all of those issues, but it's a start.

University of Texas at Austin
TURNING LEARNING INTO A GAME

College students have been known to neglect their Facebook pages because of RTTP, a game that is so powerful it can also push beer pong competitions aside and make students forget to download the World of Warcraft. In a dorm at Pace University in New York City, RTTP generated such an obsession with seventeenth-century Boston Puritanism that nonplayers complained sullenly that it was ruining the dorm's ambience. "How do you party when half the dorm is talking Puritanism?" a resident assistant asked.

RTTP stands for Reacting To The Past, the brilliant invention of Barnard College professor Marc Carnes and others, that is engaging students passionately in history, political philosophy, and similar academic pursuits at three hundred colleges and universities across the country. At the University of Texas at Austin, Larry Carver, director of the liberal-arts honors program, first came upon the game at a workshop in 2003 when forty academics like himself played RTTP. "I've never seen academics have so much fun," Carver says. "And they were in it to win."

Carver brought the concept back to the Austin campus, where his classes play RTTP as often as three times a semester. Classes of two dozen students are separated into teams and each team defends in heated but thoughtful debate an ideological position or positions during various critical times in history, such as the Peloponnesian Wars, India during the partition in 1947 at the end of British rule, or Paris during the French Revolution.

Each student is given the role of a participant in the struggle and has to research that participant's biography and perspective thoroughly and argue that perspective. "They end up understanding and internalizing these points of view in a way that I couldn't get them to do in a lecture or even a seminar," Carver says.

In re-creating the French legislative assembly of 1791, one student plays the Marquis de Lafayette as head of the national guard trying to maintain order; another King Louis XVI trying to hold on to his crown and his life; a third Georges Danton, the dominant revolutionary of the moment; others might be minor players, such as merchants, or peasants, but with strong points of view based on their stakes in the revolution. "One of the things students learn is that much of history is not inevitable," observes Carver. "If Louis XVI had been smarter, France might have wound up with a constitutional monarchy."

Including the time that it takes the students to do the initial research, the games run on for weeks, during which the student teams become highly competitive. "Everything on the surface is polite," says Carver, "but underneath it is daggers." Teams meet late into the night, members write papers, exchange e-mails, and in some cases set up Web sites. At the end of the oral debates and the presentation of the supplementary papers, the judge — generally the professor — decides the winning team and also distributes individual grades.

Wake Forest University (North Carolina)
A FOCUS ON CAREER DEVELOPMENT

Wake Forest puts students on a career path before they even begin classes their first year on campus. During orientation, Andy Chan, the university's vice president for personal and career development, introduces students to the services his office provides over the course of their undergraduate career to get them thinking from day one about their interests and passions.

Most colleges segregate the person in Chan's position in an office in some corner of campus. The fact that Wake Forest has given Chan a vice president's title shows just how important they find the job of helping their students settle on a career. Chan has raised more than $8 million to support the work of his office.

At orientation, students get a Career Passport, a small booklet that lists the steps students should take each year to prepare them for a successful career after college. Those activities might include an assessment test that helps students find a major that best fits them, or confirm the field they have already chosen. The biggest question that liberal-arts majors often have is "What can I do with a major in . . . ?"

"The feeling is that if it's not a practical major they are unemployable and that's sad," Chan says. He works with faculty in various departments to collect the jobs that graduates went on to pursue with their degrees. They conduct Web-based panels of graduates who talk about how they got their jobs with degrees that some might find impractical. "The students come to realize that what they are doing in and out of class contributes to an experience that is important to employers," Chan says. "One of our jobs is to help them develop a strong sense of self and confidence."

Wake Forest's career-development program is seen as a leader in higher education, and one big reason for that is the classes it offers on the job search, life skills, such as budgeting, and career exploration. While other campuses might offer similar courses, Wake Forest is unique in giving students academic credit for taking these classes, another sign for students that the university takes their postgraduate lives seriously.

Wake Tech Community College (North Carolina)
AN EARLY START ON A DEGREE

Each year, Wake Early College of Health and Sciences in Raleigh, North Carolina selects seventy-five eighth graders from the greater Raleigh area and puts them through an accelerated program that in four years, or sometimes five, gives them a high-school diploma plus a community-college degree, diploma, or certificate in the health sciences field.

They are solid students, says principal Lisa Cummings, but not academically, artistically, or athletically gifted. What sets them apart from others their age is that they have a goal: a career in health sciences. "Other high schools allow kids a lot of time to discover themselves and develop their interests to find out where they belong," Cummings says. "We don't do that." Although the school, which opened in 2006, provides a general high-school curriculum, Wake Early clearly focuses on courses that will prepare them for jobs in the health care field. Nor are there a lot of distractions like sports teams and other extracurricular activities.

The students attend classes at Wake Technical Community College, along with older students of college age. When they graduate, roughly 85 percent of Wake Early students enter four-year colleges with credit for two years of community college. The other 15 percent or so remain at the community college and with a few more courses become certified for such occupations as nursing assistants, emergency medical technicians, and phlebotomists.

Wake Early is one of seventy similar programs in North Carolina, which is the leader in the early-college movement. Programs are also under way in California, New York, and Texas. Early college might not be right for every thirteen-or fourteen-year-old. Some do have to sample college before they can decide on a course of study. But for determined teenagers, especially those with parents struggling with finances, this fast track might be just the right speed.

Westminster College (Utah)
A LOOK INSIDE THE RÉSUMÉ

Most hiring managers take only a few minutes to scan applicant résumés. Often it is difficult for them to know by simply looking at a résumé whether the prospective employee can actually do the work required.

For graduates of Westminster College, that will no longer be a problem. Beginning with the freshman class that entered in the fall of 2011, all undergraduates are required to build an electronic portfolio. Think of it as a personal Web page that allows someone viewing the site to see the work behind it, whether it's a video, a paper, or an art exhibit. Students also write essays that explain how the evidence in the portfolio connects to the learning goals the college has established.

"The portfolios show the competency of a student in a way grades and transcript can't," says Kerri Carter, Westminster's e-portfolio coordinator.

Employers in certain industries like them, too. In communications, for example, hiring managers can see actual examples of the work performed by applicants rather than just a description. Frequently, at some point in the hiring process, companies want to see work samples, and the e-portfolio provides them plenty to choose from, Carter says. "It gives our students an edge in the job market because the employer has access to the portfolio," she says.

Worcester Polytechnic Institute (Massachusetts)
A PROJECT-BASED DEGREE

Generations ago, engineers were known to be loners working in a corner solving a complex problem. But modern engineers operate in teams, sometimes with nonengineers, collaborating across time zones, and communicating regularly with clients. To better prepare graduates for that world, Worcester Polytechnic Institute puts its students through a rigorous project-based curriculum. Beginning in the first year with the Grand Challenges Seminar that focuses on the big problems facing society in the twenty-first century (energy, aging, water, and food), students work on project teams designing potential solutions to the toughest engineering problems.

The two significant projects come in a student's junior and senior years. The junior-year project is designed to address problems that use science to solve societal problems. This project is equivalent to three courses at WPI, and student groups work with outside organizations or abroad. For her junior-year project, Rebecca Sharpe traveled with other students to Namibia for seven weeks, where they evaluated a project to increase trade routes through the African country. Now, in her senior year, Sharpe is working on her capstone project in her professional discipline, biomedical engineering. Working with two other students, they are trying to figure out a way to deliver stem cells to regenerate muscle tissue and increase mobility after a traumatic injury. "The projects have definitely taught me about troubleshooting and problem solving in the moment," Sharpe says. "You never really have to solve a problem, per se, while you're in class."

In all, the project-based curriculum covers several of the high-impact teaching and learning practices that have been shown to benefit students: first-year seminars, collaborative projects, undergraduate research, global learning, and a capstone experience.

David Cyganski, a professor of electrical and computer engineering, who graduated from WPI in the 1970s when the senior requirement was put in place, says the projects makes graduates from the institute ready for the workforce because they are able to hit the ground running. "This is true problem solving," he says. "It's only by real problem solving that you mature."

The projects also have real impact. A few years ago, a project team in their junior year designed a wind generator to help a local school with its energy needs. The following year the team built the generator. "It's not a matter of lecturing and telling them how it works," Cyganski says. "They have to go and figure it out."

CHECKLIST FOR THE FUTURE

The reporting for this book led me to nearly two dozen college campuses throughout 2012, and whenever I saw a prospective student tour in progress, I tagged along on as many as I could inconspicuously join.

On one tour, I met a father who had been on some six tours in the previous two months with his daughter. "Practice makes perfect," he told me. By now, he was an expert and carried a notebook full of questions he picked up from parents and students on other tours.

Most of them were about the type of campus his daughter was seeing that day, not the one she would arrive on in a few years. This book is a campus tour of sorts — it gives you the lay of the land in the current higher-education system and shows how it's likely to change in the future. The questions on the following checklist are based on the findings and predictions in the book, and are meant as a guide, especially for parents and prospective students, as you consider the college of the future.

As I warned in the introduction, don't let the bells and whistles distract you on a campus visit. Colleges and universities have benefited by confusion in the marketplace: They know more about the prospective student than the prospective student knows about them. It's in your interest to change that balance and learn as much about the school you're considering as possible.

Calculate the Return on Investment

A college education is an investment. Consider going to the most selective college you can get into because the research shows students from those schools end up making it through to graduation and earning more over their lifetimes. While there is no single way to determine if the school you selected is worth the price tag, by weighing various available measures you can better assess if a college is worth at least the debt you might take on to go there. (Chapter 8)

- What is the school's gradation rate for students with family and academic backgrounds similar to yours?
- How many first-year students with backgrounds like yours return for their second semester and then for their second year?
- What is the job-placement rate of the college's graduates? How is it calculated?
- Besides the famous alumni that every school likes to tout, where are last year's graduates working? How about five years ago? Ten years ago?

Check Out the Mobility of Credits

Students in the future will move among colleges, nontraditional providers, and countries more than ever before as they cobble together their degree. Find out if the institution you're considering is open to validating your various learning experiences toward a degree. (Chapter 7)

- What is the percentage of students who transfer in each year?
- What percentage of transfer credits does the college take each year? For those it denies, on what basis does it not take the credits?
- Does the college have partnerships with other institutions to accept credits?
- Would the college accept credits through the American Council on Education credit service if a student took a massive open online course (MOOC) approved by the association?
- Any options for competency-based degrees or credits, where students earn credit for what they know, not how much time they spend in class?

How Tech-Savvy Is the College?

Forget about whether the school gives out iPads to all incoming students or the wireless network covers every single square inch of campus. The power of technology in the future is about the promise to improve learning and lower costs. If the school offers a MOOC, take it to get a taste of a professor and a class. (Chapters 5 and 6)

- Is adaptive learning technology used in any courses to personalize the experience so that students focus on what they don't know?
- Do any of the classes use open courseware content from Carnegie Mellon University's Open Learning Initiative or other providers?
- Can students take a variety of course formats? For example, how many students take hybrid courses (face-to-face and online) or purely online courses at the same time they are taking traditional face-to-face courses?
- Do professors mostly lecture or mix in technology so that most lectures can be viewed outside of class and in-class time spent on mastering difficult concepts?

Get a Sense of the College's Priorities and Academic Rigor

Find out if the school's priorities are more about gaining prestige or in educating students. Sit in on a class or two. Ask for a sample course evaluation to see how students judge their professors. And read the student newspaper. (Chapters 1 and 2)

- Did an accreditor ever take action against the school or was accreditation ever denied for any reason?
- What is the percentage of students who get A's? B's?
- What is the percentage of full-time faculty? What percentage of first-year classes do they teach?
- How much writing and reading is required in classes? What percentage of classes assign more than forty pages of reading a week or more than twenty pages of writing over the course of a semester?

- Does the institution participate in the Collegiate Learning Assessment? Ask about average scores — which are rarely publicized — to see how seniors compare with freshmen.
- What percentage of the college's budget is spent on instruction compared with student services?

Find Out If the College Prepares Students for Their Fifth Job, Not Just the First

Employers want workers who have the ability to learn how to learn. In other words, the capability to find the answers to the questions of tomorrow that we cannot envision asking today. The hot jobs of today might be extinct in twenty years, so investigate how the college develops the skills necessary to succeed in the workforce of tomorrow. (Chapter 9 and 10)

- Do students work on deep research projects outside of class?
- How many students participate in internships or field work?
- Do students have an opportunity to participate in community-based projects?
- How many students have more than one major? What is the most popular combination of majors?
- What percentage of students study abroad?
- Are there any structured, off-campus opportunities for students who want to delay the start of college to get more life experience?

Study the Financial Aid Offer Closely

By the time students reach their senior year of high school they often have their hearts set on a particular campus. But families know little about what they will actually pay for college and, more important, exactly how they will finance it until a few weeks before a final decision needs to be made. The financial-aid offers from colleges do not follow a common template, so be sure to take a close look. (Chapter 3)

- What percentage of students graduate with debt?
- What is the average debt of students at graduation?

- When do applicants typically get notified about how much aid they might expect? Ask to see a sample aid award letter.
- What percentage of last year's graduates owe more than $25,000 in student-loan debt? More than $50,000?
- What is the average amount of the parent loan?
- How does the institution evaluate an applicant's "financial fit"?

Assess the Financial Health of the College

One-third of all colleges and universities in the United States face financial statements significantly weaker than before the recession and are on an unsustainable fiscal path. Another quarter of colleges find themselves at serious risk of joining them. Applicants should know the financial strength of the schools they are considering. (Chapter 4)

- What is the college's tuition discount rate? Has it been increasing?
- Has the college made its enrollment target the past few years?
- Is the revenue the college is receiving from tuition after it awards financial aid (net tuition) going up, holding steady, or dropping?
- What is the college's bond rating? Remember, however, that not all colleges are rated. If they are, ask for a copy of the latest bond-rating report.
- How much debt has the college taken on in the last ten years? What has that paid for?

ACKNOWLEDGMENTS

A high-quality education starts with engaged teachers, and I've been blessed throughout my life with great teachers, both in formal and informal settings. They have all in some way contributed to this book.

For the last fifteen years, I've had the honor of working alongside some of the best journalists in the country at the *Chronicle of Higher Education.* What I know about higher education mostly comes from the *Chronicle,* both the opportunities it gave me to travel the world in pursuit of good stories and the reporters and editors who care so deeply about the issues they cover and who shared their knowledge with me. I learned so much in preparing for and writing this book in lengthy conversations with colleagues Goldie Blumenstyk, Scott Carlson, Tom Bartlett, Sara Hebel, Marc Parry, Scott Smallwood, Karin Fischer, Jeffrey R. Young, Eric Hoover, Sara Lipka, and former colleague Paul Fain. They listened to my ideas, provided advice and sources, and in some cases, read chapters. The *Chronicle* also supported this project from the beginning. Its editor, Liz McMillen, strongly encouraged me every step of the way and provided insights into the publishing industry, and the *Chronicle's* editor-in-chief and president, Phil Semas, gave me the flexibility to follow disruption and innovation wherever they led. Parts of this book previously appeared in somewhat different forms in the *Chronicle,* and I'm thankful for permission to reprint the material here.

My interest in the future of higher education was first provoked by a day-long session I attended at Harvard Business School in the summer of 2011. It was hosted by Clay Christensen and I secured an invitation to the small gathering through Paul LeBlanc of Southern New Hampshire University. I'm thankful for that invite and for Paul's feedback on the manuscript. The Harvard meeting led to several other gatherings where I was able to collect details for this book and test ideas. Other reporting and writing projects emerged for me from those meetings that in the end helped contribute to the thinking in this book. All those projects proved invaluable to me, both for the people I met and the research I collected. For that, I'm indebted to Andrew Kelly of the American Enterprise Institute; Hilary Pennington, formerly of the Bill & Melinda Gates Foundation; Mark Schneider of the American Institutes of Research; Jeff Denneen of Bain & Company; and Tom Dretler of Sterling Partners.

The reporting for this book took me to college campuses across the United States, where I met interesting and helpful administrators, professors, and students. Several of them went out of their way to set up meetings, gather data, or introduce me to key sources and deserve special thanks: Randy Bass, John Burness, Anthony Carnevale, Dan Porterfield, and Jeff Strohl. I'm grateful also to Peter Cherukuri of the Huffington Post, for his friendship and his kindness in introducing me to some of the most interesting people in Washington, DC, several of whom were valuable to the thinking that went into this book.

I received great feedback on chapters and the entire manuscript from Sheila McMillen, Paul Heaton, Kathleen Santora, Mark Kantrowitz, Jay Lemons, and Tracy McPherson. Two researchers, Meg Handley and Imran Oomer, went the extra length to find sources and track down numbers. But any errors of fact or interpretation are mine alone.

This project got its start over lunch several years ago with a good friend, mentor, and former neighbor, Lee Smith, who had a distinguished career as a senior writer and editor at *Fortune* magazine and served as the publication's bureau chief in Tokyo and Washington. Lee assisted me in gathering the profiles of colleges at the back of this book, kept my spirits up during some challenging stretches of writing, and most important, launched this book by introducing me to my literary agent, John Thornton at the Spieler Agency. A new writer couldn't ask for a more thoughtful advocate.

Before I started writing this book, I asked other authors for advice. Many told me stories about difficulties with editors. But when I first met Katie Salisbury at Amazon, I knew that my book would be in good hands. She was fascinated by the topic, kept me well aware of my audience, and shepherded the manuscript through many thoughtful edits. Indeed, the entire team at Amazon, and its New Harvest imprint with Houghton Mifflin Harcourt, was terrific to work with. I thank them all.

Two people I know would have contributed to my thinking about this project are no longer around: Al Sanoff of *U.S. News & World Report* and Doug Toma of the University of Georgia. Both taught me so much about higher education, but their lives were cut short by cancer. Their influence is felt throughout this book.

This book was written whenever I could find time, in the mornings, late at night, on wefiends, and on vacation. I could have never done it without the support of a network of friends and babysitters who helped at home, especially Maria Orozco. Cheering me along throughout the process were my parents, Jim and Carmella, my sister, Jamie, and brother, Dave, who have encouraged, motivated, and supported me throughout my life, especially when it came to my education. I'm also incredibly lucky to have a supportive extended family too numerous to mention. I'm particularly grateful to my father-in-law and mother-in-law, Gene and Sandy Salko, who helped pinch-hit at home and on vacation while I was off writing. And as I struggled for a title, my sister-in-law, Tracey Selingo, and her talent for words came to the rescue.

No one deserves more thanks for the sacrifices they made for this book than my family. My daughters, Hadley and Rory, are too young to appreciate why their dad spent so much time away reporting and writing. They didn't get a say on whether I wrote this book, so I can only hope that they will understand one day when they read this.

Finally, my wife, Heather, listened to me talk about this book for every waking moment we spent together for an entire year and a half. She provided useful feedback on early versions of chapters and later as my research evolved. She encouraged me whenever I was anxious about a deadline and questioned my theories, ideas, and conclusions, even if it meant more time away to check them out. She held down the fort at home, with a newborn and a toddler, while I was away on reporting trips or just off writing. But most of all, her love and support as my life partner has made me a better person all around.

NOTES

Introduction

1. This number is estimated for students who entered college in 2009 and were still there in 2010. Determining exactly how many students drop out of college each year is complicated by the method the federal government uses to track graduation rates at U.S. colleges and universities. The official graduation rate of a college excludes many students, including those who attend part-time and those who transfer. The graduation rates listed throughout the book are for 2010, unless otherwise noted and come from the College Completion web site (collegecompletion.chronicle.com).

2. According to the Organisation for Economic Co-operation and Development (OECD). There is widespread agreement that the United States has fallen behind other countries on attainment, but exactly where the U.S. ranks is subject how the OECD numbers are interpreted and whether all degrees and age groups are included.

3. Pew Research Center. *Is College Worth It?* (Washington, D.C.: Pew Research Center, 2011).

4. U.S. Department of Education. *Test of Leadership: Charting the Future of Higher Education.* Washington, D.C.: U.S. Department of Education, 2006.

5. "State Fiscal Support for Operating Expenses of Higher Education per $1,000 of Personal Income." *Postsecondary Education Opportunity.* February 2012.

6. Tanya Caldwell, "Harvard, Yale and Other Ivy League Schools Are Most Selective This Year," *The Choice* (blog), *New York Times*, March 29, 2012, http://thechoice.blogs .nytimes.com/2012/03/29/ivy-league-college-admission-rates/

7. David Leonhardt, "Top Colleges, Largely for the Elite," *New York Times*, May 24, 2011, http:// www.nytimes.com/2011/05/25/business/economy/25leonhardt.html

1. The Great Credential Race

1. "The Top 1 Percent: What Jobs Do They Have?" *New York Times*, January 15, 2012, http://www.nytimes.com/packages/html/newsgraphics/2012/0115-one-percent -occupations/index.html

2. Sabrina Tavernise, "A Gap in College Graduates Leaves Some Cities Behind," *New York Times*, May 30, 2012, http://www.nytimes.com/2012/05/31/us/as-college -graduates-cluster-some-cities-are-left-behind.html

3. As quoted in Scott Carlson, "Sprawling Mesa, Ariz., Aims to Become a College Town," *Chronicle of Higher Education,* March 18, 2012, http://chronicle.com/article/Sprawling-Mesa-Ariz-Aims-to/131230/

4. Carl L. Blankston III, "The Mass Production of Credentials: Subsidies and the Rise of the Higher Education Industry," *The Independent Review* (Winter 2011): 325–49.

5. David Glenn, "Discipline by Discipline, Accreditors Multiply," *Chronicle of Higher Education,* July 24, 2011, http://chronicle.com/article/As-Accreditors-in-Particular/128377/

6. Eric Kelderman, "Struggling Colleges Question the Cost—and Worth—of Specialized Accreditation," *Chronicle of Higher Education,* October 5, 2009, http://chronicle.com/article/Struggling-Colleges-Question/48685/

7. J. Douglas Toma, "Institutional Strategy: Positioning for Prestige," in *The Organization of Higher Education: Managing Colleges for a New Era,* ed. Michael N. Bastedo (Baltimore: The Johns Hopkins University Press, 2012), 119.

8. Elizabeth F. Farrell and Martin VanDerWerf, "Playing the Rankings Game," *Chronicle of Higher Education,* May 25, 2007, http://chronicle.com/article/Playing-the-Rankings-Game/4451/

9. Robin Wilson and Jeffrey Brainard, "The Research Drain," *Chronicle of Higher Education,* May 8, 2011, http://chronicle.com/article/Universities-Ante-Up-Own-Money/127428/

10. Katherine Mangan, "A Growth Spurt for Medical Schools," *Chronicle of Higher Education,* January 12, 2007, http://chronicle.com/article/A-Growth-Spurt-for-Medical/4846/; Peter Schmidt, "Florida's Board of Regents Wings a Reprieve (for Now) From the Legislature," *Chronicle of Higher Education,* May 19, 2000, http://chronicle.com/article/Floridas-Board-of-Regents/15069/; Karin Fischer, "Florida's Board of Governors Approves 2 New Medical Schools," *Chronicle of Higher Education,* April 7, 2006, http://chronicle.com/article/Floridas-Board-of-Governors/5423/

11. "ABA-Approved Law Schools," American Bar Association, accessed April 8, 2012, http://www.americanbar.org/groups/legal_education/resources/aba_approved_law_schools.html

12. Jeffrey F. Milem, Joseph B. Berger, and Eric L. Dey, "Faculty Time Allocation: A Study of Change over Twenty Years," *The Journal of Higher Education* (2000), 454–75.

2. The Customer Is Always Right

1. David Glenn, "A Professor at Louisiana State Is Flunked Because of Her Grades," *Chronicle of Higher Education,* May 16, 2010, http://chronicle.com/article/A-Professor-at-Louisiana-State/65555/

2. Hemi H. Gandhi, "Combating the Facebook Index," *Harvard Crimson,* October 24, 2011, http://www.thecrimson.com/article/2011/10/24/facebook-class-phenomenon/

3. Stuart Rojstaczer and Christopher Healy, "Where A Is Ordinary: The Evolution of American College and University Grading, 1940–2009," *Teachers College Record,* Volume 114, Number 7, accessed April 12, 2012.

4. David Glenn, "A Professor at Louisiana State Is Flunked Because of Her Grades."

5. Patrick Healy, "Harvard's Honors Fall to the Merely Average," *Boston Globe,* October 8, 2001, http://www.hsj.org/modules/lesson_plans/article.cfm?ArticleId=184&menu_id=&submenu_id=&module_id=2

6. Richard Arum and Josipa Roksa, *Academically Adrift: Limited Learning on College Campuses* (Chicago: The University of Chicago Press, 2011). Kindle edition.

7. Richard Arum, Esther Cho, Jeannie Kim, and Josipa Roksa, *Documenting Uncertain Times: Post-Graduate Outcomes of the Academically Adrift Cohort* (New York Social Science Research Council, 2012), 3–4.

8. Based on interviews with Jane Wellman and Delta Cost Project on Postsecondary Education Costs, Productivity, and Accountability, *Trends in College Spending 1999–2009: Where Does the Money Come From?* (Washington, DC: Delta Cost Project, 2011).

9. Gary Rhoades, "The Study of American Professionals," in *Sociology of Higher Education: Contributions and their Contexts,* ed. Patricia Gumport (Baltimore: Johns Hopkins Press, 2007), 128.

10. As quoted in Beckie Supiano, "Swanky Suites, More Students?" *Chronicle of Higher Education,* April 11, 2008, http://chronicle.com/article/Swanky-Suites-More-Students-/33537

11. As quoted in Tracy Jan, "BU dorm offers a study in luxury," *Boston Globe,* September 2, 2009, http://www.boston.com/news/education/higher/articles/2009/09/02/bu_dorm_offers_a_study_in_luxury/

12. Buildings & Grounds (blog), *Chronicle of Higher Education,* http://chronicle.com/blogs/buildings/, accessed May 15, 2012.

13. The story of the changes in campus tours is adapted from Eric Hoover, "Golden Walk Gets a Makeover From an Auditor of Campus Visits," *Chronicle of Higher Education,* March 6, 2009, http://chronicle.com/article/Golden-Walk-Gets-a-Makeover/21806/; Eric Hoover, "Campus Tours Go Disney," *Washington Monthly,* April 2011, http://www.washingtonmonthly.com/college_guide/feature/campus_tours_go_disney.php?page=all; Jacques Steinberg, "Colleges Seek to Remake the Campus Tour," *New York Times,* August 18, 2009, http://www.nytimes.com/2009/08/19/education/19college.html?_r=1

14. Greg Winter, "Jacuzzi U.? A Battle of Perks to Lure Students," *New York Times,* October 5, 2003, http://www.nytimes.com/2003/10/05/us/jacuzzi-u-a-battle-of-perks-to-lure-students.html?pagewanted=all&src=pm

15. Elizabeth Armstrong and Laura Hamilton, research to be included in a forthcoming book from Harvard University Press, http://www-personal.umich.edu/~elarmstr/research.html.

3. The Trillion-Dollar Problem

1. The story of Kelsey Griffith was based on author interview and adapted from Andrew Martin and Andrew W. Lehren, "A Generation Hobbled by the Soaring Cost of College," *New York Times,* May 12, 2012, http://www.nytimes.com/2012/05/13/business/student-loans-weighing-down-a-generation-with-heavy-debt.html?pagewanted=all&_r=0; Kelsey Griffith, interview by Robin Young, *Here & Now,* WBUR, May 15, 2012, http://hereandnow.wbur.org/2012/05/15/student-loans-debt

2. Meta Brown, Andrew Haughwout, Donghoon Lee, Maricar Mabutas, and Wilbert van der Klaauw, "Grading Student Loans," Liberty Street Economics (blog), Federal Reserve Bank of New York, March 5, 2012, http://libertystreeteconomics.newyorkfed.org/2012/03/grading-student-loans.html

3. History of tuition and financial aid policies adapted from Michael Mumper, *Removing College Price Barriers* (Albany, NY: State University of New York Press, 1996); Donald E. Heller, "The policy shift in state financial aid programs." *Higher Education: Handbook of Theory and Research,* Volume XVII. Ed. J. C. Smart (New York: Agathon Press, 2002).

4. William J. Bennett, "Our Greedy Colleges," *New York Times,* February 18, 1987, http://www.nytimes.com/1987/02/18/opinion/our-greedy-colleges.html

5. Name has been changed to protect the family's privacy.

6. Jonathan D. Glater, "A Cruise, and in Turn, Perhaps a Loan?" *New York Times,* May 9, 2007, http://www.nytimes.com/2007/05/09/us/09cruise.html

7. "Illegal Inducements and Preferred Lender Lists," accessed July 16, 2012, http://www.finaid.org/educators/illegalinducements.phtml

8. Beckie Supiano, "When a Student's First-Choice College Is Out of Financial Reach," Head Count (blog), *Chronicle of Higher Education,* May 11, 2011, http://chronicle.com/blogs/headcount/when-a-students-first-choice-college-is-out-of-financial-reach/28205

9. Story of Katherine Cooper adapted from lawsuit filing, *Alexandra Gomex-Jimenez, Scott Tiedke and Katherine Cooper v. New York Law School,* Supreme Court of the State of New York, County of New York, August 10, 2011, and Matthew Shaer, "The Case(s) Against Law School," *New York Magazine,* March 4, 2012, http://nymag.com/news/features/law-schools-2012-3/index1.html

10. David Segal, "Law School Economics: Ka-Ching!" *New York Times,* July 16, 2011, http://www.nytimes.com/2011/07/17/business/law-school-economics-job-market-weakens-tuition-rises.html?pagewanted=all

11. David Segal, "Is Law School a Losing Game?" *New York Times,* January 8, 2011, http://www.nytimes.com/2011/01/09/business/09law.html?pagewanted=all

12. "Grading Student Loans," Liberty Street Economics (blog).

4. The Five Disruptive Forces That Will Change Higher Education Forever

1. Story of Teresa Sullivan from author interview and Paul Schwartzman, Daniel deVise, Anita Kumar, and Jenna Johnson, "U-Va. upheaval: 18 days of leadership crisis," *Washington Post,* June 30, 2012, http://www.washingtonpost.com/local/education/u-va-upheaval-18-days-of-leadership-crisis/2012/06/30/gJQAVXEgEW_story.html

2. Eric Hoover and Beckie Supiano, "This Year Colleges Recruited in a 'Hall of Mirrors,'" *Chronicle of Higher Education,* May 29, 2009, http://chronicle.com/article/This-Year-Colleges-Recruited/47490/

3. Audrey Williams June, "After Costly Foray Into Big-Time Sports, a College Returns to Its Roots," *Chronicle of Higher Education,* May 18, 2007, http://chronicle.com/article/After-Costly-Foray-Into-Big/22156/

4. Paul Fain, "Birmingham-Southern's President Resigns While Trustees Explain College's Financial Meltdown," *Chronicle of Higher Education,* August 11, 2010, http://chronicle.com/article/Birmingham-Southerns/123880/

5. Jeff Denneen and Tom Dretler, "The Financially Sustainable University," Bain Brief, July 6, 2012, http://www.bain.com/publications/articles/financially-sustainable-university.aspx

6. Kelly Field and Alex Richards, "180 Private Colleges Fail Education Dept.'s Latest Financial-Responsibility Test," *Chronicle of Higher Education*, October 12, 2011, http://chronicle.com/article/180-Private-Colleges-Fail/129356/

7. "Moody's downgrades Drew University's (NJ) long-term rating to Baa1 from A3; outlook is stable," accessed July 29, 2012, http://www.moodys.com/research/Moodys-downgrades-Drew-Universitys-NJ-long-term-rating-to-Baa1--PR_249768

8. Thomas G. Mortenson, "State Funding: A Race to the Bottom," *The Presidency*, Winter 2012, http://www.acenet.edu/the-presidency/columns-and-features/Pages/state-funding-a-race-to-the-bottom.aspx

9. Tom Bartlett and Karin Fischer, "The China Conundrum," *New York Times*, November 3, 2011, http://www.nytimes.com/2011/11/06/education/edlife/the-china-conundrum.html?pagewanted=all

10. Eric Hoover and Josh Keller, "More Students Migrate Away From Home," *Chronicle of Higher Education*, October 30, 2011, http://chronicle.com/article/The-Cross-Country-Recruitment/129577/

11. As quoted in Mara Hvistendahl, "Asia Rising: Countries Funnel Billions Into Universities," *Chronicle of Higher Education*, October 5, 2009, http://chronicle.com/article/Asia-Rising-Countries-Funnel/48682/

12. Sara Lipka, "Student Services, in Outside Hands," *Chronicle of Higher Education*, June 13, 2010, http://chronicle.com/article/Student-Services-in-Outside/65908/

13. Penelope Wang, "Is college still worth the price?" *Money Magazine*, April 13, 2009, http://money.cnn.com/2008/08/20/pf/college/college_price.moneymag/

14. Frederick Rudolph and John Thelin, *The American College and University: A History* (Athens, GA: University of Georgia Press, 1990), 219.

5. A Personalized Education

1. As quoted in Dan Berrett, "How 'Flipping' the Classroom Can Improve the Traditional Lecture," *Chronicle of Higher Education*, February 19, 2012, http://chronicle.com/article/How-Flipping-the-Classroom/130857/

2. National Association for College Admission Counseling, "Early Notification Study," September 2010, http://www.nacacnet.org/research/research-data/nacac-research/Documents/EarlyNotificationStudy2010.pdf

3. Steve Cohen, "What Colleges Don't Know About Admissions," *Chronicle of Higher Education*, September 21, 2009, http://chronicle.com/article/What-Colleges-Dont-Know-About/48487/

4. "How a Match.com for Students Could Make College Admissions Obsolete," *The Atlantic*, accessed June 28, 2012, http://www.theatlantic.com/business/archive/2011/09/how-a-matchcom-for-students-could-make-college-admissions-obsolete/245970/

5. Robert Bardwell, "A Veteran High School Counselor Responds to a Report Critical of the Profession," The Choice (blog), *New York Times*, March 5, 2010, http://thechoice.blogs.nytimes.com/2010/03/05/bardwell/

6. Complete College America, "Time is the Enemy," September 2011, http://www.completecollege.org/resources_and_reports/time_is_the_enemy/

6. The Online Revolution

1. William Poundstone, "How to Ace a Google Interview," *Wall Street Journal*, December 24, 2011, http://online.wsj.com/article/SB1000142405297020455230457711252298 2505222.html

2. Kevin Carey, "Stanford's Credential Problem," Brainstorm (blog), *Chronicle of Higher Education*, May 14, 2012, http://chronicle.com/blogs/brainstorm/stanfords-credential -problem/46851

3. As quoted in Jeffrey R. Young, "Inside the Coursera Contract: How an Upstart Company Might Profit From Free Courses," *Chronicle of Higher Education*, July 19, 2012, http://chronicle.com/article/How-an-Upstart-Company-Might/133065/

4. Steven Leckart, "The Stanford Education Experiment Could Change Higher Learning Forever," *Wired*, March 20, 2012, http://www.wired.com/wiredscience/2012/03/ff_aiclass/

5. Dan Berrett, "3 Colleges' Different Approaches Shape Learning in Econ 101," *Chronicle of Higher Education*, June 18, 2012, http://chronicle.com/article/Econ-101-From -College-to/132299/

6. William J. Baumol, "Health care, education and the cost disease: A looming crisis for public choice," *Public Choice*, Volume 77, Number 1 (1993), 17–28, DOI: 10.1007/ BF01049216.

7. The Sloan Consortium, "Going the Distance: Online Education in the United States, 2011," accessed August 15, 2012, http://sloanconsortium.org/publications/survey/ going_distance_2011

8. Pew Research Center, *The Digital Revolution and Higher Education* (Washington, D.C.: Pew Research Center, 2011).

9. Marc Parry, "Tomorrow's College," *Chronicle of Higher Education*, October 31, 2010, http://chronicle.com/article/Tomorrows-College/125120/

10. William G. Bowen, Matthew M. Chingos, Kelly A. Lack, and Thomas I. Nygren, "Interactive Learning Online at Public Universities: Evidence from Randomized Trials," Ithaka S+R, May 2012.

11. As quoted in Tamar Lewin, "Harvard and M.I.T. Team Up to Offer Free Online Courses," *New York Times*, May 2, 2012, http://www.nytimes.com/2012/05/03/ education/harvard-and-mit-team-up-to-offer-free-online-courses.html/

12. As quoted in David Wessel, "Tapping Technology to Keep Lid on Tuition," *Wall Street Journal*, July 19, 2012, http://online.wsj.com/article/SB10001424052702303942 404577534691028046050.html

7. The Student Swirl

1. Sara Lipka, "Ambitious Provider of Online Courses Loses Fans Among Colleges," *Chronicle of Higher Education*, September 18, 2011, http://chronicle.com/article/ Ambitious-Provider-of-Online/129052/

2. Don Hossler, Doug Shapiro, and Afet Dundar, *Transfer & Mobility: A National View of Pre-Degree Student Movement in Postsecondary Institutions* (Herndon, VA: National Student Clearinghouse Research Center, February 2012).

3. As quoted in Lee Gardner and Goldie Blumenstyk, "At Calif. Public Colleges, Dreams Deferred," *Chronicle of Higher Education*, August 13, 2012, http://chronicle .com/article/For-Golden-States-Public/133565/

4. John Gravois, "The College For-Profits Should Fear," *Washington Monthly*, September/ October 2011, http://www.washingtonmonthly.com/magazine/septemberoctober _2011/features/the_college_forprofits_should031640.php

5. Council for Adult and Experiential Learning, *Moving the Starting Line Through Prior Learning Assessment (PLA)* (Chicago: Council for Adult and Experiential Learning, August 2011).

6. Jeffrey R. Young, "A Conversation With Bill Gates About the Future of Higher Education," *Chronicle of Higher Education*, June 25, 2012, http://chronicle.com/article/ A-Conversation-With-Bill-Gates/132591/

8. Degrees of Value

1. Anthony P. Carnevale, Stephen J. Rose and Ban Cheah, *The College Payoff* (Washington, DC: The Georgetown University Center on Education and the Workforce, 2012).

2. Higher Education Research Institute, "The American Freshmen: National Norms Fall 2011," *Research Brief*, January 2012, http://www.heri.ucla.edu/PDFs/pubs/TFS/ Norms/Briefs/Norms2011ResearchBrief.pdf

3. Melissa E. Clinedinst, Sarah F. Hurley, and David A. Hawkins, *2011 State of College Admission*, National Association for College Admission Counseling, http://www .nacacnet.org/research/research-data/Documents/2011SOCA.pdf

4. Higher Education Research Institute, "The American Freshmen: National Norms Fall 2011."

5. Stacy Berg Dale and Alan B. Krueger, "Selective College: An Application of Selection on Observables and Unobservables," *The Quarterly Journal of Economics* (November 2002): 1491–1527.

6. Caroline Hoxby, "The Return to Attending a More Selective College: 1960 to the Present," in *Forum Futures: Exploring the Future of Higher Education*, eds. Maureen Devlin and Joel Meyerson (Jossey-Bass Inc., 2001): 13–42.

7. Mark Hoekstra, "The Effect of Attending the Flagship State University on Earnings: A Discontinuity-Based Approach," *The Review of Economics and Statistics* (November 2009): 717–24.

8. As quoted in William G. Bowen, Matthew M. Chingos, and Michael S. McPherson, *Crossing the Finish Line: Completing College at America's Public Universities* (Princeton, NJ: Princeton University Press, 2009). Kindle edition.

9. Joshua Goodman and Sarah Cohodes, *First Degree Earns: The Impact of College Quality on College Completion Rates* (Cambridge, MA: Harvard Kennedy School, August 2012).

10. As quoted in Elizabeth F. Farrell and Martin VanDerWerf, "Playing the Rankings Game."

11. As quoted in Doug Lederman, "The Secretary Offers a Preview," *Inside Higher Ed*, September 8, 2006, http://www.insidehighered.com/news/2006/09/08/measure #ixzz25bAr4ASe

12. As quoted in "Q&A: Former Secretary of Education Margaret Spellings Discusses the Impact of Her Commission," *Chronicle of Higher Education*, September 17, 2011, http://chronicle.com/article/Q-A-Former-Secretary-of/129065/

13. As quoted in Doug Lederman, "Campus Accountability Proposals Evolve," *Inside Higher Ed,* June 26, 2007, http://www.insidehighered.com/news/2007/06/26/accountability#ixzz25nK2G4hM

9. The Skills of the Future

1. Carl Bialik, "Seven Careers in a Lifetime? Think Twice, Researchers Say," *Wall Street Journal,* September 4, 2010, http://online.wsj.com/article/SB10001424052748704206804575468162805877990.html

2. Sarah E. Turner and William Bowen, "The Flight from the Arts and Sciences: Trends in Degrees Conferred," *Science* 250 (1990): 517–21; Steven Brint, "The Rise of the Practical Arts" in *The Future of the City of Intellect: The Changing American University,* ed. Steven Brint (Stanford, CA: Stanford University Press, 2002), 222.

3. William Damon, *The Path to Purpose: How Young People Find Their Calling in Life* (New York: Free Press, 2008), 5.

4. Association of American Colleges and Universities, "Raising the Bar: Employers' Views On College Learning In The Wake Of The Economic Downturn," accessed August 5, 2012, http://www.aacu.org/leap/documents/2009_EmployerSurvey.pdf

5. Roger Schank, *Teaching Minds: How Cognitive Science Can Save Our Schools* (New York: Teachers College Press, 2011): 46.

6. Mark C. Taylor, "End the University as We Know It," *New York Times,* April 26, 2009, http://www.nytimes.com/2009/04/27/opinion/27taylor.html?pagewanted=all

7. As quoted in Lila Guterman, "What Good Is Undergraduate Research, Anyway?" *Chronicle of Higher Education,* August 17, 2007, http://chronicle.com/article/What-Good-Is-Undergraduate/6927/

8. Institute for International Education, *Open Doors 2012: Report on International Educational Exchange* (Washington, D.C.: Institute for International Education, 2012). Previous annual editions of this report also consulted.

9. Karin Fischer, "Short Study-Abroad Trips Can Have Lasting Effect, Research Suggests," *Chronicle of Higher Education,* February 20, 2009, http://chronicle.com/article/Short-Study-Abroad-Trips-Can/1541

10. Sue Shellenbarger, "Better Ideas Through Failure," *Wall Street Journal,* September 27, 2011, http://online.wsj.com/article/SB10001424052970204010604576594671572584158.html

11. A. G. Lafley, "Keynote Speech" (speech, Wake Forest University, Winston-Salem, NC, April 12, 2012).

12. As quoted in Ron Daniels, "Deep, smart, and diverse," *Johns Hopkins Magazine,* Spring 2012, http://hub.jhu.edu/magazine/2012/spring/deep-smart-and-diverse

13. Eric C. Wiseman, "The Current and Future World of Work" (panel discussion, Wake Forest University, Winston-Salem, NC, April 12, 2012).

10. Why College?

1. Claire Cain Miller, "Want Success in Silicon Valley? Drop Out of School," Bits (blog), *New York Times,* May 25, 2011, http://bits.blogs.nytimes.com/2011/05/25/want-success-in-silicon-valley-drop-out-of-school/

2. Anthony P. Carnevale, Tamara Jayasundara, and Andrew R. Hanson, *Career and Technical Education: Five Ways That Pay Along the Way to the B.A.* (Washington, D.C.: The Georgetown University Center on Education and the Workforce, 2012).

3. Harvard Graduate School of Education, *Pathways to Prosperity: Meeting the Challenges of Preparing Young Americans for the 21st Century* (Cambridge, MA: Harvard Graduate School of Education, 2011).

4. Sabrina Tavernise, "A Gap in College Graduates Leaves Some Cities Behind."

5. Andrew Delbanco, *College: What It Was, Is, and Should Be* (Princeton, NJ: Princeton University Press, 2012). Kindle edition.

6. Michael Mumper, *Removing College Price Barriers* (Albany, NY: State University of New York Press, 1996).

7. Pew Research Center, *Is College Worth It?*

Conclusion

1. Thomas Bartlett, "Phoenix Risen," *Chronicle of Higher Education,* July 6, 2009, http://chronicle.com/article/Phoenix-Risen/46988/

2. Indiana University Center for Evaluation and Education Policy, *Charting the Path from Engagement to Achievement: A Report on the 2009 High School Survey of Student Engagement* (Bloomington, IN: Indiana University Center for Evaluation and Education Policy, 2010).

3. Marc Prensky, "Digital Natives, Digital Immigrants," *On the Horizon* (Vol. 9, No. 5), October 2001.

4. Marc Prensky, "Digital Natives, Digital Immigrants, Part II: Do They Really *Think* Differently?" *On the Horizon* (Vol. 9, No. 6), December 2001.

5. Peter Cookson Jr., *Blended Learning: Creating the Classrooms of Tomorrow Today,* forthcoming from ASCD book.

6. John Seely Brown, "Growing Up Digital: How the Web Changes Work, Education, and the Ways People Learn," *USDLA Journal* (Vol. 16, No. 2), February 2002.

SOURCES

Unless otherwise noted, all quotations come from author interviews or presentations by sources at meetings and conferences.

Graduation rates

The graduation rates listed throughout the book are six-year rates from 2010, unless otherwise noted, and come from http://college completion.chronicle.com.

Tuition, Fees, and Financial Aid

College Board, Trends in Higher Education
http://trends.collegeboard.org/

Income by Education and Attainment

U.S. Census, Current Population Survey
http://www.census.gov/cps/

Other National Education Statistics

National Center for Education Statistics
http://nces.ed.gov/
Integrated Postsecondary Education Data System
http://nces.ed.gov/ipeds/

Earnings and Unemployment by Major

Georgetown Center on Education and the Workforce
http://cew.georgetown.edu/

Attitude Surveys of College Students

Higher Education Research Institute, University of California at Los Angeles
http://www.heri.ucla.edu/

ABOUT THE AUTHOR

Jeffrey J. Selingo is editor at large for the *Chronicle of Higher Education,* where he has worked in a variety of roles for more than fifteen years, including four years as the top editor. He frequently speaks before national higher-education groups and appears regularly on regional and national radio and television programs, including NPR, PBS, ABC, MSNBC, and CBS. His writing on higher education and technology has appeared in the *New York Times,* the *Washington Post,* and the *Huffington Post.* The National Magazine Awards, Education Writers Association, Society of Professional Journalists, and the Associated Press have recognized him for his work. He is also a senior fellow at Education Sector, an independent education policy think tank. He previously worked for the *Wilmington Star News* in North Carolina, *The Arizona Republic,* the *Ithaca Journal,* and as an intern, for *U.S. News & World Report,* where he contributed to the magazine's Best Colleges guide. He received his bachelor's degree in journalism from Ithaca College and his master's degree in government from Johns Hopkins University. He lives with his wife, Heather Salko, and two daughters, Hadley and Rory, in Washington, D.C.

www.jeffselingo.com

INDEX